100 THINGS
BULLDOGS FANS
SHOULD KNOW & DO
BEFORE THEY DIE

Jon Nelson

TRIUMPH
BOOKS

Library of Congress Cataloging-in-Publication Data

Nelson, Jon, 1968–
    100 things Bulldogs fans should know & do before they die / by Jon Nelson.
        p. cm.
    Includes bibliographical references.
    ISBN 978-1-60078-413-2
    1. Georgia Bulldogs (Football team)—History 2. University of Georgia—Football—History. 3. Football—Georgia—History. I. Title. II. Title: One hundred things Bulldogs fans should know and do before they die.
    GV958.G44N45 2010
    796.332'630975818—dc22

                                            2010018846

This book is available in quantity at special discounts for your group or organization. For further information, contact:
    Triumph Books
    542 South Dearborn Street
    Suite 750
    Chicago, Illinois 60605
    (312) 939-3330
    Fax (312) 663-3557
    www.triumphbooks.com

Printed in U.S.A.
ISBN: 978-1-60078-413-2
Design by Patricia Frey
All photos courtesy of AP Images unless otherwised noted

For Bulldogs fans everywhere. Your passion reminds everyone what the Red and Black mean to college football Saturdays.

Contents

Foreword

To set this up for you, the idea was to produce this book using someone who knows the history of the Bulldogs program, someone who's involved in the program today, and someone who is familiar with the city of Athens and the University.

This way, we can get away with saying what a lot of others wish they had the chance to say over the years to one particular individual…

"Loran, whaddayagot?"

* * *

The passion for college football continues to gain momentum with each passing year. The bowl games end, and college fans across the country focus on signing day, hoping their favorite team will bring in a bumper crop of recruits. Then they intently follow the developments of spring practice, casting a hopeful eye to the forthcoming season.

After the spring game, you begin to hear greetings on telephone recorders like, "Only 116 days before kickoff." Call the same number a week later, and you get, "Only 109 days left before kickoff."

At Georgia, passionate fans can't wait to flock to Athens each fall. Many arrive the day of the game for the tailgate scene that lasts from early morning to kickoff. Some spend their weekends in the Classic City, and others—like the RV aficionados—stay for the entire week.

If you are a newcomer to Georgia football, you can follow the lead of the television networks that dote on the tailgate scene—featuring everything from beer and barbecue to burgers on the grill to high-end gourmet dishes and Dom Perignon. Touch football games for the kids abound, and the sounds of highlight tapes from the Bulldogs' signature victories, like smoke from the grill, waft upward, fostering exalted feelings that don't abate until the chapel bell rings into the night. Fans stuff kids, grills, coolers, and video accessories in their SUVs for the all-day ritual. Everything is red and black. If it ain't—it ain't official.

Walk the campus with its tree-lined canopy and stroll by buildings whose architecture reflects the notion that much has taken place since that day in 1892 when Georgia played its first game, defeating Mercer 50–0. I suggest that was also the first tailgate party.

Years after the lopsided victory, a player said that the referee missed two Georgia scores when he took a break and walked across the street to buy some booze.

Herty Field, where the game took place, is easy to find on North Campus. You might be inspired to read the plaque, which not only tells you about that initial football scrimmage but also about the man who originated football at Georgia, Dr. Charles Herty, who invented a process for making paper from pine pulp. In that era, scholarship and sportsmanship were given the highest priority.

Come early and find your way to a scene just outside the main gate where Uga, Georgia's beloved mascot, tailgates. Have your photo made with him. He won't mind.

Enter the main gate, take an immediate right, and you will find the Uga cemetery. Georgia is probably the only school that buries its mascots inside its stadium. Uga VIII, the current all-white male English bulldog, knows interment space has been reserved for him.

Uga has his own air-conditioned Dawg house. Uga is always in the company of pretty cheerleaders. Even opposing cheerleaders cotton to Uga and delight in a photo op.

Game day is a little bit of everything cloaked in a spirited hospitality held in a social setting that renews itself each week in the fall. There's plenty to savor. A reunion with an old classmate. Visiting the buildings where you took classes, and stopping by your fraternity house where nostalgia overwhelms. Grabbing a chili dog at the Varsity. Returning to the scene where you first met your favorite coed, especially if she became your lifelong companion. Listening to old game tapes where Larry Munson breathlessly counted down the seconds to another scintillating victory. Munson has retired, but his voice and the memories of his years live on. Throughout the day, joyful sounds from the Redcoat Band remind you that game-day memories are a balm for the soul.

I'm a campus collector. Never met one I didn't like, but the crown jewel is the beautiful campus of the University of Georgia where football games are played between the hedges that are as famous as Uga. More often than not, when the Bulldogs exit those hedges on game day, victory will be toasted back in the parking lots with the chapel bell ringing. On those days, we borrow a time-honored phrase from the society editors of weekly newspapers:

"A good time was enjoyed by all."

—Loran Smith

Introduction

When you're presented with this challenge, much like the other authors in this series, you think that it'll be easy…at first.

Then you come up with 100 items…so far, so good.

Now all you have to do is rank them…that's where the fun starts.

Then, someone you talk to during your research asks if you've included Item *A*, *B*, or *C*. If you haven't, the whole process of putting the jigsaw puzzle back together is like the Humpty Dumpty nursery rhyme, and you're asking for the rest of the king's horses and king's men to put the jumble back into order.

Talking to Bill Hartman about his dad led to a lot of suggestions and items that were easy to add when he reminded me about their importance. For that education (and reminder), I'm eternally grateful.

And I also knew going in that a book like this will start a boatload of arguments when it comes to placement and storylines. I'm more than ready to accept that, too. But remember, we're only talking about 100. Yes, this could have easily been 200 and a second volume. You can always suggest it to the publisher, right?

Go ahead and have those arguments…they're healthy.

I've grown up around the program. I listened to the games while acting like a football player in my grandfather's backyard on Saturdays—tossing touchdown passes to backups and third-stringers instead of the stars. I remember Larry Munson as an integral part of what we sometimes refer to as the soundtrack of my youth. There were the Munson sound-alike contests that happened every year. There were all those moments that, before the advent of around-the-clock television, we all had to imagine the scene that was being painted by that voice coming from the speakers.

Being involved in television, I've seen the program up close, and I've seen its ups and downs. There have been coaching changes that have led to nothing short of a lynch-mob mentality toward a university president. There have been wins that surprised and losses that shocked. There were a lot of late nights where I waited on bowl game highlights coming across on the satellite, and was reminded once again what it meant for local kids who grew up watching the Georgia Bulldogs to be part of the history of the program.

You remember, "I covered that kid in high school. I covered that kid in high school." And as you keep pointing and keep adding, it turns into a lot of kids making their mark.

Either that, or I'm really old.

Yeah, I'll admit that a lot of these items were what we called when I was growing up a bunch of "well, duh" items. But when you hear the stories around why or when these 100 became important, it fills in some holes. It also makes the background of all this history fill in the spaces around everything we always knew.

Every university and athletic program has its history, traditions, and impact—and all that keeps growing over time. But as you read the *100 Things Bulldogs Fans Should Know & Do Before They Die*, remember one thing—it's just the road map as we all travel the road.

Enjoy the drive.

1 Sanford Stadium

I guess that you have to start a book like this somewhere, so why not start a book on Georgia football at the place where it all begins, the home of the Bulldogs…Sanford Stadium.

First and foremost, to appreciate the history of Sanford Stadium, you've got to understand the history of the land itself. It may now be the sixth-largest capacity on campus stadium in college football, with a 92,746 capacity, but the stadium didn't get that big overnight.

Ground was broken on the stadium, named for former UGA president Dr. Steadman Vincent Sanford, in 1928. It took a little work and some engineering due to the fact that the site of the stadium had a creek running through it. The first game in that 30,000-seat stadium was played in October 1929 against Yale which, believe it or not, was the first time that Yale had played a game in the South.

Much like everything else in college football history, there's a story as to why the stadium was built in the first place. Legend has it that the folks at UGA were frustrated at having to play their archrival, the Georgia Tech Yellow Jackets, at Tech's stadium every year. According to the stadium's Wikipedia page, then University President Sanford vowed to "build a bigger stadium than Tech" after the teams played in Atlanta in 1927 and the Yellow Jackets shutout the previously undefeated Bulldogs 12–0 to effectively end their season.

In 1940, the school put up field-level lights and added seats, growing the capacity to 36,000. Georgia played Kentucky to a 7–7

1

Artist's conception showing how Sanford Stadium at the University of Georgia in Athens will look after a $2.96 million renovation in November 1966. (AP Images)

tie that season in the first night game in Sanford Stadium history. That lighting was removed in 1964 when the University began expanding the stadium in order to compete with the other teams in the Southeastern Conference. By the end of that season, the capacity had grown to 43,000 plus.

The year 1967 brought another round of expansion. The upper deck was put in along with the press box and club seats—something pretty common now but not so much back in the 1960s. Capacity was now up to 59,000 seats.

More growth arrived in 1981. The school had the east end zone enclosed and lights were put back in, though obviously not at field level. Adding those 19,000-plus seats grew the stadium to an

82,000-seat capacity and delivered night football back to the Athens area. Five more additions from 1991 through 2004 grew the stadium to its current capacity of more than 92,000 fans, making it the second-largest stadium in the SEC.

As big as the stadium has grown, it has become even harder to get a ticket. Routinely, the games sell out whether it is a non-conference game or one of several Bulldog rivals; it is extraordinarily hard to get a ticket. If you aren't a student, a member of the faculty, or a fairly large donor, you are going to have a hard time getting into a game.

However, if you have the opportunity, take advantage of it. Sanford Stadium is truly one of the more scenic and historic

Sanford Stadium

Did you know that the stadium has a creek underneath it?

Tanyard Creek is the body of water that is fenced off on the north end by the player's entrance of Sanford Stadium.

In 1976, Prince Charles of Great Britain was set for a visit during UGA's Homecoming. A week before, the U.S. Secret Service was in the tunnel underneath the stadium, sweeping it for any kind of explosives. Before Tanyard was fenced off, you could actually walk down the creek bed and be underneath all the action…literally.

Sanford Stadium Facts

All-time Record: 344–88–12
Original Stadium Cost: $360,000
First Lights Added on Field Level: 1940
First Night Game: October 26, 1940 vs. Kentucky
Field Level Lighting Removed: 1964
Second Deck Added: 1967, cost $3 million
East End Zone Enclosed: 1981
Full Light Poles Installed: 1981
Current Capacity: 92,746, 6th largest college stadium in the country
Hosted Olympic Soccer Medal Rounds: 1996
One of two SEC stadiums that sits east to west

stadiums in college football. The game-day atmosphere and the pomp and circumstance make it an experience that not only should be enjoyed by anyone who considers themselves a Georgia Bulldog fan but a must-do for anyone who considers themselves a fan of college football.

2 The Hedges

Like this particular topic would be way down the list?

If you really want to get an entire nation mad, all you have to do is talk about the removal of the Hedges from their birth place, growth place, and rightful place in the universe. That's what happened in 1996 when one of the most recognizable pieces of shrubbery was booted from its roots so soccer could be played at Sanford Stadium for the 1996 Summer Olympics.

We'll get to that story in a bit.

How did the hedges get to be that all-important, all-imposing signature to Sanford Stadium? Back in 1929, President Steadman Sanford wanted the "best football stadium in Dixie." Charlie Martin, who held pretty much every job in the athletic program at one time or another, had seen the roses at the Rose Bowl three years earlier and thought that the flower would make a great addition.

One problem...roses wouldn't last, so they settled on hedges that were installed just hours before the Georgia Bulldogs–Yale Elis game (notice the reference wasn't Bulldogs-Bulldogs game) on October 12, 1929, which UGA won 15–0.

More than 30,000 fans showed up for the game itself, and nine southern governors were also in attendance. Coach Dan

Magill said it was the biggest athletic event ever held in the South at the time.

As the story goes, Grantland Rice, the legendary sportswriter who spent time at the *Atlanta Journal-Constitution* in his early years, used the phrase "between the hedges" first. According to Coach Magill, Rice said that Georgia would "have its opponent between the hedges" when describing a game in Athens.

There is some debate as to what kind of hedge was actually planted at Sanford—some sources say it was an English privet hedge, while others claim it is Chinese privet. Frank Henning, penning a column in the *Athens Banner-Herald* in 2003, said that there are actually two sets of hedges inside Sanford Stadium. The inner hedge is Chinese privet with the outer hedge being a Chinese mix that yields "Bulldawg red" leaves in the fall.

While the hedges certainly look pretty, they actually serve another purpose: keeping ticket-paying customers from getting on to the field itself to celebrate a Georgia win. The storming of the turf only happened once in recent memory. On October 7, 2000, when the Bulldogs beat Tennessee for the first time in twelve years, not even the hedge and low-lying chain-link fence could keep fans off the field.

The hedges, if left unattended, will grow 3 feet per year and grow for eight out of the twelve months in the calendar. Kenny Pauley, UGA's director of sports turf and grass, oversees a staff of ten full-time employees and three students that get to trim the hedges when they need it, which is fairly regularly.

Now, to the removal of the hedges for the Olympics.

No one was told that the hedges needed to be removed to accommodate the width of the soccer pitch, and when the news was broken, plenty of fits were pitched instead—even when it was later discovered that the hedges were diseased.

They were stored in two separate locations. Close to 1,200 of the cuttings from the hedges were kept in a nursery in Quincy,

Florida, while the other half were in the Dudley Nurseries in the town of Thomson—one exit west of the Augusta metropolitan area. People lined the highway to take pictures as the hedges left McDuffie County and headed home.

But Quincy, Florida, for the hedges? Housing them out of state? Isn't that sacrilegious or something?

George Hackney, owner of Hackney Nurseries in Quincy, was based 10 miles from the Georgia state line and 25 miles west of Tallahassee. He had to keep the whole thing a secret.

"It was really tough," said Hackney, who had the clippings since April 1994, told the *Augusta Chronicle* when he was interviewed in 1996. "We have about 30 employees, and most of them didn't know where [the hedges] came from or what they were for.

"It's a tremendous honor to take care of them, but we're glad to get rid of them."

"That's South Georgia, not Florida," Dooley told C. Jemal Horton of the *Chronicle*. "They were grown with Georgia soil and Georgia horticulturalists. These were South Georgia hedges. But we didn't want to let it out that they were in Florida."

But the bottom line was that they were returned in just as good a shape as when they were cut up and exported from Athens.

"The hedges are back where they belong," Coach Dooley said when the hedges were replanted, almost immediately after the Olympics left town. "Now we know the hedges are safely out of Florida. We welcome Hedges II.

"These are the sons and daughters of the original hedges," Dooley said. "They're home now."

Billy Payne was part of the group at the re-planting. "It's no secret of the affection I hold [for] this stadium and these hedges," Payne said. "It's a great experience taking part in this new era. I'll make good on my final Olympic responsibility, which is putting these hedges back where they belong."

All this attention for a 5' tall, 5' wide, 3,000-sq. ft. weed? One that has its own security system, alarms, and surveillance cameras? You bet—especially when it's an Athens-based Privet Ligustrum.

The Georgia G

For years, the headgear worn by the players of the Georgia Bulldogs was just a plain silver helmet. A block red "G" was introduced in 1963—placed in the middle of those shiny silver helmets and only seen for home games. That year, the Bulldogs finished the season 4–5–1, and Johnny Griffith was relieved of his head coaching duties.

Vince Dooley was hired off the Auburn coaching staff in 1963, and he made an immediate cosmetic impact in Athens. Dooley redesigned the Georgia uniforms, choosing a red helmet with a black G on a white background as the dominant feature.

Coach Dooley was impressed with the look of the G emblem on the Green Bay Packers helmets and wanted something similar for the new UGA red helmets. He had hired John Donaldson, who played for the Bulldogs from 1945–48, as backfield coach. Donaldson volunteered his wife, Anne, who had a bachelor of fine arts degree in commercial art from UGA, to design the new logo to Coach Dooley's specifications. Anne Donaldson's oval G fit Dooley's vision and was similar to Green Bay's G but different in design and color.

Before the Bulldogs ran onto the field sporting the new oval G logo on their new bright red helmets, Dooley wanted to make sure it wouldn't ruffle any feathers up in Green Bay. The Packers first used their oval G in 1961. Joel Eaves, UGA's athletic director at the time, called the Packers to get their stamp of approval, which was granted by the team.

If you read the Green Bay Packers' story of their logo, it mentions that their G design has been borrowed by numerous colleges and high schools. When you read UGA's history of its G logo on georgiadogs.com, it mentions that the Green Bay Packers have redesigned their G several times, and it now looks like Georgia's original 1964 design.

Today the Georgia G is one of the most recognized logos in college sports and is used by virtually all athletic teams at the University of Georgia. The red helmet with the Georgia G has become a classic helmet in college football.

Most importantly, the G has brought good luck to the Bulldogs. Since its inception in 1964, Georgia has won seven SEC championships on the football field plus the 1980 National Championship.

UGA has always been dressed for success.

4 It Was Almost Over Before It Began

The Georgia Bulldogs' remarkable record of success in college football, including 12 SEC championships and five national championships, may not have happened if it wasn't for a grieving mother who stepped in to prevent the sport from being banned permanently in the state of Georgia.

Tragedy struck the Georgia football team in 1897 during a game against the University of Virginia at Atlanta's Brisbane Park. During the Bulldogs' 17–4 loss to the Cavaliers on October 30, 1897, Richard Vonalbade Gammon was severely injured on a play. Gammon was taken by horse-drawn ambulance to a nearby hospital, but he died from his injuries the next day.

UGA immediately disbanded its football program along with in-state rival Georgia Tech, who Georgia had defeated for the first time the week before, and Mercer University. The headline that ran in the *Atlanta Journal* proclaimed the "Death Knell of Football."

Then the Georgia legislature got involved, passing a bill to outlaw football in the state of Georgia. That bill sat on the desk of Governor William Yates Atkinson waiting to be signed into law when a letter arrived from Rosalind Gammon, the mother of Von Gammon.

In the letter, Mrs. Gammon wrote:

"It would be the greatest favor to the family of Von Gammon if your influence could prevent his death being used for an argument detrimental to the athletic cause and its advancement at the university. His love for his college and his interest in all manly sports, without which he deemed the highest type of manhood impossible, is well known by his classmates and friends, and it would be inexpressibly sad to have the cause he held so dear injured by his sacrifice. Grant me the right to request that my boy's death should not be used to defeat the most cherished object of his life."

After reading that letter from Mrs. Gammon, Governor Atkinson vetoed the bill to outlaw football in the state of Georgia.

The sport received a pardon at the eleventh hour.

5 1980 National Championship Team

No discussion with a longtime Georgia Bulldogs fan would be complete without talking about 1980, the last time the Bulldogs won the national championship. To any Georgia fan during that time period, it was a true moment to behold, a moment that probably will never be eclipsed.

For the Georgia Bulldogs, 1980 began in dramatic fashion. Finishing the 1979 season at 6–5 didn't do much for expectations in Athens. The team started out at No. 16 on the Associated Press rankings going into the season. The Bulldogs began their odyssey with a road game versus Tennessee in front of what was then an SEC-record 92,000-plus screaming fans. Trailing 15–2 late in the third quarter, the Bulldogs came back and won the game, 16–15. Certainly, the game was memorable because of the comeback. Had they lost, they wouldn't have been undefeated, and wouldn't have won the National Championship. The game was, to most Georgia fans, more memorable because it was the freshman debut of Herschel Walker.

A little-known tidbit about this team was that even to this day, it still holds the record for most yards rushing in an SEC season. Of course, Walker played a big role in that record, running for 1,616 yards. But without some other notable players, the season couldn't possibly have played out the way that it did.

Those players included quarterback Buck Belue, wide receiver Lindsay Scott, safety Scott Woerner, offensive lineman Hugh Nall, and kicker Rex Robinson. Nine All-SEC players and three National All-Americans headlined this group. You also can't have a conversation about the 1980 team without mentioning head coach Vince Dooley and his defensive coordinator Erk Russell.

The 1980 squad didn't always win pretty, but they won.

After the Tennessee win, they had no problem shutting out Texas A&M 42–0. But the next week they held on to beat Clemson 20–16 in Athens. The team won its next four games relatively easily before outlasting South Carolina 13–10. The next

Georgia coach Vince Dooley, left, and Notre Dame coach Dan Devine give the Sugar Bowl Trophy a look-over during a news conference Monday, December 29, 1980, before their January 1 game. (AP Images)

1980 Championship Team

The biggest surprise about the 1980 University of Georgia football team was the fact that they had gone into the season without even being ranked.

They had a couple of close calls over the course of the season. The season-opening win against Tennessee was a comeback. The Dogs trailed 15–2 at one point in the second half before coming back to win 16–15. In the 20–16 win over Clemson, they had to rely on defensive back Scott Woerner and a punt return to defeat the Tigers. Relying heavily on Herschel Walker, this was also the year that the Buck Belue-to-Lindsay Scott play happened in the game versus Florida. Had fortunes been a little different, the 1980 squad would have been 9–2 and would never have been part of the national championship discussion.

week, they took care of the Florida Gators 26–21 in a game that will always be remembered in Georgia football history—but more on that a little later.

The team climbed to No. 1 in the AP poll after that and finished off the regular season with wins over Auburn and Georgia Tech. Making it through the season 11–0 and No. 1 in the polls, the Bulldogs earned the right to play in the Sugar Bowl. Remember, these were the days before conference championships.

In the 1980 Sugar Bowl, the Bulldogs squared off with Notre Dame and its coach, Dan Devine. It was the first, and thus far, the last game the two teams played. The game was a low-scoring, physical contest that the Bulldogs won despite passing for a grand total of 7 yards. In fact, they were outgained on the day and outplayed for the most part by the Fighting Irish.

Herschel Walker earned the Most Valuable Player Award, running for 150 yards and a touchdown. At the end of the day, it was the Georgia Bulldogs pulling out a hard-fought victory that is remembered by many with the image of coach Vince Dooley being carried off of the field on the shoulders of his team.

The 1980 Georgia Bulldogs will always be remembered as the first national championship team in school history. There were other teams that won the title but had to share it with others. As has happened quite often in the past, there were disagreements between the various polls as to the best team in college football.

The funny thing to those who follow college football closely is that the 1980–81 version of the Dawgs is legendary in NCAA circles as quite possibly the most talented team in the modern era.

6 The World's Largest Outdoor "Whatever-They-Call-It-This-Year"

The annual game between Georgia and Florida has fallen victim to political correctness.

The rivalry is known today as the Florida vs. Georgia Football Classic, but the majority of Bulldogs and Gators fans call the annual game in Jacksonville, Florida, The World's Largest Outdoor Cocktail Party.

The origins of the nickname trace back to the 1950s when Bill Kastelz, a former sports editor at the *Florida-Times Union* in Jacksonville, saw a drunken fan stumble over to a uniformed police officer and offer him a drink. Kastelz coined the phrase, and it stuck for more than 50 years.

Officials from the City of Jacksonville never liked the moniker attached to the Georgia-Florida game but tolerated it until 1984. After Florida shut out Georgia 27–0, Gator fans stormed the field, tore down the goalposts, and contributed to some damage to the Gator Bowl Stadium. Jacksonville police arrested 65 people, and there was talk of moving the game back to an on-campus site.

Florida tight end Aaron Hernandez is tackled by Georgia linebacker Christian Robinson in the second quarter of the hard-hitting annual game on Saturday, October 31, 2009, in Jacksonville, Florida. (AP Photo/Stephen Morton)

Two years later, the City of Jacksonville chose to stop calling the game The World's Largest Outdoor Cocktail Party and began cracking down on alcohol abuse. Nobody followed Jacksonville's lead and The World's Largest Outdoor Cocktail Party continued. That changed in 2004 when two people died—and alcohol abuse was the leading cause.

University of Georgia president Michael Adams and University of Florida president Bernie Machen began a campaign against the nickname. Florida athletic director Jeremy Foley got involved, writing a letter to Southeastern Conference commissioner Mike Slive requesting he get involved.

"I understand fully that this game has carried this moniker for a number of years and that the networks had nothing to do with creating this phrase," Foley wrote to Commissioner Slive. "However, the two institutions and the City of Jacksonville have worked very hard to curb the alcohol abuse that is associated with this game, and by labeling this game in this manner an inconsistent message is being sent to all fans, especially our respective students."

Later, Commissioner Slive sent a letter to executives of the SEC's television partners requesting that they not make any alcohol references.

Georgia actually first played Florida on October 15, 1904, in Macon, Georgia, with the Bulldogs defeating the Gators 52–0. Naturally, Florida doesn't recognize that game as official, but Georgia does.

The Bulldogs wouldn't meet the Gators again until 1915 in Jacksonville. That game was a big deal for the city back then. Jacksonville's mayor, J.E.T. Bowden, declared the Friday before the game a "half" holiday for local business. Georgia prevailed in the 1915 game 37–0.

It would be 18 years before the Georgia-Florida game would find a permanent site. The game moved around from Tampa in 1919 to Athens and Gainesville and even Savannah, Georgia, which hosted the game in 1928. In 1933, the game retuned to Jacksonville, and from then on the city has been the permanent site for the Georgia-Florida game.

There have been many memorable games in the Georgia-Florida rivalry, and the ones that became legendary even earned their own moniker. There's the game simply know as "The Blowout" when Georgia crushed a Florida team decimated by World War II, 75–0. It's the largest margin of victory in the series.

In 1966, Florida entered the Georgia game 7–0 and in position to clinch the program's first SEC Championship. Steve Spurrier was having a Heisman Trophy season.

"It will take 13 men at the very least to stop Spurrier," Georgia head coach Vince Dooley told *Sports Illustrated* before the game.

The Georgia defense played with 11 men and held Spurrier to 133 yards passing—almost 100 yards below his average at the time. Spurrier didn't throw a touchdown pass as the Bulldogs rained on the Gators coronation 27–10.

In 1976, Florida head coach Doug Dickey decided to go for a first down on fourth-and-1 in the second half. Gator running back Earl Carr was stopped by Georgia's Johnny Henderson. Georgia then ran off three straight touchdowns in a 41–27 rout of Florida. That play became forever known as Fourth and Dumb.

Of course, Run Lindsay Run—perhaps the most famous play in Bulldog football history—happened in 1980.

Georgia has always had a knack of ruining Florida's great seasons—case in point 1985. Florida entered the game unbeaten and ranked No. 1 in the nation for the first time in school history. The Bulldogs ran over the Gators thanks to a pair of Georgia freshman, Keith Henderson and Tim Worley. Henderson rushed for 145 yards while Worley had 104 yards, 89 of them coming on a touchdown run late in the game that sealed the Gators' fate. Georgia prevailed, 24–3.

Then there is the game simply known as The Gator Stomp in 2007. After Georgia's Knowshon Moreno barely broke the plane for Georgia's first score of the game against Florida, the entire Georgia bench emptied onto the field. It turns out that was a premeditated move ordered by head coach Mark Richt. He wanted his offense to receive an unsportsmanlike conduct penalty after their first score, and if they did not follow orders, the team would run at 5:45 in the morning.

"I told them we were going to liven it up and create some excitement," Richt said after the game.

Georgia followed Coach Richt's orders. However, he didn't intend for the *entire team* to run out to celebrate. By the way, it did rain penalty flags.

What that move did was fire up a Georgia team that needed it. It also ramped up the intensity of the rivalry. And Georgia won the game 42–30.

The Georgia-Florida rivalry is a classic but it is as much fun as a cocktail party.

7 Dr. Charles Herty

Without Dr. Charles Herty, there would be no Georgia football, period.

To trace the roots of the Bulldogs program, look no further. It all comes back to Dr. Herty—who was also the first coach of the team that played what is widely considered the first college football game in the Deep South; played against Mercer University on January 30, 1892.

His only other game as head coach was a game against Auburn, which was played on February 20 of the same year, and arranged by Herty and an old classmate from Johns Hopkins.

Believe it or not, football was not the first sport Herty began at the university. In 1890, he returned to Athens after earning his doctorate at Johns Hopkins. He almost immediately began raising money to get athletic facilities on campus. You will be surprised to find out that he coached and played center field on the university's first baseball team. Shortly thereafter, he became a chemistry instructor and spent his next 10 years at the school.

Herty also helped get funding for the construction of the first tennis courts on campus. A portion of that money helped improve the original athletic fields that would later become the area where Sanford Stadium currently stands.

Born in the Georgia town of Milledgeville in 1867, there was no indication that Herty would have such a great influence on athletics—Georgia athletics to be specific. He grew up to become a widely known chemist, who was also a driving force in the creation of the National Health Institute. He would later create the Savannah Paper and Pulp Laboratory, which would become a pioneer in the use of Southern pine trees to create paper.

The lab's location was, of course, Savannah.

Dr. Herty would become known at many of Georgia's colleges and universities. There are buildings named for him at Savannah State University, Georgia State University in Atlanta, and the University of Georgia.

If you happen to find yourself in Milledgeville, look around. If you are lucky, you will pass by a monument put up to recognize perhaps the single most important person in the history of Georgia football. In time, perhaps the school would have started a football program, but without the push from Herty, it would have taken quite a long time for that to happen.

8 Herschel Walker

Pretty much any conversation about Georgia football and its history will start with one name. Though there are quite a few famous alums and coaches, anybody you talk to will more than likely start talking to you about that one name, the biggest legend in the history of that team. They won't use his full name; they will just say his first name—Herschel.

The legend of Herschel Walker had an inauspicious start in the small town of Wrightsville, Georgia. Freakishly strong, he swore

SEC Top 10 Rushing Yards in a Season

1. 1,891 Herschel Walker, Georgia (385 rushes) 1981.
2. 1,830 Darren McFadden, Arkansas (325 rushes) 2007.
3. 1,786 Bo Jackson, Auburn (278 rushes) 1985.
4. 1,752 Herschel Walker, Georgia (335 rushes) 1982.
5. 1,686 Charles Alexander, LSU (311 rushes) 1977.
6. 1,658 Mark Ingram, Alabama (271 rushes) 2009.
7. 1,647 Darren McFadden, Arkansas (284 rushes) 2006.
8. 1,616 Herschel Walker, Georgia (274 rushes) 1980.
9. 1,600 Moe Williams, Kentucky (294 rushes) 1995.
10. 1,599 Emmitt Smith, Florida (284 rushes) 1989.

that he never lifted weights; his workouts consisted of 5,000 push-ups and 3,000 sit-ups. At Johnson County High School, he set a then-state record with 3,167 yards rushing and 45 touchdowns as a senior and was recruited by every major college in America. He decided to stay close to home and attend the University of Georgia.

And the legend would continue to grow.

There are precious few athletes who made a better first impression as a freshman than Herschel Walker. From the very beginning of his first game, he had perhaps one of the most memorable moments in Georgia football history as he plowed over Bill Bates of Tennessee, leading Georgia to a 16–15 win that we'll discuss a little later in the book.

That began a freshman season that saw Walker run for an NCAA record 1,616 yards with 15 touchdowns and the Dawgs going undefeated and winning not only the Sugar Bowl against Notre Dame but the national championship. By the time he finished, Walker ran for 5,259 yards and 52 touchdowns.

Though they would not win another championship during Walker's three years in Athens, the Dawgs had an incredible run of success, going 32–1. Herschel set 11 NCAA, 16 SEC, and 41 Georgia records and won a Heisman Trophy before he was through.

He was selected as an All-American three times during his career as a Bulldog from 1980–83. He was also elected to the College Football Hall of Fame in 1999.

That three-year stretch as a Bulldog made Herschel Walker a legend forever, not only in Athens but also on a national collegiate level. But that legend only marked the beginning of his story.

Herschel Walker established his formidable reputation in Athens, and he took things a step further when he became a professional football player. He began his career in the upstart United

Herschel Walker (No. 34) moves the ball as Penn State's Steve Sefter (No. 41) tries to stop him during Sugar Bowl action on Saturday, January 1, 1983, in New Orleans. (AP Photo)

States Football League as one of their high-profile signees, leaving school after his junior year and achieving instant success. In the 1985 season, he ran for what is still a single-season professional record 2,411 yards while playing for Donald Trump and the New Jersey Generals.

When the USFL folded, Walker landed with the Dallas Cowboys in the NFL. He played in two Pro Bowls and finished his career as one of the league's all-time leaders in all-purpose yardage. But he will probably be remembered professionally as being part of the NFL's largest player trade in history. Without going into the *very* lengthy details, the trade was Walker and four draft picks heading to the Minnesota Vikings for five players and eight draft picks. The Cowboys used that trade to rebuild the team for their successful run in the 1990s. The Vikings, however, got Walker on the downside of his career and did not do well with the draft picks. The trade would go down as one of the biggest fleecings in the history of the sport.

Herschel Walker retired from football in 1997, and the accolades were still coming. *Sports Illustrated* picked him for its All-Century Team, and other sports outlets named him the greatest college football player of all time. His jersey was retired at the University of Georgia.

Walker has moved in and out of the public eye since his retirement. He has been a successful businessman, owning a large food service company, and he has appeared on multiple television shows. He was on the U.S. Bobsled team in the 1992 Winter Olympics and has competed as a fighter in Mixed Martial Arts (MMA).

Walker has accomplished quite a lot in his life—everything from football star to Olympic competitor to television star to successful businessman, and he even had a go as a successful author. Even if he wasn't as public a figure after his college years, he will always be considered a legend in Athens, Georgia. There are few people who can duplicate what he has done, and there have been none like him, before or since.

Herschel Walker is an original.

Herschel Walker is a legend.

More importantly, Herschel Walker will always be a Georgia Bulldog, and his is a story from which legends are made.

9 The 1942 National Champs

Head coach Wally Butts had been steadily upgrading the talent on the Georgia Bulldogs football team throughout the late 1930s and early 1940s. All of Coach Butts' hard work came to fruition in 1942.

Georgia was led by seniors George Poschner, who would earn All-American honors at the end of that year, and Frank Sinkwich, the 1942 Heisman Trophy Winner. New to the team was freshman Charley Trippi—giving Georgia one of the most potent offenses in the country in 1942.

The Bulldogs opened the 1942 season in Louisville, Kentucky, against the Kentucky Wildcats and held on to win 7–6. From then on, the Bulldogs cruised with double-digit wins over Jacksonville NAS, Furman, Ole Miss, Tulane, and Cincinnati.

By that time, Georgia was ranked No. 2 in the nation and prepared for a showdown with third-ranked Alabama. The Bulldogs and Crimson Tide met at Grant Field on the Georgia Tech campus in Atlanta on October 31, 1942. With World War II raging in Europe and the South Pacific, fuel rationing was in effect, so Atlanta was the neutral site.

It had been 13 years since Georgia had defeated powerful Alabama, and it looked like the losing streak would continue after Alabama raced out to a 10–0 lead at halftime. By the fourth quarter, Georgia's offense suddenly came alive thanks to the pitch-and-catch from Frank Sinkwich to George Poschner. Poschner's first touchdown catch was from five yards and cut the lead to 10–7.

Later in the fourth quarter, the Bulldogs had a second-and-11 on the Alabama 15-yard line when Sinkwich fired in the end zone to Poschner, who, as he caught the ball, was simultaneously hit high and low and was flipped upside down. Poschner came down on his head but still secured the ball to his chest. Those who saw it say Poschner caught the ball "standing on his head." Georgia had the lead 14–10, and Poschner's remarkable catch became part of Georgia Bulldog lore.

Georgia added another touchdown to win the game 21–10. "You're the greatest bunch of battlers I have ever seen," Coach Butts told his players after the win.

The following Monday, Georgia was ranked No. 1 in the nation. The Bulldogs went on to thrash the Florida Gators 75–0 in Jacksonville, Florida, then whipped UT-Chattanooga 40–0 on the road. The roll ended on a late November afternoon at Memorial Stadium in Columbus, Georgia, against the Auburn Tigers. The Bulldogs were beaten 27–13 for their only loss of the season.

With the loss to Auburn, Georgia tumbled from the top of the polls to No. 5 for their showdown with Georgia Tech in Athens. The Yellow Jackets were undefeated at 9–0 heading into the game and ranked No. 2 behind Boston College, who took the top spot in the polls following Georgia's loss to Auburn.

The 1942 Georgia–Georgia Tech game was huge. The winner would have a shot at the national championship, and to make it more interesting, the day before the game, the Rose Bowl committee announced the winner of the Georgia–Georgia Tech game would be invited to play UCLA on New Year's Day 1943 in Pasadena.

There was a great demand for tickets for the game in Athens. Thousands of extra seats were added in Stanford Stadium to accommodate the large crowd. What they witnessed was a Georgia domination. Georgia routed Georgia Tech 34–0 to earn the trip to the Rose Bowl and a shot at the national championship.

On January 1, 1943, the Bulldogs went up against the best team in the West, the UCLA Bruins. Heisman Trophy winner Frank Sinkwich played the game with two sprained ankles and scored the game's only touchdown as the Bulldogs shut out the Bruins 9–0. Georgia finished the 1942 season 11–1.

After the game, Georgia was declared the national champions by the six polls recognized by the NCAA at that time: DeVold, Houlgate, Litkenhous, Williamson, Poling, and Berryman.

10 The 1927 National Champs

After a couple of mediocre seasons, head coach George "Kid" Woodruff finally saw the fruits of his labor come to fruition. When Woodruff became UGA's head coach in 1923, he introduced the South to the Notre Dame "Box 4" shift offense. He had witnessed that particular offense earlier that season when he watched the Fighting Irish rout Georgia Tech 35–7.

Woodruff decided then and there to implement that offensive system at Georgia. He hired three Knute Rockne disciples: Frank Thomas, who would later gain fame during his tenure as head coach of the University of Alabama; Harry Mehre, who would succeed Woodruff as head coach of the Bulldogs; and Jim Crowley, who was part of the famous Notre Dame Four Horseman.

From 1923 to 1926, Georgia compiled records of 5–3–1, 7–3, 4–5, and 5–4. Those seasons set the stage for a watershed year for the Bulldogs.

The Bulldogs opened the 1927 season hosting the University of Virginia and blanked the visiting Wahoos 32–0. Next up for Georgia was a trip up north to face one of college football's powerhouses in the 1920s, Yale. On that October afternoon at the Yale Bowl, the Bulldogs scored a pair of touchdowns and held on to defeat Yale for the first time in school history, 14–10.

The win over Yale not only propelled Georgia into the national spotlight but gave the Bulldogs confidence. Georgia rolled to four shutout wins in five games—first blanking Furman 32–0, then defeating Auburn down in Columbus, Georgia, followed by consecutive shutouts of Tulane in New Orleans, Florida in Jacksonville, and at home against Clemson.

Mercer traveled up to Athens from Macon and finally put points up against the stout Georgia defense by scoring a touchdown. But that game belonged to the Bulldogs as Georgia won, 26–7.

Next came a trip to Birmingham, Alabama, to christen the newly completed Legion Field in a game against the Alabama Crimson Tide. The Tide had taken five straight from the Bulldogs, but the visitors from Athens found the new accommodations to their liking, defeating Alabama 20–6 and ending the losing streak.

The Bulldogs had won nine straight games and were called the "Dream and Wonder Team." The only obstacle that stood in the way of an undefeated season was in-state rival Georgia Tech.

Rain fell through that December afternoon at Grant Field in Atlanta, and Georgia Tech dampened Georgia's mood. Tech ruined UGA's dream of an undefeated season by shutting out the Bulldogs 12–0. The win by Georgia Tech gave them a share of the Southern Conference title with NC State and Tennessee.

Yet Georgia's dream of a national championship remained. Two polls were recognized back in the 1920s. Boand and Poling voted the Bulldogs No. 1, thus giving Georgia its first national championship. Tom Nash earned consensus All-America honors in 1927 at end, and team captain Chuck Shiver, also an end, received All-America honors, as well.

The 1927 season was the last year George "Kid" Woodruff served as head coach. Woodruff stepped down and was replaced by Henry Mehre, who would go on to a legendary coaching career at UGA.

Woodruff compiled a 30–16–1 record and a .649 winning percentage.

11 Vince Dooley

On November 22, 1963, the same day President John F. Kennedy was assassinated, the University of Georgia hired Joel Eaves as the new director of athletics. Eaves' first order of business was to hire a new head football coach. Johnny Griffith had resigned after three seasons—not one game over .500.

Eaves came to Georgia after a highly successful tenure as Auburn's head basketball coach. During his time on the Alabama plains, Eaves had crossed the path of Vince Dooley many times as a Tigers player and later as an assistant coach. Eaves and Dooley even scouted opponents together.

Although he was only 31 years old, Eaves offered the Georgia head coaching job to Dooley. The cries back in Athens were, "Vince who?"

Auburn head football coach Ralph "Shug" Jordan, who Dooley had played for in the early 1950s and later served as an assistant, knew Georgia had found a diamond in the rough. Jordan told the

Penn State head football coach Joe Paterno, left, talks with Georgia head coach Vince Dooley prior to the Sugar Bowl game on Saturday, January 1, 1983, at the Superdome in New Orleans. (AP Photo)

Associated Press, "He will be a great head coach. He has a keen mind and is a great competitor with a tremendous desire to excel."

The early 1960s was a low point in the Georgia football program. The program had fallen on hard times under Johnny Griffith's direction. Bulldogs followers were not pleased about losing to Georgia Tech three years in a row.

"There was great turmoil here. But I didn't care," Dooley said many years later to the *Athens Banner-Herald.* "I came in and went to work and put together a good staff. We all were very close to each other and stayed close and had to establish credibility, and the way you establish credibility is to win football games."

Dooley's first Georgia football team was beat up by Alabama 31–3 in the 1964 season opener. That Crimson Tide team went on to win the national championship.

The 1964 season turned out better. The Bulldogs went on to win six games, including victories over two of their three traditional rivals—Florida and Georgia Tech. Georgia finished the 1964 regular season 6–3–1, placed second in the SEC, and received an invitation to the Sun Bowl in El Paso, Texas, where the Bulldogs defeated the Texas Tech Red Raiders 7–0.

Credibility had been established.

Georgia opened 1965 against Alabama at Sanford Stadium and got a program-establishing win over the Crimson Tide thanks to a little trickery. With just more than two minutes left in the game and the Bulldogs down 17–10, quarterback Kirby Moore completed a pass to Pat Hodgson, who immediately lateraled to halfback Bob Taylor, who raced 73 yards for the touchdown.

Sports Illustrated reported in its September 27 issue that Taylor "moved so fast that no official was able to detect what a sequence camera later showed—Hodgson's knee on the ground while he had possession of the ball. The play should have been dead on the 35. Instead, Taylor raced untouched down the sideline for the touchdown."

Instead of going for the tie, Dooley went all-or-nothing and called for a two-point conversion. Moore completed to Hodgson again in the end zone, and Georgia recorded a shocking upset of the Crimson Tide of Alabama 18–17.

Dooley was quoted in the same *Sports Illustrated* article referring to the flea-flicker play, "Four years ago, [Georgia] Tech used it on us when I was at Auburn, and I thank them very much. We practiced it for two weeks, but I thought it would be 1980 before I'd have the nerve to call it in a game."

Dooley wouldn't need the flea flicker then. He had Herschel Walker.

Leading up to the 1980 season, Georgia, who closed the decade of the 1960s with two SEC Championships, was at a crossroads. After winning Dooley's third SEC Championship in 1976, the

Coach Dooley

During Vince Dooley's more than 40-year association with the University of Georgia, he was tempted to leave a few times. Following the 1965 season, Gomer Jones stepped down as head football coach at the University of Oklahoma but stayed on as athletic director. Vince Dooley was in Jones' crosshairs for the job, and Dooley seriously considered it.

Meanwhile, Georgia fans wanted coach Dooley to stay and let him know it by any means necessary.

Dooley told the *Athens Banner-Herald* years later, "When I went out there, I saw a pretty good situation, and they made an attractive offer. If it had not been for the outpouring of affection wanting me to stay, plus raising my salary a little bit, I might have gone."

Dooley stayed in Athens.

The next courting of Vince Dooley came from his alma mater, Auburn. During the 1980 season, Auburn let Doug Barfield go and went after Dooley, who was in the middle of a national championship season at Georgia. Alabama governor Fob James was a roommate of Dooley's when the two attended and played for Auburn, and he made the initial contact.

It looked like Dooley was on his way to Auburn after he confided with defensive coordinator Erk Russell that Auburn had made him an offer he couldn't refuse. That offer was head coach and athletic director.

Dooley explained his decision to stay at Georgia in Tony Barnhart's book, *What It Means To Be A Bulldog*, "Had that come earlier in my career, I would have been very tempted to take it. But by then, I had been at Georgia for 17 years. My family had grown up in Athens and knew nothing about Auburn. By then my roots were too deep, and my love for Georgia was too great."

Dooley stayed, but Auburn did get a Georgia man to lead the Tigers, Pat Dye.

Bulldogs dropped to 5–6 in 1977, Dooley's only losing season as head coach. A nice 9–2–1 rebound in 1978 was followed by a 6–5 campaign in 1979.

During the late 1970s, Dooley was building a talent base to make another SEC championship run. Signing Herschel Walker in 1980 made all the difference in the world.

Walker was a coveted running back out of Johnson County High School in Wrightsville, Georgia, where he rushed for more than 6,000 yards. Once he put on the Georgia uniform, Walker became the cornerstone to Georgia's special 1980 season.

The 1980 season found Georgia on top of the world. The Bulldogs won all of their games, earned their fourth SEC Championship, and defeated Notre Dame 17–10 to claim the undisputed national championship.

After the game, Dooley told *Sports Illustrated* in its January 12, 1981, issue, "I don't know how good we are, but I do know we're 12–0 and nobody else is."

The early 1980s was, record-wise, Dooley's finest moment as head coach. From 1980 to 1983, Georgia was 43–4–1, including three SEC championships and a national championship. Dooley coached for five more years and stepped down following the 1988 season to concentrate on his other duties at the university.

Joel Eaves retired as athletic director at the University of Georgia in 1979, and Dooley was appointed his successor. For nine years, Dooley wore both hats, but by 1988 he felt it was time to move on to athletic director full time. During his time as athletic director, Vince Dooley oversaw what has been called the golden age of Georgia athletics.

Millions of dollars had been raised to build and maintain state-of-the-art facilities at the University of Georgia. Because of the facility upgrades under Dooley's watch, the Georgia athletic program became one of the best across the board. In Dooley's 25 years as athletic director, Georgia won 18 national championships and 75 SEC titles, competing in 21 sports.

"Every school needs an athletic director like Vince Dooley," said former University of Arkansas athletic director and Georgia Tech alum Frank Broyles. "His expertise and his vision and his judgment are unsurpassed by anyone I've ever known."

Dooley's tenure as athletic director came to an end in 2004 following a highly publicized power struggle with University of Georgia president Michael Adams after which his contract was not renewed.

Dooley told the *Athens Banner-Herald*, "People ask me if I miss coaching and I say no because I did what I wanted to do and left when I wanted to. It's not true in this situation, but I'll not let the decision of one person I disagree with affect 40 wonderful years at Georgia. That's a regret, and it always will be, but it's not something that will affect me in any way. I'm not about that."

12 Larry Munson

Generations of young Georgia Bulldogs fans have dreamed of doing something great wearing the red and black with the voice of Larry Munson describing it.

That's how much Larry Munson is woven into the fabric of the Georgia sports culture. Like most southern announcers, Munson connected with the Bulldogs fans who listened to him on the radio and, like his peers, Munson was a homer. While describing the game on the radio, Munson lived, died, and sweated out close games each Saturday like every Bulldogs fan.

Broadcasting was in Munson's blood, and after stops in Cheyenne, Wyoming, and Oklahoma City, Oklahoma, Munson was on his way to Nashville, Tennessee, to announce minor league baseball. That job evolved into calling Vanderbilt games for several years.

When the Milwaukee Braves moved to Atlanta for the 1966 season, Munson was hired along with Milo Hamilton to become the new broadcast team. Later that year, Munson recognized another opportunity.

Munson told Dan Magill in 2007 in an article published by the *Athens Banner-Herald*, "Early in 1966 I read that Ed Thilenius [Georgia announcer prior to Munson] had given up his job doing the Georgia football games. So I immediately phoned [Joel] Eaves [Georgia athletic director], whom I had known when he was Auburn's basketball coach. His teams played Vandy twice a year. He gave me the job."

In those early years, Munson was not a homer, and he wasn't popular with the fans. Munson still lived in Nashville and commuted to Athens on Friday, then drove home late Saturday.

"He met more State Troopers than Georgia fans," longtime radio sidekick Loran Smith said.

By the mid-1970s, the connection between Munson and the Georgia fans was still distant. That changed on an autumn afternoon in Knoxville, Tennessee, in 1973. Munson had rarely witnessed a win in Knoxville by one of his teams. On November 3, 1973, the Bulldogs took on the then No. 11 Vols at Neyland Stadium and although Georgia was 3–3–1 and the Vols were 6–1 heading into the game, the Bulldogs kept the game close.

Late in the fourth quarter with Georgia down 31–28, the Bulldogs were on the Volunteer 8-yard line when quarterback Andy Johnson and reserve tailback "Glidin'" Glynn Harrison failed to make the handoff exchange. The ball bounced perfectly off the Astroturf into the hands of Johnson, who ran around the left end and into the end zone for the touchdown. Georgia had a 35–31 lead and went on to win.

Munson told the radio audience at the end of the play, "My God! Georgia beat Tennessee in Knoxville. Georgia's defeated Tennessee 35 to 31 in Neyland Stadium!"

Larry Munson's passion for the Bulldogs finally connected with the Georgia fans.

Larry Munson, the Georgia football team's legendary radio announcer on October 2, 2004, during a broadcast from Athens, Georgia. (AP Images)

When Larry Munson debuted as the voice of the Georgia Bulldogs on September 17, 1966, Georgia was at the beginning of Vince Dooley's highly successful run as head coach. That first year with Munson behind the microphone, Georgia went 10–1 and won the SEC Championship. Munson witnessed five more championships during the Dooley era and eight overall.

Munson's career also benefited from two sources—the keen marketing savvy of Dan McGill and WSB radio.

McGill and Billy Joe Brown took the tape of the game broadcast and edited highlights onto a cassette tape to sell to the public. Georgia fans bought those cassettes and enjoyed reliving Bulldogs moments through Munson's voice.

WSB radio began to capitalize on Larry Munson's growing popularity among Bulldog fans and promoted his radio calls, as well. WSB's strong AM signal carried Munson's voice well beyond the Georgia state borders.

In the end, Larry Munson was a one-of-a-kind broadcaster who developed a sense for the dramatic while calling the Georgia games on the radio. You would be hard pressed to find another sports announcer, college or professional, that has as many signature calls as Larry Munson.

"Announcers become part of the fabric," Loran Smith said. "Larry Munson was the ultimate in connecting to his audience."

13 Mark Richt

To the current generation of Georgia Bulldogs fans, Coach Mark Richt could do no wrong...at least up until the 2009 season.

To say that it would be worth the time of every Bulldogs fan to meet Coach Richt would be a gross understatement. The reason for that? He is widely considered to be one of truly good people both in college football and in life.

The funny thing is that Richt wasn't even recommended for the job by his former boss, Bobby Bowden. Said Coach Bowden, "Mark may just be too nice to be a good head coach."

That nice guy has brought Georgia back into the national spotlight and helped place the team among the most highly regarded programs in Division 1/FBS Football.

His accomplishments include 90 wins, two SEC championships, six 10-win seasons including four straight 10-win seasons, and two Sugar Bowl victories. And he was named SEC Coach of the Year twice.

It's not just all on-the-field with Coach Richt. He's very active within the Athens community and lends his name to a lot of Athens-area charities. Two seasons ago, he helped sponsor a bowling league for the general students at the university. He had the students pair up with some of his players to help build camaraderie.

He's also known for doing relief work in poor countries. He and his family have made several trips to Honduras to help rebuild some of the poor communities in the Central American nation. Richt requires his players to give a significant amount of time to charities in the Athens and Atlanta area. One of them is Camp Twin-Lakes, a camp for underprivileged kids.

Richt, who was born in Boca Raton, Florida, was a college quarterback at the University of Miami. Most of his early coaching experience came at Florida State with the exception of a brief stay at East Carolina in 1989.

Georgia head coach Mark Richt watches from the sidelines as the Bulldogs play Vanderbilt in Nashville, Tennessee, on Saturday, October 17, 2009.
(AP Photo/Mark Humphrey)

Little-Known Mark Richt Information

Born: Omaha, Nebraska
High School: Boca Raton H.S.
College: Miami
Backed Up in College: Hall of Fame QB Jim Kelly
Other QB's Backed Up: Vinnie Testaverde, Bernie Kosar
First Coaching Job: Volunteer assistant at Florida State
First Coordinator Job: Offensive coordinator at East Carolina
Heisman Trophy Winners Coached: Charlie Ward and Chris Weinke
Famous Relatives: Brother-in-law of former NFL QB Brad Johnson
Movie Appearances: *Facing the Giants* (as himself)
Favorite Lunch Item After a Win: Scalloped potatoes

To get a chance to speak with the coach (or to listen to him speak at an event) is something that all Georgia fans should do. It is for most, a humbling experience and for many a motivational one. It's easy to say that the Bulldog Nation's love affair with the coach continues.

Whether the Bulldogs win or not, they will be able to take comfort in the fact that they have a coach the players, the administrators, the fans, and the media all love.

14 Uga, the Damn Fine Dawg

The face of the Georgia Bulldogs is broad, wrinkly, white, and sometimes has drops of slobber hanging from his mouth. However, Uga always looks dapper in his red sweater and spiked collar.

Since 1956, a lineage of pure English Bulldogs owned by Frank W. "Sonny" Seiler of Savannah, Georgia, has served as the mascot of the Georgia Bulldogs.

Before Uga came along, several other mascots represented Georgia. The first in 1892 was actually a goat. It appeared for the first-ever meeting against Auburn. The goat wore a black coat with red U.G. letters on each side.

Two years later, a female bull terrier named Trilby, named after a novel by George Du Maurier and owned by a student, Charles H. Black Sr., won the hearts of the Georgia football team. Legend has it Trilby and her 13 puppies would go on their own to football practice, darting through the player's legs and barking. The players adopted Trilby as their mascot with one claiming she brought the team a name, "Bulldogs." Trilby and her 13 pups would show up at the games with the players dressing them up in red and black ribbons.

It wasn't until 1946 when the English Bulldog became Georgia's mascot. From 1944–46, Mr. Angel, owned by Eastman, Georgia, physician Warren Coleman, started it all. He was followed by Butch in 1947, owned by Mabry Smith of Warner Robins, Georgia. Mike came along in 1951, owned by C.L. Fain, and served as Georgia's mascot for five seasons.

In 1956, the Seiler lineage began and all bore the name Uga—derived from the abbreviation for the University of Georgia. Uga I, named Hood's Ole Dan, began the line. During Uga I's tenure, the Bulldogs went to a pair of bowl games, the 1960 Orange Bowl and the 1964 Sun Bowl, and earned one SEC championship while compiling a 53–48–6 record.

Uga I was succeeded by his son, Uga II, officially named Ole Dan's Uga. During a pregame ceremony at Homecoming 1966, Uga II's reign officially began when the student body shouted, "Damn Good Dawg," which was picked up by the entire stadium.

Any father, dog or human, wants his son to surpass his achievements, and this dog did just that. Uga II witnessed five bowl games plus two SEC championships. Uga II's record of 42–16–3 is arguably the best among the lineage.

Uga II retired during the 1972 season, and Uga III, officially named Seiler's Uga Three, took over. Uga III had his paw prints on six bowl games, a pair of SEC championships in 1976 and 1980, and a consensus national championship in 1980, becoming the most decorated dog in the lineage. After the season opener in 1981, Uga III retired with a record of 71–32–2. He passed away a few weeks later.

Next came Uga IV in 1981, and he lived a colorful life. Uga IV became the first mascot invited to the Downtown Athletic Club in New York City, and he attended the Heisman Trophy presentation when Herschel Walker received the honor in 1982. This dog lived the high life, adding a collar and black tie to his jersey "G" ensemble for the occasion. He was even an invited guest to the Heisman Trophy banquet and was escorted by the president of the Downtown Athletic Club.

Uga IV became the first of the line to miss games due to injury. Before the Vanderbilt game in 1986, Uga IV jumped off a hotel bed and ended up damaging ligaments in his left hind knee. This caused him to miss four games during the season. Uga IV's older brother, Otto, stepped out of the dog house and went 3–1 the rest of the way.

After Georgia won its first two games, the fans chanted "Two and 0 with Otto!"

Head coach Vince Dooley loved Otto's commitment off the bench. "I have always had a great affection for those who came off the bench and performed, and he did that and had a great time." Coach Dooley truly enjoyed his team's depth at "dog."

Uga IV worked for three more seasons, compiling an impressive 77–24–4 record, including nine trips to bowl games—the most in the lineage.

In 1991, Vince Dooley declared Uga IV "Dog of the Decade" for his tremendous service in the 1980s and was posthumously awarded a varsity letter, the highest honor for mascots at the University of Georgia.

Uga VII, the English bulldog mascot for the University of Georgia football team, surveys the sidelines prior to the game against Arizona State on Saturday, September 20, 2008, in Tempe, Arizona. The Bulldogs defeated the Sun Devils 27–10.
(AP Photo/Ross D. Franklin)

Uga V is widely thought of as the most famous dawg. He gained national attention when he lunged at Auburn receiver Robert Baker during a game in 1996. The next year, Uga V appeared on the cover of *Sports Illustrated*, which declared him the "best mascot in college sports." Later that year, Uga V hit the silver screen, appearing in the movie *Midnight in the Garden of Good and Evil*, which was filmed in his hometown of Savannah, Georgia.

During his term, Uga V compiled a nice record of 65–39–1 and oversaw national championships in women's swimming and diving, women's gymnastics, men's tennis, and men's golf.

Uga VI was only a year old when he was anointed successor in 1999, but he became the winningest mascot in the lineage. Uga VI was 87–27 during his reign and witnessed three SEC Eastern Division titles and two SEC championships.

By the way, Uga VI was one big dawg, literally. At 65 pounds, Uga VI is the biggest dog in the lineage. The 2007 season was Uga VI's last, and on New Year's Day 2008, Uga VI went out in style with the Bulldogs crushing Hawaii 41–10 in the Allstate Sugar Bowl to finish No. 2 in the final AP poll.

Before Georgia opened the 2008 season against Georgia Southern, Uga VII was introduced. Sadly, Uga VII's tour of duty was a short one. He died unexpectedly on November 19, 2009, just days before the Bulldogs were to play their last game of the season at Samford Stadium against Kentucky—a game Georgia lost.

Uga VII passed away from a heart attack, which is not uncommon in the bulldog breed. While they look like they are built like a tank, the breed is medically delicate. Heart and lung problems are common within the breed. Uga VII's abbreviated tour ended with a 16–7 record.

After mourning the death of Uga VII, Georgia Tech was next on the schedule. Uga VII's 5½-year-old half brother, Russ, filled in successfully. While Georgia Tech was considered the superior team, the Bulldogs ran over the Yellow Jackets 30–24 with Russ on the sidelines.

15 The Bulldog Name

So how were they named the Bulldogs, anyway? All true sons and daughters of the South may have to cover their eyes and ears for this one. It may have come from a Northerner and, worse yet, a Yale guy.

The University of Georgia's founder and first president, Abraham Baldwin, was a Yaley, and the mascot at Yale University is a white English bulldog. Baldwin even modeled the UGA campus after Yale's for its official opening in 1801 after its initial 16-year planning phase.

But most attribution for the nickname Bulldogs and an association with the University of Georgia starts in November 1920. Morgan Blake of the *Atlanta Journal-Constitution* newspaper thought that the "Georgia Bulldogs" would "sound good because there is a certain dignity about a bulldog, as well as ferocity." Three days later, after a scoreless tie played against the University of Virginia, *Atlanta Journal-Constitution* writer Cliff Wheatley used the term a handful of times in an article, and the nickname has stayed Georgia Bulldogs ever since.

Hey, it could have gone two other directions. Georgia was simply known as the "Red and Black"—the traditional colors, and there is also a story that a goat was prevalent in the early days of the program as a frequent spectator from the sidelines. But thankfully, no one has pictures or proof.

So Bulldogs will just have to do. Could you imagine the Georgia "G" standing for "Goats?"

16 The Dog Walk

College football is all about tradition. Going to see a game in Athens at the University of Georgia is one of the more tradition-laden things that any college football fan, but especially Georgia Bulldog fans, could ever do.

The "Dog Walk" itself is a Georgia tradition that was revived in 2001. There is some debate as to when and how it actually started. Since Coach Mark Richt arrived, however, the walk has been what truly starts the countdown to every kickoff.

The walk itself is fairly simple, though very crowded. Part of that is due to the 100,000 or so Georgia football fans there for the game, and in some cases, just there to soak in the atmosphere. The other part is that the team traditionally enters between the Tate Student Union Center and a parking lot. There isn't a whole lot of room between the two.

If you go, you'll want to get there early. The tailgating in Athens usually starts early, regardless of the kickoff time. Since the Dog Walk starts about 90 minutes to two hours before kickoff, you will want to be in place with at least 30 minutes or more of lead time so that you can get the best viewing position.

The team makes the short bus trip from the Butts-Mehre Athletic Heritage Hall down Lumpkin Street to the side of the Tate Center facing the road. You'll know when the team arrives because you will hear the Georgia Marching Redcoat Band crank it up and begin the march toward Sanford Stadium.

The buses will then empty, and out will come the head coach with Uga the Bulldog mascot right behind him. They will follow the band and lead the team through the crowd.

Know this—you won't get an autograph, nor will you be able to have much conversation with the players. If you are lucky enough to get to the front of the line, you might get a high five, but that will be about it. The walk will be crowded—very crowded— and will last for five to ten minutes.

Here is our suggestion:

Wait on the bridge between the student center parking lot and the football stadium. You will also need to get there early, but there will be more room for you to stand. The biggest thing you will notice is the scope of it all. You will be above the crowd, but you will see the immense amount of fans lining up and creating the small, narrow pathway that the Bulldogs will traverse as they make their way to the game. You won't get to be up close and personal with the players, but you will get to see everything.

It's an experience that is part of the game-day atmosphere. It's a tradition, like many others. There are a lot of schools that do similar things, and for each school it is a special, defining moment in the entire game-day experience.

Standing outside in Athens on a cool, clear, and crisp fall afternoon and taking in the pageantry, history, and tradition of it all is well worth the time and effort. Once you do it, you truly will never forget this unique experience.

17 Georgia–Georgia Tech

The game against the North Avenue Slide-Rule Jockeys—otherwise known as Georgia Tech—nothing stirs the passions of a Georgia fan like facing their in-state rival. It doesn't matter if it's on the football field or in a corporate board room, the Bulldogs want to best the Yellow Jackets.

Georgia competes against Georgia Tech for just about everything. It's on the field. It's recruiting student athletes. It's attracting potential students, state funding, and academic recognition in the State of Georgia and nationally. And that's just the beginning.

The Georgia–Georgia Tech rivalry has the elements of most rivalries involving in-state institutions. Jealousy is the most basic element.

You have the big-city engineering research university (Georgia Tech) against the liberal arts institution located in the boonies (Georgia). Insults between the two are plentiful. Bulldog fans like to refer to Georgia Tech as the "North Avenue Trade School" (Georgia Tech is located on North Avenue in Mid-Town Atlanta). Since Georgia Tech is an engineering school, UGA fans have no problem calling Tech students "nerds," "dorks," and "Techies."

Teams with a History

The University of Georgia suspended its football program in 1917 and 1918 as many able-bodied male UGA students went on to fight in World War I. Georgia Tech continued to field a football team during the war, and this became a bone of contention between the two in-state institutions.

It came to a head in 1919 when Georgia reinstated the Bulldogs football team. The Georgia student body staged what they called their Annual Senior Parade that coincided with the rebirth of Bulldogs football. The parade featured UGA students pulling a plywood replica of a World War I tank with a big banner on the turret that read "1917 Georgia in France 1918" with the intention of celebrating the University of Georgia's involvement in World War I.

Just behind that plywood tank was a Model A Ford carrying a banner that read "Tech In Atlanta 1917-1918". It was meant as an insult to Georgia Tech students who were living it up in Atlanta while Georgia students were fighting in the European theater in World War I.

The following Monday, Georgia Tech athletic director Dr. J.B. Crenshaw demanded a public apology from the Georgia senior class or athletic relations between the two schools would be severed forever.

Georgia didn't respond with an apology.

The *Atlanta Journal-Constitution* reported, "If the boys can't agree to conduct their sports in a friendly manner—more than that, in a sportsmanlike manner—then it is time to sever athletic relations and for the two schools to look elsewhere for rivals on the gridiron, the field, and diamond."

A.M. Thornton, president of the University of Georgia senior class, wrote in the *Atlanta Journal-Constitution* in 1919, "Day by day we have been taunted by Tech students and supporters because we did not play football in 1917. They said we showed a 'yellow streak' by not having our team play them. While the war raged, the Golden Tornadoes ran wild over its opponents in Atlanta, Georgia was up to ridicule because its athletic authorities refused to permit football to be played. The senior who carried the offending banner in the parade has a brother at Tech and only a wide stretch of the imagination can enable Tech to be angry at a prank that was purely boyish."

With Georgia not coming forth with an apology, the two schools went six years without playing each other on the football field. In 1925, Georgia and Georgia Tech renewed the series in front of 35,000 fans at Grant Field, then the largest crowd to watch an athletic event south of the Mason-Dixon Line. Georgia Tech won that game 3–0.

Some even claim Georgia Tech students sleep in Star Trek pajamas.

While Georgia competes against Georgia Tech in other sports, the football game defines their rivalry. Georgia first battled Georgia Tech in 1893 in Athens and lost 28–6. Bulldogs fans were so disgruntled over the loss they reportedly threw stones and whatever else they could get their hands on at the Georgia Tech players and chased them back to their waiting train.

Clean old fashioned hatred had begun.

From that initial meeting, Georgia has dominated the series except from 1949–56 when Georgia Tech won eight straight over the Bulldogs, and the period was known as "The Drought" in Athens. Since then, Georgia is 38–15 against Georgia Tech. That includes a pair of seven-game winning streaks in 1991–97 and 2001–07.

18 Frank Sinkwich

Frank Sinkwich became a Georgia Bulldogs legend. But if it wasn't for a chance stop at an Ohio gas station, history might have been different. Back in the summer of 1939, backfield coach Bill Hartman was on a recruiting trip in Ohio that didn't go well—at least not initially.

Hartman made the long trip by car from Athens to Youngstown, Ohio, to recruit a running back the coaching staff thought was the best back in Ohio. When Hartman arrived, he was too late. That particular back was Ohio State bound.

On the way back into town, Hartman stopped at a gas station to fill up and struck up a conversation with the attendant, who informed Hartman that the best back in Ohio lived a few blocks down the road.

It was Frank Sinkwich.

Sinkwich was a star athlete at Chaney High School in Youngstown where he played running back on the football team. Hartman got some boys together to see Sinkwich for himself and discovered a diamond in the rough. The Georgia coaching staff knew that Sinkwich could be a special player, and was determined to convince him to attend the University of Georgia and play for the Bulldogs.

All Sinkwich asked was that his friend from Ohio, George Poschner, receive a scholarship, as well. It was a done deal.

When Sinkwich suited up for Georgia's freshman football team—known as the Bullpups—he became an instant star. Sinkwich and the rest of the Georgia freshman scored at will and became known as the Point-a-Minute Bullpups. But Sinkwich was clearly the star of the group. After an unbeaten freshman season, Sinkwich moved to the varsity team.

Sinkwich started slowly as a sophomore. Head coach Wally Butts decided to go with experience for the season opener against Oglethorpe University. Sinkwich only carried the ball one time for 15 yards as a second teamer.

The next week against South Carolina, Sinkwich ran for two long touchdowns and threw for another. It was becoming apparent that Butts needed to put Sinkwich in the starting lineup. After strong performances against Columbia and Kentucky, Sinkwich

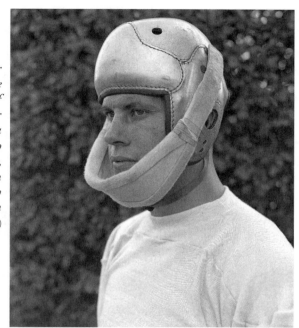

Frank Sinkwich, star left halfback of the University of Georgia, on October 24, 1941, wore a special brace to protect his jaw, which was broken in a game with North Carolina earlier in the season. (AP Photo)

was finally inserted into the Bulldogs starting lineup that November against Auburn where he threw a touchdown pass in the game.

Sinkwich ended his sophomore season of 1940 with a great game against arch-rival Georgia Tech. A couple of days before the game, Sinkwich was laid up in his dorm room with a high fever, but against the Yellow Jackets he showed no effects of the illness. Sinkwich ran for 128 yards on 28 carries and threw for a pair of touchdowns as the Bulldogs defeated the Jackets 21–19. Until then, Georgia's last win over Georgia Tech was back in 1936. UGA won the next week over Miami, and the Bulldogs ended the 1940 season 5–4–1.

Much was expected from Sinkwich for the 1941 season, and those expectations were met—but not without some hardship. In Georgia's second game of the year against South Carolina,

Sinkwich ran into Gamecock end Steve Novak, who gave the Georgia back a hard lick to the jaw. Late in the game, as Sinkwich ran out of bounds, he took a late hit to the jaw again. When asked about it years later, Sinkwich thought the second hit was from Novak as well, and that hit out of bounds knocked him out of the game.

But Sinkwich didn't miss any games.

Team dentist Dr. Jerry Allen wired his jaw shut, and for Georgia's next game against Ole Miss, a local machinist made a metal chin strap for protection. Sinkwich ran for 98 yards and threw a touchdown as the Bulldogs and Rebels ended in a 14–14 tie.

For the next game against Columbia, Sinkwich received a special helmet with a large jaw protector attached. Sinkwich wore this helmet for the remainder of the 1941 season.

Frank Sinkwich enjoyed a record-breaking year in 1941, gaining 1,103 yards rushing to set the SEC record. He also set the NCAA total offense record with 2,187 yards. Sinkwich led the Bulldogs to an 8–1–1 record and UGA's first postseason bowl game.

On New Year's Day 1942, Sinkwich and the Georgia Bulldogs were in Miami to face Texas Christian University in the Orange Bowl. In that game, he put on a show. In front of 35,786 fans (an attendance record at the time), Sinkwich went 9-for-13 passing for 243 yards and three touchdowns and added another score with a 43-yard touchdown run in the third quarter. When the day was done, Sinkwich accounted for 382 yards of total offense with four touchdowns as the Bulldogs routed TCU, 40–26. That performance is considered one of the best in bowl history.

In 1941, Frank Sinkwich earned All-America honors and finished fourth in the Heisman Trophy voting. Due to his Orange Bowl performance, Sinkwich was noticed outside the Southeast. That would bode well for the 1942 season.

Although Sinkwich shared the offensive load with his understudy, Charley Trippi, his senior season was another great year. Georgia went on to a 10–1 season, and with a 34–0 victory over arch rival Georgia Tech to close the season, the team received a bid to the Rose Bowl to take on UCLA.

Sinkwich played his final game as a Bulldog with a pair of sprained ankles and scored the only touchdown of the game as Georgia defeated UCLA 9–0 to finish 11–1 and win the program's first national championship.

For the 1942 season, Frank Sinkwich rushed for only 795 yards but passed for 1,392 yards and accounted for 24 total touchdowns. Once again, Sinkwich earned All-America honors, but most important to Bulldog fans, he won the Heisman Trophy by unanimous vote and became the first Southern football player to receive the award.

Sinkwich's No. 21 jersey was retired following that season. He was the first Georgia Bulldog so honored.

Frank Sinkwich had a brief but outstanding professional football career with the Detroit Lions, who made him the first pick in the 1943 NFL Draft. Sinkwich was named All-Pro as a rookie in 1943, and in 1944 he was named the NFL's MVP. But his playing career ended there.

Sinkwich returned to Athens in the late 1940s where he became a beer distributor, and that success enabled him to become a major supporter of the Georgia Bulldogs. Sinkwich and his former coach, Bill Hartman, chaired the committed to raise funds for the construction of Butts-Mehre Heritage Hall, which was completed in 1987.

Frank Sinkwich died of cancer on October 22, 1990.

19 Charley Trippi

There are those who swear that Charley Trippi was the greatest all-around athlete to play for the University of Georgia. Trippi was an All-American baseball player with the Bulldogs, but it was football were he became a star.

Charles Louis Trippi grew up in Western Pennsylvania, the son of a coal miner. At Pittston High School, Trippi weighed only 160 pounds, but his athletic ability caught the eye of Harold "War Eagle" Ketron. Ketron ran the Coca-Cola bottling plants in Western Pennsylvania, but he had played for the Bulldogs in the early 1900s and scouted area prospects for his alma mater.

In the 1930s, boosters could offer scholarships—and that's exactly what "War Eagle" Ketron offered to Trippi. The 19-year-old accepted.

After completing a year of prep school, Trippi traveled south to Athens in 1941 where he played for the Bullpups—UGA's freshman team. That year the Bullpups went undefeated, and Trippi was the star of the youngsters.

The next year, Trippi joined the Bulldog varsity and shared the backfield with Frank Sinkwich, who was coming off an All-American season. It was midway through the 1942 season that Georgia head coach Wally Butts decided to put Trippi in as the halfback and switch Sinkwich to fullback. Trippi gained 1,239 yards of total offense, while Sinkwich turned in a Heisman Trophy Award–winning season.

The Bulldogs of 1942 went 11–1 and defeated UCLA in the Rose Bowl. Trippi was a huge factor in that game, rushing for 130 yards. That earned him Rose Bowl Most Valuable Player honors. Georgia won the program's first national championship that year.

World War II raged on, and the call to arms interrupted Trippi's college career. Trippi served in the Third Air Force and stayed in football shape playing service football. He missed the 1943, 1944, and part of the 1945 seasons.

By the time Trippi returned to Georgia midway through the 1945 season, head coach Wally Butts had changed the Bulldogs offense. Butts switched from the single wing to a T formation. The new offense gave Trippi the opportunity to throw the ball.

In the 1945 season finale against arch rival Georgia Tech, Trippi showed off his passing skills, throwing for 323 yards against the Yellow Jackets and set the SEC record for passing yards in a single game. Trippi also ran for 61 yards, which when added to his passing yardage, became an SEC record of 384 yards of total offense in a single game.

Trippi and the Bulldogs would go to the Oil Bowl in Houston, Texas, where he threw a touchdown pass and ran a punt back 68 yards for a score. That punt return is considered by many Bulldogs fans to be one of the most spectacular plays in UGA history.

Charley Trippi of the University of Georgia posed for a photo on November 22, 1946.
(AP Photo)

By the time Trippi entered his senior season in 1946, he was known by the writers as the "One-Man Gang." As a captain of the '46 Bulldogs, he led Georgia to an undefeated season and an SEC Championship. Trippi also led the SEC in scoring with 84 points on 14 touchdowns, in rushing with 744 yards, and in passing with 622 yards.

Georgia capped off the 1946 season with a 20–10 win over North Carolina in the Sugar Bowl to complete the Bulldogs' first undefeated season.

That year Trippi won the Maxwell Award and Walter Camp Trophies, but the Heisman Trophy eluded him. Army's Glenn Davis won it, angering Bulldogs fans and head coach Wally Butts.

Back in those days, Southern football teams didn't get much exposure. With no national television, the newspaper was the dominant media of the time, and New York was the nation's media hub. Army, Navy, and Notre Dame got most of the ink, while Southern teams might only get a few inches of type.

Trippi could have played baseball in the majors if he thought to pursue it. He was an All-American shortstop for the Bulldogs in 1946, and he played professionally for the Atlanta Crackers in the Class AA Southern Association in 1947 where he hit .331. Before he reported to the Chicago Cardinals, who had drafted Trippi in 1945 and held his rights, Trippi decided to pursue football full time.

He was the center of a bidding war between the Cardinals and the New York Yankees of the All-American Football Conference. The Yankees thought they had him, but Charles Bidwill Sr. inked Trippi to a four-year deal worth $100,000. Trippi's presence completed Bidwill's Dream Backfield along with Paul Christman, Pat Harder, Marshall Goldberg, and Elmer Angsman.

Trippi went on to a brilliant nine-year career in the NFL (all with the Cardinals) where he won an NFL championship his rookie year in 1947. His ingenuity was on display in the title game where he wore basketball shoes for better traction. He scored touchdowns on a 44-yard run and a 75-yard punt return in the 28–21 win over the Philadelphia Eagles.

In 1968, Trippi was inducted into the Pro Football Hall of Fame, and to this day he is the only Hall of Famer with 1,000 yards receiving, 1,000 yards passing, and 1,000 yards rushing in a career. Trippi was also elected to the College Football Hall of Fame in 1959 and the Georgia Sports Hall of Fame in 1965.

You can also add Trippi's jersey No. 62 to the list of numbers that have been retired in Athens.

20 Herschel Flattens Bill Bates

You have heard of incoming freshman recalling their "Welcome to the SEC" moment.

At Neyland Stadium on the night of September 6, 1980, the SEC had its "Welcome Herschel Walker" moment. The highly touted freshman from Johnson County High School in Wrightsville, Georgia, entered the game against the Vols in the second quarter and immediately made a huge impact.

With Georgia down 15–2, Walker took the handoff from Buck Belue, ran right, cut back, broke some tackles, and jetted 16 yards for the Bulldogs' first touchdown of the game to cut the Georgia deficit to 15–9.

But that run is forever etched in the memory of every Bulldog fan who saw it. It was on that run the Herschel Walker literally ran over Tennessee linebacker Bill Bates.

Interesting Herschel Walker Tidbits

- Rushed for more than 100 yards in 28 of 33 games in College
- Was on the Georgia track team where he was a two-time All-American in the 400-meter relay and indoor 60-meter dash
- In 1982, held the world record in the outdoor 60-meter dash, 6.15 seconds
- Was on the cover of *Sports Illustrated* nine times
- Has a fifth-degree black belt in Tae Kwan Do
- Has performed with the Fort Worth Ballet
- Owns two food companies, Herschel's Famous 34 and H. Walker Foods
- Appeared in the 1991 movie *Necessary Roughness*
- Appeared in the 2009 season of the Celebrity Apprentice
- Twice appeared in the TV show *Pros vs. Joes*
- Appeared in the sports documentary *Damn Good Dog*
- Won TV's *Superstars* competition show two times, 1987 and 1988

All Walker did was lower his shoulder full speed into Bates' head gear, and the helmet-to-helmet collision sent Bates tumbling head over heels. Herscel never lost stride and gave Georgia Bulldog fans a glimpse of what was to come.

Here's how Georgia's legendary broadcaster Larry Munson described the play on the radio:

Tennessee leading 15–2, the crowd roaring against Georgia trying to make them drop it so they can't hear.

We hand it off to Herschel, there's a hole, 5, 10, 12,

He's running over people! Oh, you Herschel Walker!

My God almighty, he ran right through two men.

Herschel ran right over two men, they had him dead away inside the 9. Herschel Walker went 16 yards, he drove right over those orange shirts, just driving and running with those big thighs.

My God, a freshman!

Not only did that powerful and electrifying run spark the rally enabling Georgia to defeat Tennessee 16–15 (Herschel Walker also scored Georgia's other touchdown), but it catapulted Georgia to an undefeated season and a national championship.

It was the first "wow" moment in Herschel Walker's legendary Georgia career—one that was viewed many times on the new sports highlights show on cable TV, ESPN's SportsCenter, as well as local sports highlights shows across the country. Walker's bulldozing of Bill Bates made him a household name.

Bill Bates and Herschel Walker crossed paths again during their time in the NFL. When Walker joined the Dallas Cowboys after leaving the USFL in 1986, one of his teammates on the Cowboys was the Tennessee player who took the lick, Bill Bates.

21 Georgia—Auburn Rivalry: The Oldest Rivalry in the South

Georgia's rivalries with Georgia Tech and Florida stem from bitterness and contempt. The rivalry with Auburn has the feel of a family reunion.

Former Auburn head coach Pat Dye, who played for Georgia, summed up the rivalry as brotherly love. "When Auburn and Georgia play, it's like two brothers going at it in the backyard," Dye once said. "I love my brother, but I want to whip him."

Vince Dooley, who played and coached at Auburn, said, "I believe the Georgia-Auburn series is more like feudin' cousins than any other rivalries. There are many similarities among the Georgia and Auburn people."

Family bloodlines run thick between Georgia and Auburn. The football interconnections are many, with former Bulldogs like Will

Muschamp and Hugh Nall making their name in the coaching profession as coordinators at Auburn. Shug Jordan was an assistant at Georgia when Auburn hired him as head coach where he would become a legend. Remember, Vince Dooley had a chance to return as head coach of his alma mater in 1981 but chose to stay in Athens.

Georgia's rivalry with Auburn has been based on friendship from the beginning. Georgia's trainer Dr. Charles Herty and Dr. Georgia Petrie of Auburn were classmates at Johns Hopkins and came up with the idea for the two schools to compete on the football field.

When the deal was done there, was much anticipation for the contest. "Atlanta will be the scene Saturday of the first interstate intercollegiate football game," the *Atlanta Journal* reported on February 17, 1892.

Three days later in front of 2,000 fans at Piedmont Park in Atlanta, Auburn prevailed over the Bulldogs 10–0. The oldest rivalry in the Deep South was born.

Atlanta is one of many sites for the Auburn-Georgia rivalry. After playing the first 10 games in Atlanta, the game moved to Macon, Georgia, in 1904. After four years, the game moved to Montgomery, Alabama, in 1908. And after two years in Alabama's capital city and two Auburn victories, the game moved back into Georgia and was held in Savannah.

In 1912, the rivalry shuttled between Atlanta and Athens before finding a permanent neutral site in the west Georgia town of Columbus. From 1916 through 1958, with the exception of 1929 when the two teams played in Athens, the Tigers and the Bulldogs met at Memorial Stadium in Columbus. Georgia held a 21–16–2 advantage in 39 games played in Columbus.

The Auburn-Georgia game became a home-and-home series beginning in 1959 when the game moved to Athens for the first time in 30 years. The next season, Auburn hosted the rivalry for the first time ever.

Previously, Auburn's biggest SEC rivals, Tennessee, Georgia Tech, Alabama, and even Georgia, refused to travel to the Loveliest Village on the Plains. On November 12, 1960, Georgia's cleats marked the turf at Auburn for the first time. A fired-up Tigers team defeated Georgia 9–6.

Since the home-and-home began in 1959 a quirky trend emerged: the "road team advantage." Auburn owns an 18–11 advantage over Georgia in Athens, while the Bulldogs are 14–9–2 at Jordan–Hare Stadium.

When Terry Bowden was head coach at Auburn, his Tigers teams never defeated Georgia at home in two tries (0–1–1), but they never lost to the Bulldogs at Sanford Stadium (3–0). Against Georgia, head coach Tommy Tuberville had a better record (3–2) in Athens than he did at Auburn (2–3) during his Tigers tenure. Vince Dooley's legendary career as Georgia head coach produced much more success at Auburn (7–5–1) than in his home stadium in Athens (4–8).

Georgia and Auburn have played many memorable games over the years. In the Bulldogs' 1942 national championship season, Auburn prevented Georgia from an unbeaten season with a 27–13 win.

In 1959, facing fourth down on Auburn's 13-yard line late in the fourth quarter, Georgia quarterback Fran Tarkenton ignored head coach Wallace Butts' play call and literally diagrammed a play on the turf. It was a success as Bill Herron caught Tarkenton's pass. Georgia won 14–13 and captured the SEC championship.

The 1986 game at Auburn became known as "The Battle between the Hoses" after Georgia fans stormed the field of Jordan-Hare stadium after the Bulldogs upset the Tigers 20–16, pulled up the turf, and refused to go home. Auburn doused the Georgia victory party by turning on the water hoses.

One of the most famous pictures in college football history occurred in the 100th meeting between Auburn and Georgia in

1996 at Jordan-Hare Stadium. Bulldogs mascot Uga V lunged and snapped at Auburn wide receiver Robert Baker after he caught a first-quarter touchdown pass and ran toward Uga on the sidelines.

That game also made SEC history, being the first to go overtime when, with one second left, Georgia quarterback Mike Bobo found Corey Allen, who made an unbelievable jumping, twisting catch for a touchdown to tie the game at 28.

After four overtime periods, Georgia finally prevailed when Auburn quarterback Dameyune Craig was stopped on fourth-and-3 and Georgia won this thriller 56–49 in a game that became known as the "Miracle on the Plains."

The Bulldogs pulled off another Miracle on the Plains when, down 21–17 with 1:25 left in the 2002 game and facing a fourth-and-15 on the Auburn 19-yard line, David Greene threw up a prayer and Michael Johnson outjumped Auburn's Horace Willis and made an impossible catch to win the game and clinch the SEC championship for Georgia.

Close games define the Auburn-Georgia rivalry—only 56 points separate the two teams as of 113 meetings. Two things you can almost guarantee the next time the Auburn Tigers and Georgia Bulldogs meet on the football field—the game will be close, and the home team will lose.

22 Erk Russell and GATA

It's not often that a discussion about the legendary people, places, and things at a university that is chock full of history would include an assistant coach. Particularly if that assistant coach wasn't there for his entire career.

Erk Russell at Georgia Southern

- Hired in 1982 as first Georgia Southern head coach since 1942
- Won three national championships: 1985, 1986, and 1989
- Career Record as a Head Coach: 83–22–1
- Coached only 15–0 college football team of the 20th century
- 1989 Chevy-CBS 1-AA Coach of the Year
- Inducted Georgia Sports Hall of Fame: 1987
- Elected Alabama Sports Hall of Fame: 1991 (born there)
- Coached at Grady High School in Atlanta from 1950–57 (two-time high school Coach of the Year)
- Coached at Vanderbilt, Georgia, and Georgia Southern

That being said, no discussion of Georgia football would be complete without learning about the legend of Erk Russell. Russell, though he would go on to success as head coach at Georgia Southern University, will always be a Bulldogs legend from his time as the defensive coordinator. He gained fame as the leader of the "Junkyard Dawgs," a defense that, after a run of poor seasons, found an identity with the nickname and helped Georgia to the SEC title in 1975.

Russell, an Auburn graduate, was an assistant at his alma mater and at Vanderbilt before heading to Athens to be part of Vince Dooley's first staff in 1964—a job that he held for 16 straight seasons.

Erk was a master motivator who motivated players who were often undersized or out of position to play their hearts out and do things often unheard of in college football. In the 17 seasons Russell ran the Junkyard Dawgs, they recorded a remarkable 27 shutouts.

Perhaps the most enduring image of Erk Russell is that of the bald-headed coach who butted heads with his players. With the intensity that he brought to the game and the excitement of his players succeeding, Russell would often butt heads with his players. The crazy part was that the players had their helmets on.

Erk Russell on Wednesday, August 18, 2004, in Statesboro, Georgia.
(AP Photo/Stephen Morton)

The helmetless Erk didn't care. It was all about motivating to him. He prided himself on getting the most out of "his kids," and if that is what it took, he was okay with that.

College football is full of sayings and quotes that we all hear from time to time. One of football's most widely known acronyms, GATA, can be traced back to Coach Russell.

He came up with it after playing Georgia Tech one year and noticed that they had a "GTAA" logo plastered all over their clothing. In Tech's case, that stood for "Georgia Tech Athletic Association." Erk, however, took it upon himself to come up with a new combination of words for it. In what would be considered typical Erk, he decided that they would also use an acronym.

But when he attached words to it, it meant something a little different. "Get After Their Asses" was a phrase that he used, and over the years many others have used to motivate the players.

But it was Erk's love for the game and his ability to get the most out of his players that grew his legend. The Bulldogs won their second national title in 1980, and first since 1942, in large part because of a certain freshman running back—Herschel Walker—but also because of the Junkyard Dawgs defense.

The true measure of Erk's skill as a motivator and winner came after the 1980 season. He took a job starting the football program from scratch at Georgia Southern University in Statesboro. A mere three seasons after Georgia Southern played its first football game, it won the NCAA Division I-AA National Championship—one of three that Erk would win.

A great deal of the success was attributed to Erk and a motivational ploy he often used. Erk convinced his players that the water from a drainage creek near their practice field would help them win. He took the water in a milk jug to all of the Eagles' playoff games, poured some in the end zone, and his team would somehow find a way to win. He called it the magic of beautiful Eagle Creek.

Even after leaving the University of Georgia, he was always revered by the alumni, frequently making appearances and doing some motivational speaking. He will always be considered a part of the University's history.

Erk Russell passed away in 2006 at the age of 80. He was memorialized and remembered by the fans and the administration of both Georgia and Georgia Southern along with the Georgia State Legislature and football fans around the state.

Though he is no longer here to motivate and teach, it is well worth any Georgia fan's time to look up his story and enjoy. No discussion of UGA's football history would be complete without learning about the legendary Erk Russell.

23 The Drought Breaker— Theron Sapp

Theron Sapp became a Georgia legend not for his entire body of work, but for one play that restored Georgia pride and broke a long losing streak. Sapp forever etched his name among the Bulldogs greats on the frigid afternoon of November 30, 1957, at Grant Field in Atlanta.

The Bulldogs were about to end another losing season, Georgia's third in a row, and were taking on arch rival Georgia Tech, who had dominated the series. The Bulldogs hadn't defeated the hated Yellow Jackets since 1948. Georgia had not even scored a touchdown on Tech since 1953. The balance of football power in the state of Georgia had shifted to that technical school on North Avenue in midtown Atlanta.

No one in attendance knew on that cold November afternoon at Grant Field that a legend would be born.

Sapp was Georgia's best back. He led the Bulldogs in rushing in 1957 and again in 1958. Against Georgia Tech in 1957, Sapp was getting the majority of the carries. However, both teams were finding it difficult to move the ball in the sub-freezing temperatures.

The Bulldogs got a big break late in the third quarter, recovering a Tech fumble at midfield. Georgia drove the ball down the field thanks to the hard-nosed running of Theron Sapp, who carried the ball eight times as the Bulldogs marched to the Yellow Jackets' 1-yard line. Georgia faced fourth-and-goal. Sapp had carried the load during the drive, and in this critical moment, he had the chance to end Tech's streak.

Sapp took the handoff from quarterback Charley Britt, started right, then found a gap and literally fell into the end zone for the touchdown. The score broke the eight-game drought as Georgia defeated Georgia Tech 7–0. Bulldog pride was restored, and Sapp became known as "The Drought Breaker."

It even inspired an Atlanta lawyer named Harold M. Walker to pen a poem titled, "The Man Who Broke The Drought."

You can rave about your Sinkwich
And Trippi's praises sing.
While talk about the "Bowl Days"
Still makes the welkin ring.

But to all Bulldog supporters
In every precinct in the South
I propose a hearty toast
To the man who broke the drought.

Rise up you loyal Georgians
From Tybee Light to Rabun Gap.
Here's to the Macon Mauler
The mighty Theron Sapp.

I have seen some lovely paintings
In galleries of art,
Gorgeous sunsets on the water
Which stirred the inner heart.

But of all the wonderous visions
Ever seen by eyes of mine,
I'll take old number forty
Crashing through that Jacket line.

And so down through the ages
Whenever Bulldogs meet,
Whether in the peaceful countryside
Or on a crowded street.

The word will still be carried
By every loyal mouth—
Let's stand and drink another toast
To the man who broke the drought!

In 1958, Georgia endured another losing season but ended on a high note with the Bulldogs defeating Tech 16–3 in what was Theron Sapp's final collegiate game. Sapp only scored six touchdowns in his Georgia career, but the one he scored in 1957 that broke the drought with Georgia Tech was unforgettable.

Months later at the annual G-Day game that ends spring practice, Theron Sapp became the third Bulldog to have his jersey number retired. No. 40 forever belongs the man who broke the drought.

24 The Junkyard Dawgs

Following the 1974 season, the Georgia defense didn't feel very good about itself. The Bulldogs finished 6–6 with the defense giving up 20 or more points eight times. Always looking for a motivational edge, defensive coordinator Erk Russell found one from the chorus of "Bad, Bad Leroy Brown," by Jim Croce:

And it's bad, bad Leroy Brown
Baddest man in the whole damned town
Badder than old King Kong
Meaner than a junkyard dog.

The idea came for a conversation with a Georgia alum. "I was looking for a name for our defense," Erk Russell said. "A supporter said, 'Why don't you use Junkyard Dogs?' I didn't think it was original enough, but I couldn't think of anything better, so we went with it."

Not only did Erk Russell go with it, he promoted it. To this day, the Junkyard Dawgs label has been tagged with every Georgia defense.

In Tony Barnhart's book *What It Means To Be A Bulldog,* former Georgia defensive end Dicky Clark said, "Erk was trying to come up with a catchy name to describe what was a pretty scrawny defense. None of us were really big, I think Ronnie Swoopes [at 245 pounds] was the biggest guy we had, and the rest of us barely go to 200 pounds."

Former Georgia head coach Vince Dooley described the 1975 Georgia defense as a bunch of small, tough guys who really wanted to win. The Junkyard Dawgs of 1975 played inspired football, helping the Bulldogs go 9–3 on the year and finishing with an appearance in the Cotton Bowl.

The next year the Junkyard Dawgs were awesome. That defense had a nation's-best four shutouts and led the SEC in scoring defense by allowing 118 points.

The 1976 team won the SEC Championship and went to the Sugar Bowl where the Junkyard Dawgs faced Heisman Trophy winner Tony Dorsett and the Pittsburgh Panthers. The Junkyard Dawgs couldn't handle Dorsett, who ran for 202 yards and a touchdown in Pittsburgh's 27–3 victory.

But the history of the name and the moniker still ring true every year for those eleven defenders who try to keep the other team out of the end zone.

25 Buck Belue

Imagine if you played four years of football at a major university, won a national championship, played four years of college baseball, played three years of minor league baseball, and you are remembered for one thing.

Well, not really a thing, but rather a play. One play, one game, one moment in time—*the* play.

If you wanted to know who that person was, ask any Georgia football fan about "The Catch." The 93-yard touchdown pass to Lindsay Scott to win the Georgia-Florida game in 1980 was "The Play."

The pass was thrown by Valdosta's own Buck Belue. Benjamin Franklin "Buck" Belue was the prototypical small town, heroic quarterback and the star baseball player as a kid. After his success at Valdosta High School, he landed in Athens and his success continued.

"It was a dream come true for me to be part of the program and to wear the uniform," Belue said in an interview with the *Red and Black*. "I was a big Georgia fan."

Coach Dooley admitted in the *Red and Black* that Belue was part of a "triumvirate in the offense that provided incredible fire power" and led the Dogs to those 1980 and 1981 SEC championships. He was also the captain of the 1981 squad.

All in all, Belue was 27–3 as a starter in college. Not too shabby, and he never lost to Georgia Tech.

What many Georgia football fans forget is that Belue was just as successful in baseball. A two-time All-SEC player, he was a sixth-round draft pick by the Montreal Expos and played in their system for three years.

Belue gave pro football a try, playing quarterback for the USFL's Jacksonville Bulls during their final season. He spent some time after that as an assistant coach at Valdosta State University for a couple of years before turning the page and heading into a new career—broadcasting.

If you were in Savannah in the 1990s, you might have caught Buck as the sports director at WJCL-TV. He would go on from there to Atlanta where he became the co-host of the afternoon drive

Buck Belue (No. 8) of Georgia gets ready to pass as Pittsburgh's J.C. Pelusi (No. 52) moves in on him during first-half action of the Sugar Bowl on Friday, January 1, 1982, in New Orleans. (AP Photo)

radio show on sports talk station WCNN-AM. He's been at that gig for 10 years now and is still on every day. You'll still find Buck at most Georgia games. He does the color commentary for Comcast Sports Southeast's rebroadcast of the Georgia football games. He's also their color analyst for the baseball games.

However, despite all the things he has done since "The Play," that is the one thing forever embedded in the minds of Georgia football fans. Granted, the generations have changed and the legend of "The Play" still lives on, but despite that team going on to win college football's greatest prize, it is the one enduring image that sticks with folks.

Belue hitting Scott across the middle, Scott taking it to the house, and the Dogs win.

In 1990, Belue was in Belize on a business trip. As the story goes, while inside a restaurant, a man sitting next to him kept staring and finally said, "Are you Buck Belue? You are, aren't you? My gosh, I was there that day for Lindsay Scott. One of the happiest days of my life."

It finally hit Benjamin Franklin Belue how he had impacted people's lives over the last thirty years. "Man, I was in Belize. I started thinking, 'This thing is bigger than I even imagined.'"

That would be accurate...and also an understatement.

26 Lindsay Scott

The pride of Jesup, Georgia, and Wayne County High School, Lindsay Scott was a 6'1" receiver who anchored the University of Georgia's 440-meter relay team. He had been the team's leading receiver his freshman and sophomore years, catching a total of 70 balls for 996 yards and three touchdowns. Athleticism ran in the family with his older brother, Dennis, making his way to Virginia Tech.

Lindsay would also lead the Dogs his senior year with 42 catches, 728 yards, and six scores. A running back named Walker kept the on-campus receiving numbers low in the 1980 season. Amp Arnold led UGA with only 20 catches in that season with Buck Belue at quarterback.

Scott's junior year, 1980, had been the hardest on him as a Bulldog. His scholarship had been taken away from him that fall because of an on-campus discipline issue, and he wrecked his car that summer. He suffered a concussion in the wreck itself that almost sidelined him for the entire season. When he was late to a team meeting a month before the 1980 Florida-Georgia game, Coach Dooley demoted him to the second-string offense for two weeks.

"Losing that scholarship was the hardest thing I've ever had to deal with," Scott told *Sports Illustrated's* Joe Marshall that season. "I began to think I just wasn't Coach Dooley's kind of guy."

Regrettably, the coach was thinking the same thing, too.

Scott was Belue's roommate on the road. The night before the Florida game, the two were up late talking. "I told him, 'It's been a year since I've caught a touchdown pass,'" Scott recalled in an interview with the *Athens Banner-Herald*. "'Can you believe it?' I said. I didn't even know what it felt like to catch one anymore.

"When the opportunity finally presented itself, the key for me was I was ready," Scott said.

The "Left 76" became Scott's only touchdown catch of the season. "I will always be linked to that play, that year, and that football team," Scott said. "It's something I take pride in and something I'm proud of. It's not, if not the best, one of the best experiences I've ever had."

Georgians had voted that particular play (which we'll talk about in a minute) the greatest moment in state sports history in a *Sports*

Illustrated poll. "What makes it so special is I'm able to get with those guys and we're older now with kids and families and all that good stuff," Scott said, "but you can tell even today it was a unique group of people."

These days, after years of personal ups and downs, Lindsay Eugene Scott has hooked up with Belue and other Bulldogs to run clinics across the state of Georgia, helping young athletes hone their on-field skills.

Heading into the 2009 season, Scott was still in the top five for career receiving yards in Bulldogs history. Safe to say he knows a thing or two about pass catching and route running.

Oh, and about that one route in particular…

27 "Run Lindsay Run!"

It's perhaps the most famous play in Georgia Bulldog history. It's one play that changed the lives of those who were involved, and it paved the way for the Bulldogs' national championship run.

On November 8, 1980, the second-ranked Georgia Bulldogs faced the No. 20 Florida Gators at the Gator Bowl in Jacksonville, Florida. Georgia roared to a 20–10 lead in the fourth quarter thanks to Herschel Walker's 238 yards rushing and a touchdown.

Florida rallied in the fourth quarter led by freshman quarterback Wayne Peace. The Gators scored 11 unanswered points to take the lead late in the fourth quarter 21–20.

With 1:35 left in the game, Florida punter Mark Dickert pinned back Georgia, booting one out of bounds at the 8-yard line.

On Georgia's first play, quarterback Buck Belue had to scramble away from the hard-charging Florida defense, and he lost a yard.

The next play, on second-and-11, Belue's short pass to Charles Junior was incomplete.

On third down, Belue was chased out of the pocket again. Georgia fans had little hope for a miracle. The play called "Left 76" was designed to only pick up a first down. Wide receiver Charles Jones ran a deep post pattern but was covered. As Belue avoided the rush, he spotted the other receiver, Lindsay Scott, open and running a short curl pattern underneath the deep zone coverage.

For those who listened to Larry Munson on the radio, this is what you heard:

Florida in a stand-up five, they may or may not blitz. Belue third down on the 8, in trouble, he got a block behind him, going to throw on the run, complete on the 25 to the 30, Lindsay Scott 35, 40, Lindsay Scott 45, 50, 45, 40...Run Lindsay, 25, 20, 15, 10, Lindsay Scott! Lindsay Scott! Lindsay Scott!...Well, I can't believe it. 92 yards and Lindsay really got in a foot race. I broke my chair. I came right through a chair. A metal steel chair with about a 5-inch cushion, I broke it. The booth came apart. The stadium...well, the stadium fell down, now they do have to renovate this place...they'll have to rebuild it now. This is incredible. You know this game has always been called the World's Greatest Cocktail Party, do you know what's gonna happen here tonight, and up at St. Simons and Jeckylll Island, and all those places where all those Dawg people have got those condominiums for four days? Man, is there going to be some property destroyed tonight! 26–21, Dawgs on top. We were gone. I'd gave up, you did, too. We were out of it and gone. Miracle!

Munson's call of "Run Lindsay Run!" can be recited word for word by the most passionate Bulldogs fans.

Lindsay Scott's 93-yard catch, spin, and sprint to the end zone made him a Georgia legend. That play is forever known as "The

Play" because it kept the Bulldogs' undefeated season intact as well as its national championship hopes.

"Once I caught it and got outside, I thought I'd go all the way," Lindsay Scott said after the game.

"I think it's for the ages. We couldn't have won [the national title] without it," head coach Vince Dooley told the *Athens Banner-Herald* years later.

Following Georgia's 26–21 win over Florida, the Bulldogs received some help from their in-state rival Georgia Tech. The Yellow Jackets shocked top-ranked Notre Dame, tying the Fighting Irish 3–3. Georgia moved up to the No. 1 ranking, a position the Bulldogs would not relinquish the rest of the 1980 season.

28 Dan Magill: The All-American Flunkie

When Coach Dan Magill was 10 years old in 1931, he was a batboy for the Bulldogs baseball team. His legacy includes being sports information director, Bulldog Club secretary, and men's tennis coach. His tireless efforts toward the program he spent every year building, save his four in the Marines, total 85 of his 89 years.

Trying to condense 85 years into a few pages within these covers is almost unfair and borders on the impossible. There is much to learn about the man whose nameplate on seat No. 8 in the Sanford Stadium press box reads, "Dan Magill—Legend."

And that's no understatement—despite what he'll tell you to the contrary.

"He's never done anything for himself. That hasn't been his objective," said Loran Smith in a *Red and Black* article from 2007.

"I don't think anybody's ever loved Georgia more than Dan Magill," Smith said. "A lot of people claim to, and everybody's got a fan that they think is the greatest Georgia fan—well, I can tell you there might be some great ones out there, but can't anybody top Dan."

It's said that Magill was the first baby born in the old Athens General Hospital in January 1921. His grandfather was editor of the *Hartwell (GA) Sun* newspaper and his mother's father was the editor of the old *Athens Herald*. You could say that the gift of the word was in Coach Magill's bloodlines from the beginning.

He saw his first football game when he was eight years old. The UGA business manager, Charley Martin, snuck the young Magill into the game wearing his football uniform to see the 15–0 shutout over Yale. (The young Magill through he might get to play.) Eventually, he cut the Sanford Stadium grass with a push mower before working his way to batboy, foul-ball chaser, and grandstand cleaner-upper at Sanford Field during the early years of the Great Depression.

Magill received his diploma in journalism from UGA in 1942 and worked for the *Atlanta Journal* in the mid-to-late 1940s after his tour with the Corps. Coach Butts asked him to come back to campus on September 1, 1949.

"He wanted me to be assistant athletic director, to do that, help him," Magill remembered in an interview with the university's Fran Lane in 2006. "And I was looking forward to doing it. But the first week I was here, he lost his sports information director, and he said, 'I want you to fill in for the sports information director.' Well, I did fill in...for about thirty, forty years."

Losing to Georgia Tech didn't sit well with Magill or Coach Butts. It was Magill who told him that the school's strength is "in every county in the state." They had more alumni than Tech, so they set out to organize Bulldogs clubs in all 159 counties in Georgia.

The quest started in 1953. Magill would have a breakfast meeting in one county, a luncheon in a second, and dinner in a third. "We'd start every meeting, 'Fellow Georgia Bulldogs, Chosen People, Members of the Great Majority party of this Empire State of the South.'"

In 1955, Magill was named head coach of the tennis program. Albert Jones was a law school professor on campus since the tennis coaching job wasn't a paying position. He had been a star for the team in the 1930s. But when Jones was named the assistant to then-president Davison, he had to give up the job. Magill tried to bring in two other professors, but they didn't have the time to invest. The players asked Magill to do it, and the new coach thought it would be a good stress reliever. That stress reliever meant he was now spending 15 hours a day on campus two months out of the year.

Coach Magill said he'd coach the team "for a year." That year turned into 34 seasons. His career record was 706–183 with 13 SEC Championships in addition to eight indoor and two national titles for the Bulldogs.

His associations with Mary Ann and Kenny Rogers and Kim Basinger brought tennis to the forefront on campus, getting the Collegiate Tennis Hall of Fame to UGA and lights installed for the NCAA tournaments held in Athens.

A 1977 article by Kent Hannon in *Sports Illustrated* lets us in on a few other lesser-known facts about Coach Magill. He's the world's fastest two-finger typist at 148 words per minute (the title was self-proclaimed). He's a 10-time table tennis champion, who once had a point last an hour and fifty-eight minutes. He's the son of one of the first co-eds at UGA. And he's the husband of Rosemary Reynaud and father of Daniel Hamilton Magill III, Sharon Reynaud Magill, and Molly Harvey Magill.

He would wear his wife's Phi Beta Kappa key around his neck when he would coach on the road to pass on the illusion that he might be a scholar. And by the way, he can prove the almost-two-hour-point in table tennis.

He's seen Stegeman, Butts, and Dooley coach; Sinkwich and Trippi run; Herschel run over people; and all the bulldogs roam the sidelines in sweaters—even the one named Magillicuddy in his honor (Uga V, Uga IV's Magillicuddy II).

He serves as the curator of the Dan Magill ITA Collegiate Hall of Fame and personally gives tours of the complex. The University of Georgia has named the entire tennis complex after Magill in his honor. He still writes weekly columns for the *Athens Banner-Herald* newspaper and apparently provides each sports department staffer with a Claxton fruitcake at Christmas. He's looking forward to winning a tennis tournament in the 90-year-old age bracket, which he "knows is coming soon," as he said. And he's even received a commendation from the Garden Club of America.

That really is just the beginning of the story.

Coach Magill is, Bill Hartman admits, the "Funk" in the University of Georgia's Funk and Wagnalls Encyclopedia of knowledge and history that is held so dear by the campus.

Wagnalls is next.

29 Loran Smith

For years when Georgia Bulldogs football fans listening to their beloved team on the radio heard Larry Munson bark, "Loran, whaddyagot?" Loran Smith would have plenty to say.

Smith's role for Bulldog radio is to co-host the "Tailgate Show" and add sideline color to the broadcast. Whether it's an injury report or an observation from the sidelines, Smith will pepper his commentary with a good story or two.

Francis Tarkenton, left, star quarterback for the University of Georgia, receives the Associated Press All-America certificate from Loran Smith, sports editor of the Athens Banner-Herald, *on January 11, 1961.* (AP Photo)

Loran Smith has been many things to the University of Georgia—athlete, fund-raiser, broadcaster, author, and historian.

Smith was born and raised in Wrightsville, Georgia, where he excelled in football and track. He often refers to himself as "Wrightsville's Second-Most Famous Citizen" behind that Herschel fellow. Robert Preston Jr. of *In The Game Magazine* found out what Loran wanted most when he got to school—a varsity letter. "I loved that block 'G,' and I wanted one."

Loran initially pursued a degree in the College of Agriculture in etymology but gradually gravitated toward a journalism degree. He admitted to Preston that the main reason he left the etymology degree idea behind was "because it bugged me." Smith walked on to the track team and earned his letter as team captain in 1960. He went to law school after graduation, and when the law career didn't work out, he returned to campus after a stint with the Coast Guard.

Thus began Loran Smith's long association with the Georgia Bulldogs. Among the many hats Smith has worn with the University of Georgia are assistant sports information director, business manager of athletics, and executive director of the Georgia Bulldog Club—a job he started in 1964.

Smith's greatest contribution is sharing his vast knowledge of the university he loves. He is the historian of the Bulldogs. For years, Smith has written columns published by the *Athens Banner-Herald* and printed in other newspapers statewide that demonstrate his tremendous storytelling.

Newspaper columns aside, Smith has authored several books on Georgia's rich athletic history including *Glory, Glory* with Lewis Grizzard and *Dooley Dawgs* with Vince Dooley. In all, Smith has authored 10 books on his beloved Georgia Bulldogs and five on the Masters.

Smith came close to leaving a few times in his illustrious Bulldogs career. In 1970, he left to pursue a career in the real estate market in Atlanta. He returned the next year. Smith was also offered a job as athletic director for Florida State University in the 1970s but turned down that job, as well. That offer came in the days when the Seminoles were not the successful program they have been over the last two decades or so. The Dallas Cowboys also came knocking on Smith's door to gauge any interest, but it didn't happen there, either.

There are other interests in Loran's life—golf and aiding cancer survivors are among them. While he doesn't play golf anymore, he has made efforts to attend as many of golf's majors as he can during a calendar year.

Since Smith is a cancer survivor himself, he has made efforts to reach out to other survivors and those in need when it comes to the disease. The Athens Regional Medical Center has named its treatment facility in his honor—the Loran Smith Center for Cancer Support. Because it is endowed by the Athens Regional Foundation, all of the center's services are available at no cost to anyone who needs its focus to fight cancer.

Rest assured, Bulldogs fans, Loran has no desire to retire any time soon. He probably wouldn't know what to do with himself if he did. Having Coach Magill as a role model and friend will do that for any follower of the red and black.

30 Sonny Seiler

Before you try to track down the Seiler family, make sure that you know that the senior Seiler, Frank, has "Sonny" only as his proper name. Chances are that if you ask for Frank, nobody will know of whom you speak. Make sure that you ask for Sonny.

Sonny and his family play a huge, if not the most important, role in the marketing of Georgia football. They are responsible for the raising, rearing, and the naming of Uga. (Remember, the dog's name is pronounced "uh-guh," and the university is pronounced by the letters individually: U-G-A.)

Football notwithstanding, the single most identifiable icon— what most people see as the face of Georgia football—is none other than Sonny Seiler's dog.

If you see Uga at an event or at a football game, Sonny Seiler is not very far away. Sonny is an attorney by career and a rather successful attorney at that. He is a senior partner at the Bouhan, Williams and Levy Law Firm in Savannah, Georgia—one of the state's oldest and most successful firms. Sonny was the president of the State Bar of Georgia in 1973.

Sonny has also had some success, believe it or not, as a movie actor. He was prominently featured in the movie adaptation of the book *Midnight in the Garden of Good and Evil*. Because of his and his dog's role in the book, the producers decided it would be good to cast them in the movie. If you pay attention, you will see Seiler as Jim Williams' attorney in the film.

Seiler was able to parlay that role and his celebrity status in the Savannah area and, for that matter the state of Georgia, into another couple of flicks. Both *The Legend of Bagger Vance* and *The Gingerbread Man* were filmed in the Savannah area and again, if you look closely, you'll see Seiler in the films.

Uga, as we know him, got his start purely by chance when Sonny, a second year law student at the university, decided to take his white bulldog puppy to a game in 1956. At that game, then-sports information director Dan Magill first noticed Seiler and his dog. When Magill brought a picture to Coach Wally Butts, the two decided they had their mascot.

The Seilers have taken their bulldog (or relatives of that original bulldog) to every Georgia football game since then. They always travel with the team, and they get star treatment. The Seilers and Uga get their own escort and always lead the team off of the bus and either into the visiting stadium or the beginning of the Dog Walk. On the road and at home, they stay in their own suite.

Sonny takes the role of Uga's father very seriously. Along with attending all of the football games, they are very much in demand on the banquet and promotional circuit. It isn't unusual to see them show up at an alumni gathering anywhere around the state of Georgia. You can bet, if and when they do, a crowd will gather.

During the preseason when the team has its picture day, Uga and the Seilers are there, too. In fact, they get their own room, and the line for pictures with Uga winds around the door.

Sonny and the rest of the Seiler family take a lot of pride in being the mascot's caretakers. They are as easily identified as anyone associated with the football program would be. Be it Sonny, his son, or his daughter, one of the Seilers is always leading Uga along by the leash, and you can bet Uga is always leading the cheers.

31 Jacksonville

Since 1933 when the calendar reaches late October (or early November), it means one thing for Georgia fans—road trip to Jacksonville. It's the Georgia-Florida game.

Generations of Bulldogs backers have made the 342-mile trip for a weekend of partying and, oh-by-the-way, there's a football game to attend. Call it if you will a mid-season bowl game.

Georgia fans make a full weekend in Jacksonville, spending their discretionary dollars in the town's hotels, restaurants, and bars. With the city only 73 miles from the University of Florida campus, it's usually just a day trip for the Gator Nation.

The epicenter of the party is the Jacksonville Landing, a riverfront plaza near downtown that faces the St. John's River. The horseshoe-shaped facility is full of Georgia fans getting into the "spirit" of the event. It becomes the largest tailgate party in the nation.

During Georgia-Florida week, in the parking lot across the street from Jacksonville Memorial Stadium, life takes on something of a county fair atmosphere. It's unofficially known as "R.V. City" and can accommodate around 200 of the vehicles. The carnival atmosphere includes "Bulldog Boulevard" where Georgia fans park and party.

Jacksonville, Florida, can boast of having a National Football League franchise and a yearly college bowl game—the (whoever is sponsoring it this year) Gator Bowl—but the city's largest annual sporting event is the Georgia-Florida football game.

There has been talk recently of moving the Georgia-Florida game out of Jacksonville to Atlanta. However, traditions that are more than 70 years old are hard to break.

Generations of Bulldogs fans plan their vacations around the Georgia-Florida game. Families with deep Bulldogs roots have rented houses or condominiums for years at nearby St. Simons or Amelia Island. Golf and game hype are part of the fabric of life during the week leading up to the game.

Jacksonville receives a huge economic shot in the arm from the game. An estimated $25 million is added to the city's coffers each year. While moving the game to Atlanta would be closer for Georgia fans, a long-standing tradition would die.

Tradition is more important than money or miles.

32 The Uga Mausoleum

There are all kinds of nicknames given to football stadiums and the crowds that inhabit them. You have The Swamp, two different Death Valleys, Jungles, and a bunch of other nicknames to strike fear into visiting teams.

However, not a lot of stadiums can say they actually have a mausoleum in them or, more specifically, a mausoleum on the field level. The University of Georgia actually has a mausoleum inside Sanford Stadium. Take a look in the left side of the Northeast corner of the stadium if you are sitting on the press-box side of the field. It's there in the corner.

It's the wall where the press box stands run into the stands that front the street.

Who is in this mausoleum? Why is it there? It is a tribute to Uga the bulldog—the university's beloved mascot and the school's own way of acknowledging his contributions to both the team and the school. Go ahead. If you are able to attend a game, make sure that you have a chance to walk down there and look.

You will see headstones of all of the mascots. Uga I is buried there, and so is the most recent Uga, Uga VII, who passed away during the 2009 football season, only his second one as keeper of the Seiler family tradition.

Really, the ceremony itself is quite a sight to behold. It's full of pomp and circumstance with a rather lengthy list of speakers. As for the mausoleum itself, it's quite impressive. It is cast in marble with markers that list each dog along with his birth and death date and his beginning and ending date for his run as the mascot. And yes, much like the rest of the Sanford Stadium facility, the mausoleum is kept in immaculate shape.

During home games, when you walk by you will see flowers in front of each tomb. Uga is revered in Athens and is a symbol that represents everything that the university does. When one of the dogs passes away, it is a sad, sad day in the Athens community.

A full funeral ceremony follows the passing of each dog. The ceremonies used to be open to the public and were every bit like the ceremony for the passing of anyone's loved one. Over the years, that has changed a bit. The crowds have just become too large. As Uga's popularity soared, so did the affection of those who wanted to be part of his life from beginning to end.

These days, the burial ceremonies are usually closed to the public. They will, however, allow some cameras to attend and tell the story. Generally, the Seiler family are all in attendance. Also attending is an athletic "Who's Who"—the university president, athletic director, some of the big-time boosters (by big-time we mean the bigger donors), some family friends, and a few others inside the Georgia athletic department.

As you would expect, the passing of one of the dogs and his subsequent funeral are pretty big stories within the Georgia family. Uga is revered by the whole campus and is a nationally recognized figure who is seen in virtually every broadcast of a Georgia football game.

There are plenty of things to see and do in and around Sanford Stadium on a game day. If you are fortunate enough to have tickets, take a look around, and try and enter on the field level. They will allow you to walk around on the field level outside of the gate and hedge-line. If you stay on the side where the Georgia bench is, you will get to see the mausoleum closeup in the area where you can enter the stadium from the street.

You will get a chance to see a lasting tribute to those damn fine dawgs who have served their school over the years.

33 Ringing the Chapel Bell

The University of Georgia chapel bell was cast in Medway, Massachusetts, in 1835 and is three years younger than the chapel itself. For more than a hundred years (give or take some time for repairs), it has notified everyone within earshot that the Bulldogs have pulled out another win.

Its first function was to make sure students made it to class on time and that they knew when classes started and stopped. The ringing of the 700-pound bronze bell also meant it was time for the student body to attend chapel services.

The late UGA historian John Stegeman (yes, that Stegeman) has the first-recorded ringing of the bell for football taking place in 1901 after a scoreless tie against the Auburn Tigers. The game was considered a "moral victory" as Auburn never crossed midfield in a game the visitors were supposed to win.

"It is the biggest victory Georgia has won in years," a jubilant Harry Hodgson told a reporter as the team came off the field on the shoulders of a howling mob.

"The demonstration here tonight is unprecedented in the history of the institution," wired a *Constitution* correspondent. "A large percent of the students went to Atlanta, but those who remained at home are making the night hideous. The chapel bell has been kept ringing, and the entire campus is aglow from three large bonfires."

Freshmen were, in the early days of the tradition, ordered to ring the bell until midnight after a Georgia win. Nowadays, the concept is voluntary and even gets those from the opposing side involved just to say they took part in the act. Initially, the bell hung in the belfry atop the UGA chapel, but it was removed to its own tower in 1913 when it was discovered that the belfry was rotten and couldn't support it.

The bell was cracked in 1911 and again in the 1920s by people who were too "enthusiastic" in their emotional displays.

There have been a few other minor instances of bell repair. In 1981, the rope on the bell was broken as fans celebrated the Bulldogs' national championship. The bell tower was completely redone in 1995, and the Physical Plant was called in to fix part of the bell's shaft and bearings in August 2001.

But the biggest moment necessitating bell repair happened after a win over the Florida Gators. On October 27, 2007, the Bulldogs beat Florida 42–30, and students literally broke the bell with all the ringing—making it jump from its moorings and sending it onto a platform below the rafters inside the tower.

At first, Doug Roberts, the foreman of the welding shop, and his team worked nonstop to put the pieces of the broken yoke (that's the big support piece on top that allows the bell to rock back and forth) back together just to have the bell back on display for the next home game. It was decided, however, in the spring of 2008 that it was best to take down the bell and tower for a complete overhaul.

Physical Plant workers built a new tower that closely resembled the old one at about 40 feet tall. But the tower was made of Douglas fir (a stronger wood than the predecessor) this time around with steel braces. The roof was even made to resemble that of the UGA chapel. The bell itself was refurbished, polished, and covered with a preservative.

She was ready for action before the 2008 season opener against Georgia Southern.

What used to look grey is now golden, and the clapper was changed from steel to bronze, so for those of you who have heard both versions, it now sings a different tune.

It's always a joyful noise on campus.

34 Singing "Glory, Glory"

"Glory, Glory" is the tune identified with the University of Georgia, but there was another song played before the theme song became the theme song.

In 1908, R.E. Haughey penned the "Red and Black March" when he served as the volunteer director of the university's first band. He owned a music store in Athens and led a local dance orchestra. He helped establish what is now known as the Redcoat

Band, but he retired in 1909 after five years directing the group. He died in 1963.

While completing a doctoral dissertation on "Singing in American Colleges from 1636–1860," Lloyd Winstead, a euphonium player in the band from 1984–89, was searching on eBay for old college songbooks and came across something called the "Red and Black March" in North Dakota which, according to a history of the Redcoat Band written in 1962, was "Georgia's first original school song."

Winstead tracked down an article written by Andrew Davidson where he had interviewed Haughey before his passing. He then connected the notes to determine the history on the "Red and Black March."

35 The Athens Music Scene

Anyone who was raised in the late 1970s and 1980s can tell you that aside from Georgia football, this is the big reason that people can recognize Athens, Georgia.

The "Music Scene," as it is known, hit its stride with the growth of alternative rock and new wave music. A lot of that music was heavily played on college radio. In Athens, the growth of the 40 Watt Club helped spur the music and night scene.

We'll tell you about the 40 Watt a little later.

The first local band to hit the national scene was the B-52's. They began making the rounds in Athens back in the mid-1970s with a very unique style unlike anything making the popular rounds at the time. However, the band that truly brought Athens to the national eye was R.E.M.

Dan Wall, right, talks with University of Georgia graduate student Brook Reynolds in front of his Athens Music Museum in Athens, Georgia, on Wednesday, July 27, 2005. The modest space, which Wall opens several days a week, features rare albums and CDs, posters promoting classic Athens music shows, and other items such as copies of the first T-shirts ever made for R.E.M. and the B-52's. (AP Photo/Ric Feld, File)

R.E.M's roots can be traced back to college radio and, over the course of the 1980s, the group grew to be one of rock's most successful and popular acts. As their popularity soared, the band drew national attention to the thriving "alternative music" scene while letting people know that there was some pretty good music coming out of a little college town in Georgia.

Other groups and performers arrived on the national scene seemingly at the same time. Individuals like Matthew Sweet and groups such as Dreams So Real and Widespread Panic all had hits and gained national followings.

Locations like Downtown Records, The Georgia Theater, and the 40 Watt were all places where you could see some of the best alternative music in the country. These clubs are still around and not hard to find encircling the downtown area, all a mere walking distance from the university. On any given night, you can choose from 15 or more restaurants, bars, or theaters where you'll find someone playing live music.

Athens has its own Music Walking Tour, a trek through the downtown district to the places that define the musical scene. Make sure to stop in at the Athens Welcome Center on East Dougherty Street to get information on it. There are several music stores downtown, as well—don't forget about them, either.

If you are coming in the fall during football season, make sure that you get there early. Leave yourself some time to explore, and make sure that you have at least one night to listen to some music. Listening to live music in Athens isn't the same as going to another town. It has a vibe, sound, and style all its own.

Check it out, you will be happy that you did.

36 Damon Evans

Whoever says that football players aren't smart never met Damon Evans.

If you want to get a feel for the Georgia "Keep it in the Family" ideal, there is probably no one better suited to talk about it than the Bulldogs' current athletic director.

It's not everyone who can say that they, at the age of 34, had the opportunity to oversee one of college athletics' top-10 revenue-producing programs. Evans was handpicked—once as a recruit by Georgia's legendary Vince Dooley, and again by Dooley as his successor as athletic director.

Said Coach Dooley, "I said often that it seemed just a short time ago that I was in his living room talking to his mother, father, and Damon about the great opportunities that he would have here at Georgia if he came. Little did I know at the time that the opportunities would include one day succeeding me as athletic director. He has done a splendid job of building on the program that he inherited."

Those who have come across Damon Evans will tell you, "He's very approachable." It's true. If you are able to attend a football game, he won't be very hard to spot. Before the game, you'll see Evans working the field…the whole field, talking to alumni and former teammates, laughing with the cheerleaders, or chatting up various members of the media—he is comfortable talking with them all.

Evans was raised in Gainesville, Georgia, where he was a star athlete and an academically gifted student at Gainesville High School. He was a four-year starting wide receiver in Athens who graduated in 1992 and received his master's degree there, as well.

Working first at SEC Headquarters and eventually making his way back to Georgia, Evans was very much on the fast track to sports management success. By 2003, he had replaced Coach Vince Dooley as the athletic director.

It's amazing to see the growth in Georgia's sports programs, and a lot of that growth can be traced back to Evans and Coach Dooley. New facilities have popped up all over the Georgia campus. Evans spearheaded the drive for the new Coliseum practice facility—a sprawling building with facilities for the basketball teams and the gymnastics team—attached to Stegeman Coliseum. He also helped spearhead the drive to expand the Butts-Mehre Athletic building.

When you come to the University of Georgia campus in Athens, take a drive around. Look at the athletic facilities. Start at the Butts-Mehre building, then head to Foley Field, the baseball stadium across the street. Check out the Tennis Center right behind it, then go down the street to the Coliseum. You will also see that practice facility. From there, make your way down a little farther and you will run into the football stadium. If you still haven't had enough, ride just outside the loop and check out the golf and softball facilities. You will see that Georgia has some of the most impressive in the country. It is no coincidence that they are all first rate.

After all, it took a smart man to make the programs successful. And it took another very smart man to raise the money to take those programs to the next level.

37 The Redcoat Band

"Ain't Nothin' Finer in the Land…Than the Georgia Redcoat Marching Band!"

More than 400 strong, the Redcoats are undoubtedly the loudest fans on a Saturday in Athens.

The band was founded in 1905 as a section of the Military Department, though the band's first non-military performance was actually at the 1906 Georgia-Clemson baseball game. In its early days, the group struggled to survive, as students split time between their studies, military drills, and band activities.

In the 1920s and '30s, the band expanded when non-military students were allowed to join. But funds were scarce, and the still-undersized band was rarely able to travel with the football team when it played on the road. This changed in 1935.

In November of that year, Georgia was set to play LSU. Louisiana Governor Huey Long was bringing his Golden Band from Tigerland to Athens. When UGA fans and officials saw the size mismatch, scholarship and operating funds were immediately pledged to make the Georgia Band comparable to the bands of other schools.

In 1955, Roger and Phyllis Dancz became the band director and auxiliary coordinator, respectively. Their arrival brought a new enthusiasm to the organization, along with a new name.

Roger Dancz felt that the band—known simply as the Georgia Marching Band—deserved a unique name. The term "Redcoat" seemed an appropriate name for a band that wished to differentiate itself from the Yellow Jacket Band of Georgia Tech. The new name was The Dixie Redcoat Marching Band, and was later changed to The Georgia Redcoat Marching Band.

Under the Danczs, the Redcoats thrived. Phyllis Dancz added the Georgettes and Bulldog Banners (now known as the Flagline) to the existing majorettes, creating a welcome visual spectacle. Mr. Dancz's likeable demeanor and musical prowess improved the band's size and performance. His imagination brought about a new era of memorable performances, including the Halloween Show complete with band members dressed in their favorite costumes, and the Wedding Show in which a couple was actually married in a halftime ceremony.

In the 1980s, the Redcoats continued to grow. The Satin Silver Sousaphones were introduced at a cost of $5,000-$6,000 each. Today's Redcoat Band boasts 30 of them.

During the 1990s, the look changed with an updated uniform. In 2000, the Redcoats became the first Southeastern Conference band to win the prestigious Sudler Trophy, awarded to "bands of particular excellence that have made outstanding contributions to the American way of life."

During the 2004–05 year, the Redcoats celebrated their 100th anniversary and became the first American collegiate marching band to tour China. The band is currently directed by Director of

Athletic Bands Dr. Michael C. Robinson and Associate Director Dr. Nikk Pilato.

The Redcoat Band experience is enjoyable but requires a lot of work. Students prepare for the honor throughout middle and high school. Once in the band, they rehearse six to eight hours per week for one hour of academic credit. Redcoats study nearly every academic field available on campus. In fact, only about 25 percent of band members are music majors.

After years of rehearsing at various sites on campus, the Redcoats now have a home. In November 2009, the former Recreation Sports Field #9 was dedicated as the Redcoat Band Practice Field. It includes a retaining wall, drainage system, and lighting. Future plans for the facility include stadium seating, storage space, an artificial surface, and an instructional tower.

At the facility's ribbon-cutting ceremony, Hugh Hodgson School of Music Director Dale Monson summed up the occasion appropriately. "This is the culmination of a tradition here today. This is what happens when you have a tradition as vital and as inspired as the Redcoat Band that exists over generations. They are a proud and a strong inspiration for all of us at this university. They combine the past, the present, and the future into something that endures across generations."

38 The McWhorter Family

According to historian Nash Boney, more than 225 McWhorters have officially passed through the University of Georgia.

Bob McWhorter, class of 1914, is widely regarded as the best football player the University of Georgia has ever known. He was named as an All Southern selection from 1910 to 1913. He was the first UGA athlete to be given All-American status and the first to be inducted into the National Football Hall of Fame and the Georgia Hall of Fame.

One All-American voter, Park Davis of Princeton, phrased McWhorter's abilities this way: "To Northern enthusiasts, McWhorter comes as a stranger, but not so in the South, where he is known as the most phenomenal backfield player the game has known for years."

His 61 touchdowns would count as the record for the Bulldog football team, but the numbers can't be backed up because of the record-keeping of the era. The official record holder is Herschel Walker with 52.

Baseball was the real reason McWhorter ended up at Georgia in the first place. In 1910, he was the starting center fielder for the Gordon Military College squad that beat the Bulldogs 11–0. His coach, W. Alex Cunningham, was hired as UGA coach the next day. McWhorter followed him.

McWhorter had the opportunity to play professionally in football and baseball, but he turned down both to pursue a law degree at the University of Virginia. He graduated Phi Beta Kappa in 1917 and may have shown Northern college football fans what all the headlines were about during his undergraduate years while in Charlottesville.

Notice the word "may."

The University of Virginia traveled to Boston to play a game against the Crimson of Harvard. Boston sportswriters mentioned a halfback that went by the name of "Bob White" who had a pretty good day for the visitors. There's talk that "Bob White" was really Bob McWhorter.

Dan McGill went to school with Bob McWhorter Jr. and was a friend of the family. "Bob never admitted or denied it to me," Magill told the *Athens Banner-Herald*. "He always merely smiled when I asked him about the story. But it is well known that in the old days schools often played 'ringers.'"

McWhorter returned to UGA to teach law from 1923 until his retirement in 1958. He was also a four-term mayor of the city of Athens from 1939 to 1947 and a member of the Georgia athletic board until his death in 1960. In 1966, the athletic dorm was renamed McWhorter Hall in his memory.

The other McWhorter who made his stamp on southern football was H. Boyd McWhorter, a 1949 graduate of the school who became dean of the Franklin College of Arts and Sciences. He also was commissioner of the Southeastern Conference from 1972–86. Under his watch, the postseason men's basketball tournament was reinstated in 1979 after a 27-year hiatus, and the SEC also agreed to send its football champion to represent the conference in the Sugar Bowl every postseason.

The Birmingham News named McWhorter in its Top 10 Most Influential Figures in the History of the SEC in 2007. Once the Universities of Georgia and Oklahoma won their anti-trust lawsuit against the NCAA in 1984, McWhorter signed an exclusive contract with Ted Turner and WTBS-TV to televise a game of the week. The first SEC Football Game of the Week was a 21–21 tie between Florida and LSU at Florida Field in Gainesville on September 8, 1984. Bob Neal and Tim Foley handled play-by-play and color commentary.

"If you live in the Southeast, the SEC is the 800-pound gorilla in the room," said Wright Waters, commissioner of the Sun Belt Conference, when asked by the *Birmingham News* about the power of the SEC. "But the influence has been tied to who was the commissioner at the time. Under Dr. [Boyd] McWhorter, the SEC was way out in front on academic issues, with a continuing progress rule before the rest of the nation knew what they were talking about."

The Southeastern Conference also continues the McWhorter legacy by recognizing student-athletes with the H. Boyd McWhorter Southeastern Conference Scholar-Athletes of the Year Award. The McWhorter Scholar-Athlete Award is the highest honor a student-athlete can receive in the SEC. Each award winner receives a $10,000 post-graduate scholarship, while 22 other finalists for the award receive a $5,000 post-graduate scholarship.

39 The Woodruff Practice Fields

When the Bulldogs practice behind the Butts-Mehre building, it used to be on four fields that were four in number and had a bunch of different drills and lessons going on at the same time. No one is resting unless there's a water break for everyone—it's constant motion, constant practice, constant chatter, and constant lesson-planning for the next game. Practice periods are timed down to the second, complete with a running clock, and a horn takes over the southwestern campus in a rhythm to send head coach Mark Richt, his assistants, and his players from station to station.

The look in 2010 is a bit different than folks have been used to viewing when driving past the chain-link fence at the corner of Pinecrest and Lumpkin Streets. Two Sprinturf fields within the Woodruff Practice Fields Facility were the only ones getting any work during spring practice in 2010. The two grass fields were occupied with construction equipment as the Butts-Mehre Building expansion was underway.

More on that in a bit.

Before construction started, the team always had to walk about 200 yards to practice in shoulder pads and shorts in the three-year-old Coliseum Training Facility on Smith Street if weather became an issue during the week. The Bulldogs have even made their way over to the Ramsey Center and the barn that the Atlanta Falcons have at their practice facility in Flowery Branch if they really needed to get things done.

Before all of those facilities existed, practice was usually indoors at the Coliseum itself. The Redcoat Band has had their time on the Woodruff fields, and Mother Nature even had her way with the practice fields in June 2004, causing them to flood.

The Athletic Department needed to update facilities to make sure that the team could compete at the highest levels within the Southeastern Conference.

The locker rooms already have a new look. The $2 million renovation a few years ago gave Bulldogs players a new lounge, equipment room, TVs, and video games. Each player has his own locker, and the lockers themselves face a common area in the center of the room that features Bulldogs legends and teams of the past—a constant reminder of their place in UGA history. And players travel through the Heritage Tunnel to get from Point A to Point B on the basement floor of the Butts-Mehre.

Usually, Bulldogs fan access to the Woodruff Fields is extremely limited, save for events like Picture Day and Countdown to Kickoff. The university even put up green tarps along the fence line to keep fans from peering through the fence.

Practice is now a serious business in college athletics—which has also become a serious business—and any Bulldogs fan can view the progress of the area's construction by going to the facilities section of Georgiadogs.com and watching the webcam's images.

40 Catfish Smith

The first and most obvious question here is, "Who is Vernon 'Catfish' Smith, and why is he important in Georgia football history?"

Here's your answer. Catfish Smith was a football, basketball, and baseball player for the University of Georgia, and from 1934–37, he was the university's baseball coach while also an assistant coach on the football team. He picked up the name "Catfish" as a kid, winning a bet in his hometown of Macon by biting the head off a catfish that he and a friend caught.

Catfish played all three sports from 1929 to 1931 and was an All-American football player and a three-time all-conference performer. He was also the captain for both the basketball and baseball teams. Perhaps his biggest claim to fame as a football player was what he did in the first game ever played at Sanford Stadium in 1929.

In that game, Smith scored all 15 of Georgia's points, leading them to the upset of heavily favored Yale that we talked about earlier in the book. Smith scored both touchdowns in the game, one by falling on a blocked punt in the end zone, and the other by catching a touchdown pass. He also kicked an extra point and tackled a Yale player in the end zone for a two-point safety.

After he graduated from the university, Catfish coached until 1941—again, not just football but baseball, as well. In 1941, he joined the United States Air Force, where he stayed until 1963, retiring as a colonel.

One of the greatest early athletes in early Georgia history, Smith was inducted into the Georgia Sports Hall of Fame in 1966.

In 1979, he was inducted into the College Football Hall of Fame. Not so coincidentally, 1979 was also the 50th anniversary of Sanford Stadium. Smith came back to his alma mater and was recognized for his achievements.

Sure, this is primarily a book about the football history at the school. Vernon Smith was certainly part of that. But he was also part of its baseball history, and it is probably safe to say that he was an integral part of the school's athletic history as one of its greatest athletes. Vernon "Catfish" Smith passed away in 1988 at the age of 80. Few athletes in university history have ever accomplished more.

41 Wally Butts

Everyone who has traveled to the UGA campus knows about the building that houses the athletic offices and the museum. We'll go into a little more detail about what you're missing if you haven't been there in a bit.

But the first half of the namesake of the building on Selig Circle was the coach responsible for item No. 9 in this book and a share of the 1946 national title in his 21 seasons on the sidelines.

James Wallace Butts Jr. was born in 1905 near the town of Milledgeville in central Georgia. He was a three-sport star in high school and made his way to Mercer University in Macon for his college years where he gained recognition as an All-Region end. After graduation, Butts coached in the high school ranks for 10 years.

Joel Hunt left the Bulldogs after a 5–4–1 season in 1938 to take the same position at the University of Wyoming. Butts was an assistant on that staff and was promoted to take over after Hunt's departure.

Top 10 Coaches Career Wins

1. Vince Dooley	1964-1988	201–77–10
2. Wally Butts	1939-1960	140–86–9
3. Mark Richt	2001-present	90–27
4. Harry Mehre	1928-1937	59–34–6
5. Ray Goff	1989-1995	46–34–1
6. W.A. Cunningham	1910-1919	43–18–9
7. Jim Donnan	1996-2000	40–19
8. George Woodruff	1923-1927	30–16–1
9. Herman J. Stegeman	1920-1922	20–6–3
10. Johnny Griffith	1961-1963	10–16–4

If you combine the wins of the first 14 coaches the University of Georgia had for the football team (through the 1909 season) and Joel Hunt, the coach in 1938, they would have 52 wins among them—good enough for fifth place.

His assistants in that first year included Bill Hartman, Spec Towns, Howell Hollis, Quinton Lumpkin, J.V. Sikes, and J.B "Ears" Whitworth. Not a bad staff for a team that was a proponent of doing something not a lot of other teams did at the time—pass.

In the 10-feet-at-a-time era of running, running, and more running, Butts wanted his team to throw as both a change-up and a staple of his offense. When you would eventually have athletes like Frank Sinkwich and Charley Trippi in those backfields, adding a passing game yielded championship results.

Butts also had another prominent Southeastern Conference coach as an assistant on his 1946 staff—Auburn legend Shug Jordan. Jordan was an assistant line coach for Jennings Whitworth starting in October 1946, but when the Plains called after a winless season in 1950, he returned to Auburn. Jordan, however, became a part of that Bulldogs' Sugar Bowl–winning staff that beat North Carolina.

Head coach Wally Butts posed for a picture in Atlanta on Saturday, December 31, 1938.
(AP Photo)

The Charley Trippi–captained team in 1946 only once scored less than 28 points in a game in the regular season (the 14–0 win over Alabama in Athens) and only once gave up more than 14 points in a game (the 48–27 shootout win over Chattanooga for win number nine). The Bulldogs put up an even 70 points in a win over Furman in Greenville, South Carolina, and blew through their regular season schedule with relative ease with wins over Clemson, Temple, Kentucky, Oklahoma A&M, Furman, Alabama, Florida, Auburn, Chattanooga, and Georgia Tech. The Dogs then faced the Carl Snavely–coached Tarheels in the 13th Sugar Bowl.

After a 7–0 lead at the half in front of a sell-out crowd of 75,000 in New Orleans, North Carolina gave up 20 second-half points to lose 20–10. John Rauch scored two touchdowns to lead the Bulldogs offense to the win.

The 1946 squad never finished higher than third in the Associated Press rankings with their 11–0 record, but the

Williamson System would give the title to the SEC co-champs. Army and Notre Dame split the title that year in the AP poll after a scoreless tie in Yankee Stadium. The four-year record of the 1941 recruiting class was a stellar 40–4–1 with two SEC and two national championships.

The 1950s weren't kind to Butts and Bulldogs history with five losing seasons, but he earned his last SEC title in 1959 behind Fran Tarkenton's quarterbacking and a 10–1 record.

The 1950s was also the era when Uga the dog became the signature mascot for the football team. Butts' bulldog, Mike, was the precursor to all the Roman numerals that the Seiler family has brought to Athens. Pictures were taken of a Seiler dog at the 1956 Florida State game and drew the attention of Dan Magill. As the story goes, pictures made their way from Magill to Butts, and Butts wanted to talk to Seiler in his office.

"Sonny, Dan tells me you've got a white English bulldog that would make a good mascot for the team," Coach Butts said. "What would you say to us using him to create some excitement?" You've read about how much excitement that dog has caused a little earlier, and you've seen it every football Saturday since.

Butts resigned as head coach in 1960 after going 6–4. Butts wrapped up his coaching career with a 140–86–9 record, going 5–2–1 in postseason bowls. He stayed on as athletic director, but one event marked his last few seasons on campus.

In March 1963, the *Saturday Evening Post* published a story claiming that Butts and Alabama head football coach Bear Bryant "fixed" the 1962 Georgia-Alabama game. The Tide won the game 35–0, and both men sued the *Post* for libel to the tune of $10 million each. They won the case, and Butts was awarded more than $3 million—the largest plaintiff award for a libel suit at the time. The award was lowered to a little less than $500,000, but Butts' reputation still took a major hit.

Coach Bryant settled out of court, as well. The verdict was even seen in some circles as the beginning of the end of the *Post*.

Butts' attorneys, William Schroder and Allen Lockerman, gave his defense. Schroder was a Notre Dame football player and received his law degree from UGA, while Lockerman was one of the FBI agents responsible for gunning down John Dillinger. In Schroder's closing remarks, as reported by Robert H. Boyle in *Sports Illustrated*, he told the jury:

"Someday, as must happen to each of us, Wallace Butts will pass on where neither the *Post* nor anyone else can then bother him. Unless I miss my guess, they will put him in a red coffin with a black lid with a football in his hands, and his epitaph will read, 'Glory, glory to Old Georgia.'"

One of the first things Butts did after returning home to Athens when the verdict came down was stop at the grocery store and pick up some stale bread to feed the birds in his backyard.

Pressure would be felt by Butts' replacement on the field, Johnny Griffith, and university President O.C. Aderhold, who testified against Butts at the trial. Aderhold was even snubbed at a local country club after his testimony. One alumnus told *Sports Illustrated* that they were "dusting off a chair for a president emeritus."

Butts eventually resigned as AD, and his Bulldogs era came to a close. He died of a heart attack after coming home from a walk in 1973 at the age of 68, and he is buried in Oconee Hill Cemetery.

"The Little Round Man" was elected to the Georgia Sports Hall of Fame in 1966 and to the College Football Hall of Fame in 1997. But he'll always be known for bringing Bulldogs football off the ground and into the air and for bringing the program's first national titles to Athens.

42 Glenn "Pop" Warner

No, we aren't talking about a youth football league, but we are talking about the guy that it is named after. If you are like most fans, you're probably looking at this name and asking yourself, "What did he have to do with Georgia football?"

Glenn "Pop" Warner was the fourth football coach in University of Georgia football history. Dr. Charles Herty, who is considered the father of Georgia football; Ernest Brown, a graduate student who played and coached the team in 1893; and Robert Winston, who was the first paid coach at the university, all preceded Warner, but none matched his accomplishments.

In this day of younger and younger football coaches, you might be surprised to know that "Pop" Warner was 24 years old when he became the coach. He was three years removed from his alma mater, Cornell University, where he graduated with a law degree. He actually played football at Cornell, where he earned his nickname for being the oldest guy on the team. After he graduated, he practiced law for a short time in Buffalo, New York, before he landed in Athens.

Can you guess how much money Georgia paid Warner to coach in 1895? It was a modest $340 for a 10-week season.

The university at the time had a student body of only 248 students, 13 of whom played on the football team. The team, playing in an empty, open field on campus, was 3–4. Warner coached the team again in 1896, getting his pay boosted to $40 per week. That team was the first undefeated team in school history, going 4–0.

Warner left Georgia after that season, heading to back to his alma mater as its head coach. From there, he headed over to the Carlisle Indian School in Pennsylvania where he coached for the

This is a 1942 photo of football legend and coach Glenn S. "Pop" Warner.
(AP Photo)

next five seasons. He came back to Cornell for three seasons before he went back to Carlisle and got the opportunity to coach the legendary Jim Thorpe.

Warner's coaching career would find him at the University of Pittsburgh in 1914. His Pittsburgh team won its first 33 games in a row and two national championships. He would coach in three Rose Bowls at Stanford and took his last coaching job at Temple University before he retired in 1938. He retired with 319 career coaching wins, a record that placed him behind only Joe Paterno, Bobby Bowden, and Bear Bryant. In 1997, he got his own stamp from the United States Postal Service who honored Warner, Bear Bryant, Vince Lombardi, and George Halas with their own stamps.

You might be surprised to find out that Warner brought several innovations to football—some of which are still used today. The screen pass, the single- and double-wing formations, the use of shoulder and thigh pads are all plays, sets, and equipment that he drew up.

The legacy of Glenn "Pop" Warner lives today, vicariously through Pop Warner Football leagues (the leagues are officially called "Pop Warner Little Scholars"). The league's history can be traced back to 1929 in Philadelphia, Pennsylvania, where it began as "The Junior Football Conference." In 1934, after speaking at a Junior Football Conference event in Philadelphia, the league renamed itself after Warner, calling itself the Pop Warner Conference.

Warner's name was an instant draw for the league, and the four teams that began in 1929 grew to 157 by 1938. Although the league struggled during the 1940s, much of that was due to World War II. By the time the 1950s came around, Pop Warner Football became a growing institution.

Today, more than 400,000 kids from ages five through 16 participate in these leagues, all of which have both an academic and a weight requirement in order for the kids to participate. The group also has cheerleading and dance competitions, as well. There is now a Pop Warner Football National Championship/Super Bowl played in December at the Disney Sports Complex in Orlando, Florida.

43 William Porter Payne

The son of Porter Otis Payne, captain of the 1949 Bulldogs football team, is known to the rest of us as Billy Payne—two-way player for Vince Dooley, the man who brought the 1996 Summer Olympics to Atlanta, and the current Chairman of the Augusta National Golf Club.

But what you may not know is that some neighbors played a key role in the upbringing of one of the most driven individuals you'll ever meet.

Bill Hartman's mother, Ruth, used to tell the story of how she played a hand in Billy becoming the man that he is. When the Paynes and the Hartmans lived in the Mathis Apartments in the late 1940s on Lumpkin Street in Athens (the buildings still stands today), the Hartmans had an ice box. Billy's parents did not. The young Payne's baby formula was kept cool by the Hartmans, helping the future Olympic dreamer get the nourishment he needed for greatness.

Payne was born in Athens but was raised in Atlanta. He attended Dykes High School where he was president of the student body and played baseball and football. He was recognized as an All-State quarterback and was the leading hitter on the baseball team.

Off the field at UGA, he was student body vice president, vice president of the campus chapter of the Fellowship of Christian Athletes, winner of the distinguished service award from the business school, and recipient of an honorary doctor of laws.

On the field, he started out as a tight end. But before the 1968 season, Coach Dooley asked him to switch over to defensive end since the team was thin at the position. Payne did, received All-SEC honors at end, and helped lead the team to its Sugar Bowl berth.

"I said many times that I've seen some individual specialists at different skills, but I've never seen a better 60-minute man," Dooley said to Loran Smith for his statewide newspaper column. "If there's one guy you want in the game playing the whole time—offense, defense, and kicking—it would be Billy Payne."

Payne was also a motivator off the field and a bit of a cut-up. Billy created a poet persona, "Lamar" (his wife's maiden name), and posted verses in the locker room as the team neared the end of spring practice one year. He was counting down each day with a new verse.

"They couldn't catch me," Payne told Loran, "because I might go into the locker room at midnight or 3:00 AM." He didn't remember any of the poems themselves, but he did recall the tag line:

"Oh the coaches are sad, but gee, I'm glad."

There's also talk that someone wrote motivational words on the chalkboards during the Sugar Bowl run. That's also linked to Payne, but it's still a mystery.

Payne credits Erk Russell as his on-field motivator in a *Georgia Trend* magazine article from 2009. "His enthusiasm was contagious. He would mix it up with us head to head. He would get into a scrimmage and come at us full speed with no headgear."

Motivation to succeed also came from the early death of his father. Porter Payne passed in his early 50s, so Billy lost (from his point of view) not only a father but also a brother.

He's also driven himself so much that he has had three heart procedures performed on him since the age of 26, but that hasn't stopped his desire to compete, succeed, and thrive.

"My daddy always said, 'Never was a horse that couldn't be rode or a rider that couldn't be throwed,'" Payne said in a 1990 *Sports Illustrated* article. "He would say, 'Billy, if you're not smarter than a lot of people or a better athlete than somebody, you can always outwork 'em.'"

That work ethic carried him far. He has received four honorary doctorates from four Southern schools. He was inducted into the Georgia Sports Hall of Fame. He was named Georgian of the Year by multiple groups, and Payne is a recipient of the Theodore Roosevelt Award—the highest honor given by the NCAA—for all the work he's done.

Payne admits there are no more fields left to conquer—even as the chairman at Augusta National. But he is always thankful to the University of Georgia for three things: meeting his wife, Martha; meeting fellow students that he is still friends with, and playing college football like his father did before him.

He has always tried to, as Payne phrases it, "Play every play to the fullest extent of my ability," and we've all seen the results across the state of Georgia. And the gut feeling is we will for quite some time to come.

44 1984 Cotton Bowl

In the late 1970s and early '80s, Georgia football had a hugely successful run in the college ranks. The team was a Top 10 contender almost every year and played in one of the big bowl games each of those seasons.

In the stretch between 1976 and 1984, the team played in the Sugar Bowl four times and the Cotton Bowl twice. Some of those games were more successful than others, but very few of Georgia's bowl games before or after the 1984 Cotton Bowl would qualify as more successful or more significant.

The 1983 Georgia Bulldogs completed the regular season at 9–1–1. They didn't win the SEC title or the right to play in the Sugar Bowl, but the record was good enough for the Dogs to make the top five in some polls. The Nebraska Cornhuskers finished the regular season ranked No. 1, and they played in the Orange Bowl against the University of Miami. The No. 2 team at the end of the season was Texas. They drew seventh-ranked Georgia for the Cotton Bowl, located a mere 90 minutes from the Longhorns' home in Austin.

The '83 Dogs were not a flashy bunch. The team was just three seasons removed from the Herschel Walker–led national championship and just one season after Walker left to turn pro. The group relied heavily on a very strong defense led by All-American safety Terry Hoage and an offense with John Lastinger running an efficient ground-based attack. They scored enough for the Dogs to pull off the nine wins and the tie versus Clemson.

The Dogs were 8–0–1, rolling through most of the schedule, winning non-conference games against UCLA, Clemson, and Temple, and beating Mississippi State, Ole Miss, Kentucky, South

Carolina, Vanderbilt, and Florida in the SEC. That set up a home game against the undefeated Auburn Tigers and Bo Jackson. Jackson ground out a 13–7 win over Georgia, catapulting the Tigers to the SEC title and the Sugar Bowl game. Georgia, though ranked in the top 10 at the time, would have to settle for that Cotton Bowl berth against Texas.

The Longhorns thought they might still have a shot at the national title going into the 48th Cotton Bowl. Georgia was playing for the pride of the SEC. The game itself wasn't pretty. Mostly the game was a defensive battle. Tied 3–3 at the half, neither team was able to solve the other's defense. The Bulldogs' defense kept Texas somewhat at bay, and the Longhorns tacked on two more field goals in the third quarter, taking a 9–3 lead with just 15 minutes to play. Through the fourth quarter, Georgia got the ball across mid-field twice. The Bulldogs were forced to punt in Texas territory with

Georgia quarterback John Lastinger runs behind Keith Montgomery (No. 23) on a keeper during the first half of the Cotton Bowl Classic against the University of Texas in Dallas, Texas, on Monday, January 2, 1984. (AP Photo/Mike Murphy)

less than five minutes to go in the game. Thinking that Georgia might go for the fake, the Longhorns put in a different punt return unit and the return man, Craig Curry, fumbled the punt. Gary Moss recovered it for the Bulldogs.

Three plays later, Georgia finally crossed the goal line. John Lastinger, running the option, kept the ball and went 17 yards for what would be the game-winning touchdown.

The loss for Texas ended up costing them the national championship. Later in the day, No. 1 ranked Nebraska lost to Miami in the Orange Bowl. That was the game where Nebraska went for a two-point conversion after scoring late in the game rather than kicking an extra point.

The game itself was not one for the ages, but it certainly changed the final poll for the 1983 season. Texas fell to fifth after losing, one spot behind the team that upset them—the No. 4 Georgia Bulldogs.

45 "Look at the Sugar Falling Out of the Sky…"

The greatest era of Georgia football was rolling full speed in 1982. By the time Georgia met Auburn on November 13, the Bulldogs were ranked No. 1 in the major polls and were on their way to a possible second national championship in three years.

Auburn was also on the way to its first winning season in three years and, with a win over Georgia, would be in the driver's seat for an SEC championship—the Tigers' first conference title since 1957.

Georgia had Herschel Walker on its side en route to winding down his Heisman Trophy season. Auburn had a pair of outstanding tailbacks in its wishbone formation, junior Lionel "Little Train" James and a young freshman who was leading the team in rushing— you might have heard of him, Bo Jackson.

Auburn-Georgia games are always tense, and the 1982 version was a nail-biter. Early in the fourth quarter with Auburn down 13–7 and pinned on its own 12-yard line, James took the ball and raced 87 yards for a touchdown to give the Tigers a 14–13 lead.

Georgia started its next possession on the 20-yard line and used its biggest weapon, Herschel Walker, to lead the Bulldogs back in front. Walker capped off a 13-play, 80-yard drive with a 3-yard touchdown run with 8:42 left in the game. Georgia regained the lead 19–14.

While Herschel Walker carried the load, rushing for 37 yards on eight carries, the biggest play of Georgia's scoring drive was a critical third-down completion by Bulldogs quarterback John Lastinger to Herman Archie for 17 yards. It was one of only three passes completed by the Bulldogs all day, but it was a big one. Walker capped off what turned out to be his last SEC game with 177 yards on 31 carries for Georgia.

All Georgia needed now to secure its third SEC Championship in a row was a defensive stand.

Auburn took possession on its 20-yard line and soon crossed the 50-yard line into Georgia territory. With 3:04 remaining in the game, Auburn reached the Georgia 14 after a run by Auburn fullback Ron O'Neal. It was then that legendary Georgia broadcaster Larry Munson implored the Bulldogs defense to hold Auburn again.

After an Auburn penalty, Georgia's defense did hunker down. First, Tony Flack stopped Bo Jackson two yards behind the line. Then Bulldogs defensive end Dale Carver made one of the biggest plays of the year, sacking Auburn quarterback Randy Campbell for a nine-yard loss and knocking the Tigers back to the Georgia 30-yard line.

That brought up third-and-26 for the Tigers. Campbell made up for the loss and completed a nine-yard pass to Auburn tight end Ed West. Now it was fourth-and-17 for Auburn.

Those listening to the game on the radio heard Munson beg for one last stop: "Hunker down, you guys! If you didn't hear me, you guys, hunker down! I know I'm asking a lot of you guys, but hunker it down one more time!"

Auburn faked to Bo Jackson, who curled around and was open across the middle. However, Georgia defensive lineman Freddie Gilbert was pressuring Campbell, who was forced to make a fast decision and get rid of the ball quickly. Campbell spotted split end Mike Edwards and threw the ball toward the end zone. Under duress from Georgia's blitz, Campbell didn't get everything into the throw, so it became a desperation heave.

Edwards was double-covered by Georgia safety Jeff Sanchez and cornerback Ronnie Harris. The Bulldogs duo broke up the pass, and the Bulldogs defense did "hunker down."

When John Lastinger put down his knee for the final time to run out the clock, the celebration had already begun. From his radio booth, Larry Munson said it was raining sugar in the Alabama plains. "Oh, look at the sugar falling out of the sky! Look at the sugar falling out of the sky," he said as the clock reached double zeros.

Georgia fans stormed the field at Jordan-Hare Stadium, and the players carried head coach Vince Dooley off the field on their shoulders. Georgia's 19–14 win over Auburn secured the Bulldogs' third SEC Championship in a row and another trip to the Sugar Bowl in New Orleans.

46 Fran Tarkenton

Fran Tarkenton didn't have to stray too far from home to play college football.

After his family moved to Athens from the Washington D.C. area in 1952, Tarkenton became a tremendous athlete at Athens High School. During his career with the Athens High Gladiators, Tarkenton earned All-State honors in basketball, baseball, and football. As the Athens High quarterback, Tarkenton led Athens High to a 41–20 victory over state power Valdosta for the 1955 state championship.

Tarkenton stayed in town and enrolled at the University of Georgia in 1957 and led the Bullpups to an undefeated season.

Although 1958 was supposed to be a redshirt year for Tarkenton, that notion wasn't in his plans. Georgia hosted the Texas Longhorns to open that season and were trailing 7–0 midway through the third quarter. Without telling the Georgia coaching staff, Tarkenton inserted himself into the lineup, replacing starting quarterback Tommy Lewis.

"They wanted to redshirt me, and I didn't want to because I thought I could help the team," Tarkenton told the *Athens Banner-Herald* years later. "So I just bolted onto the field. I put myself in."

Beginning from Georgia's own 5-yard line, Tarkenton led a 21-play, 95-yard drive ending in a 3-yard touchdown pass to Jimmy Vickers. When Georgia head coach Wally Butts sent in the kicking unit for the extra point, Tarkenton waved them off, taking it upon himself to go for two. The sophomore completed a pass to Aaron Box for the two-point conversion.

Following a stellar career at Georgia, quarterback Fran Tarkenton put together a Hall of Fame career in the NFL. (AP Photo/NFL Photos)

It was that kind of risk-taking that defined Fran Tarkenton.

The next season, Tarkenton took another risk that paid off by drawing up a play on the turf against Auburn in Athens. Trailing the Tigers 13–7 late in the game, Coach Butts sent in a play, and Tarkenton ignored it.

"I knew we needed something different," Tarkenton said. "I told the left end, Bill Herron, who was in tight, to really go ahead and make a block. I told him, 'Count to a thousand-four and then run to the left corner of the end zone.'"

Herron followed Tarkenton's instructions and made the catch to defeat Auburn 14–13 and win the 1959 SEC Championship.

Georgia met the Missouri Tigers in the Orange Bowl. Tarkenton played great, throwing two touchdowns as the Bulldogs shut out the Tigers 14–0.

As a senior in 1960, Tarkenton lead the SEC in total offense (1,274 yards) and passing (1,189 yards) and earned All-American honors. The Bulldogs finished a disappointing 6–4.

Tarkenton went on to a Hall of Fame career in the NFL with the New York Giants and the Minnesota Vikings, and he led the Vikings to three Super Bowls.

47 Tailgating: Large and Small

Tailgating has become a bit of an art form in college football circles.

It's best enjoyed with friends, groups of friends, friends of friends, fellow alumni, and people you may have just met for the first time who were passing by and offered you a spare beverage because you share the same interest—the game you're about to go watch in one, two, or six hours.

Tailgating has evolved into one of those "can-you-top-this" social experiments where everyone in your posse brings something to your spot, whether it's food, drink, portable satellite dishes, an industrial sized grill on wheels big enough to rotisserie a small barnyard animal, or a large inflatable representation of your mascot.

It isn't just a trip to the grocery store anymore, and it has gotten expensive. Not to the point where you've had a coin-flip decision on cashing in a 401k to pay for something on game day, but it's close.

The most recent example of that is the recreational vehicle. This movable home on multiple wheels carries everything the modern tailgater needs (or thinks he or she needs) to survive the ordeal...short of flying over traffic to get out of town. It'll even tow your four-wheeled vehicle behind so you can get around town in a different manner before game time should you need to make one of those runs to the store.

College campuses have seen the influx of this beast and have taken advantage of their popularity. Some enterprising souls off-campus are making a killing by charging RV owners to use vacant, grassy lots. At the University of Georgia, they let you park at certain points on-campus.

Two points are for the RV drop-off and camp-out: N01 and N02, and that's it. You can't just roll up your RV anywhere close to the stadium, set up base camp, and party. And the only way you get to go to the RV lots is if you're a donor to the school.

If you drive a normal, four-wheeled horse, don't feel left out. To be able to park on campus yourselves, it's first-come, first-served. But you've got to be a donor to either the school or the athletic department to make that happen, as well.

Prestige Parking in Athens is in charge of the RV lots, and they need your car to be out of the N01 and N02 lots by Friday at 5:00 PM if you're there on any kind of official business. Depending on the lot, season permits in the 2009 season ran from $325 to $650, and single-game permits fell in the $100-$150 range.

And just how popular has this idea become?

Prestige now renews season ticket holder plans in April.

See what you've gotten yourself into? If you're into walking or cabbing it from another lot and trekking to campus, that's another possibility. Just make sure you cover all your options, decide whether you want to bring a second car, make sure all of your personal amenities are covered in the cost of your choice of lot, and above all—enjoy yourself—remember, it's the SEC we're talking about here.

48 Watch a Game from the Bridge

Football stadiums are unique places in American culture. Often they can be called monuments to excess, many can be called scenic, and others in some form or another can be called home.

In college football, the stadiums often have personalities of their own. They almost all have character, and many have some unique traits that make them as much a part of the football experience as the game itself. We've talked about Sanford Stadium in an earlier chapter. We spoke about its history and place as a structure and how it came to be. We also spoke about some of its unique quirks, such as the Uga Mausoleum.

One of the many things that stick out about the game-day experience is the Bridge.

More specifically, the Bridge is part of Sanford Drive—a fairly short road that runs less than a mile and links the two ends of the University campus. The Bridge itself is nothing fancy. It's not ornate, and it doesn't pass over much other than the ground-level entrance to the football stadium.

The Bridge is a link to many things on the University campus, however, and a crucial part of the game-day experience. You might ask, "Why would a bridge be so important?" Well, it's because said bridge runs behind the west end zone of Sanford Stadium.

You can actually stand there and watch a game. You won't see the whole game, but you will see at least part of it—and from a somewhat unique perspective.

Not only is the Bridge a way to watch the game, it's the place to be seen before the game. Sanford Drive runs from the west corner of the stadium north toward Baldwin Street. It also passes near the Tate Student Center and the Bookstore—two of the more popular places for folks to hang out before the game. Because it is closed to street traffic on game days, you can walk across it. Though keep in mind that if you do, you are likely to have 50,000 or so friends walking around the area with you. Most of them have tickets but are probably arriving early and looking to take in some of the unique game-day atmosphere.

Please note while on the Bridge that you will be able to see quite a bit from there.

We spoke in an earlier chapter about the Dawg Walk, and we can tell you from experience that although you won't be able to get up close and personal with the players, you will get a unique view of how big an event the walk is. You'll see how far the fans line up just to see the players from your perch on the Bridge.

The key is to get to the game early. It's not something that is always easy to do when heading to Athens for a game, but if you can, the Bridge is well worth your time. Walk around, observe, and let it all soak in. And if you are one of the many who aren't able to actually score a ticket to the game, just hang out up there, watch the crowd, and hope that there is some action on the other end of the stadium.

You'll be a bit far away, but you can see it. Take pictures if you can. In part because it's a cool place to be and in part because there is no telling how much longer that view will be there.

Several message boards have mentioned a discussion about putting another row of seating in that end zone. Let's hope that doesn't happen because watching a game from the Bridge is a true Georgia experience that makes the university one of the most respected and most honored within the college football community.

49 Eric Zeier

If you ask Eric Zeier's high school coach, Dexter Wood, to name the best player he ever coached, he'll say Eric because he had all the tools in high school—the quick release, the velocity on the football, the footwork, and the ability to read coverages at a level beyond his high school years.

But the top prospect in the country almost never made it to Athens. "Georgia, at the time Eric was being recruited, didn't throw the football," Wood recalled. "Eric had developed a relationship with Mark Richt, who was at Florida State at the time. Richt came up and visited. I was a fan of his. Eric was a fan of his, too."

Florida State appeared to be at the top of the list. But Coach Goff had made some changes to the offense. Wayne McDuffie and Greg Davis were added to the staff, and that gave Eric a reason to go to Athens and make an official visit.

UGA was his "home" university, and Eric decided to stay at home. He started at quarterback in the middle of his freshman year and was locked into the job for the next three seasons. "He was prepared well beyond his years," Wood said. "His maturity as a high school quarterback was beyond his peers. I think it was more a tribute to his upbringing, being an army brat and all."

Wood saw Zeier was a competitive, hard-nosed player and opened up the passing game for Eric during his time at Marietta High School. Wood could tell he had someone special even at that first practice. Zeier was a three-sport star at Heidelberg American High School in Germany and had returned to the United States for his junior year in high school. His father, Rick, was a colonel in the U.S. Army, thus all the moving around. Zeier's father had requested a transfer stateside so Eric could get the chance to shine.

Georgia quarterback Eric Zeier searches for a receiver in the 43–10 victory over Georgia Tech in Atlanta, Georgia, on November 25, 1993. (AP Photo/ Charles Kelly)

"He was articulate then, too," Wood remembered. "Our philosophy was that you had to work your way up at Marietta. When he came in with that second group for the first time, he was telling them to straighten up. And you could tell in his bark and his cadence that he was in charge and in control of the situation.

"His whole approach was that, 'We were going to get this right.'"

That also applied to his schooling. He graduated from Marietta High School early so he could enroll in classes in Athens early and get a jump on his competition. The practice wasn't all that common back then, but it is fairly commonplace today.

"It was completely my decision," Zeier told *Sports Illustrated's* William Reed back in 1992. "Football is the thing I love most, not the senior prom, or spring break, or the class cruise. I looked at it not as missing out but as gaining a lot. When I came to Georgia early and got up at 6:00 AM to run and work with the other guys, I think I earned their respect, because that's the hard part of the season."

And he got it right in Athens during three-plus years of performing between the Hedges. Taking over for Greg Talley in the 1991 Ole Miss game, Zeier eventually set school records for attempts, yards, completions, and an SEC mark for interception percentage (a little more than 1 percent). He was named to both the SEC and All-American freshman squads.

After the 1992 season, Zeier was already second on school career charts in passing yardage, completions, attempts, completion percentage, third in average gain per play, as well as sixth in TD passes and total offense. He became a consensus second-team All-SEC, first-team Sophomore All-American, and an Academic All-SEC selection.

His junior year, the 1993 season, saw Eric light up the scoreboards and stat sheets to an entirely different level. He set several SEC records:

Passing Yards in a Game: 544 against Southern Miss [That performance gave him SEC Player of the Week honors. He also became the only player in SEC history to throw for more than 500 yards in a game, breaking a 24-year-old record of yards passing in a game by Alabama's Scott Hunter (484)].
Passing Yards in a Season: 3,525
Total Offense in a Season: 3,482

He had his name attached to 61 University of Georgia passing marks including:

Passing Yards in a Game: 544

Yards in a Season: 3,525

Career Yards: 7,757

TD Passes in a Game: four

TD Passes in a Season: 24

TD Passes in a Career: 43

Pass Completions in a Game: 36

Completions in a Season: 269

Completions in a Career: 579

Total Offense in a Game: 527

Total Offense in a Season: 3,482

Total Offense in a Career: 7,384

Interception Percentage in a Season: 1.39 percent

Consecutive Passes without an Interception: 130

You see where we're going with this...

In his senior season, Zeier was on a few of the preseason All-America lists and kept throwing the football all over the field. He took out Shane Matthews' records for all-purpose yards and passing yards by a quarterback in the SEC. Zeier set six school records during the year and threw for more than 400 yards four times during the season. While giving Georgia claim to seven passing records in the SEC books, he also became one of three passers to finish north of 11,000 yards all-time in the NCAA.

When Eric Zeier was through, he was responsible for 67 University of Georgia passing records and 18 SEC marks (some of which have since been broken by a Tennessee quarterback named Peyton Manning and fellow Bulldog David Greene). Zeier's trek from Pensacola, Florida, to Heidelberg, Germany, to Athens is an unquestioned exclamation mark in Bulldogs history. It was even good enough for a proclamation in the Georgia General Assembly for his service to the state.

Zeier was also one of the three finalists for the Davey O'Brien Award and finished seventh in the Heisman Trophy voting. After his college days were through, Zeier was drafted by the Cleveland Browns and bounced around the NFL for six years with stops in Cleveland, Baltimore, Tampa Bay, and Atlanta.

Zeier left the University of Georgia with a degree in Business. He has a wife and two children and spends his time working in the mortgage lending industry, but he has a pretty good side gig. Zeier and Scott Howard are now the full-time voices of Georgia football.

50 Walking Under the Arch...as Long as You're Not a Freshman

If it wasn't for Daniel Huntley Redfearn, class of 1910, every underclassman at the University of Georgia wouldn't have to worry about the idea of graduating or going sterile, depending on which version you believe…unless you believe both of them.

Redfearn, as the story is told, had only $200 with him when he came to school in Athens, but his quest was to graduate. He told himself that he wouldn't walk under the Arch facing Broad Street until he had his diploma.

When he was a freshman, he was supposed to run under the Arch in his underwear with his classmates before the Georgia Tech game. He ran, but he went around the Arch.

One of Redfearn's professors supposedly learned of his superstition (ritual, quest, or whatever you would like to call it), told his own classes about it, and the tradition was started. But remember, the tradition only applied to freshmen.

When Redfearn died, he bequeathed $1,000 to the school for the upkeep of the Arch. That $1,000 was the exact amount of its original construction in the late 1850s.

The university, at first, was surrounded by a wooden fence. That was changed when the school's botanical gardens were sold, raising the funds for the construction of an iron gate and fence structure.

The Arch was modeled after the Great Seal of the state of Georgia. The Arch itself represents the state constitution, and the three columns represent (from left to right) wisdom, justice, and moderation. Each pillar has a word wrapped around it as a reminder of the virtues discussed in Plato's *Republic*.

And you thought those columns were just "columns."

The Arch held gates that were closed when the campus needed to be secured, but those gates disappeared in 1885. No one is exactly sure why the gates were there and then suddenly gone, but a prank is the most likely explanation.

Two other changes to the Arch occurred when lights were added in 1946, and it was physically moved away from the Broad Street curbside by 6 feet or so.

The Arch has also been a gathering place for significant events over time. In 1961, when Charlayne Hunter-Gault and Hamilton Holmes became the school's first two African American students, desegregation protests (both for and against) were held there. After the Kent State shootings in 1970, students gathered to protest as well as at times during the Persian Gulf War. After the attacks on September 11, a makeshift memorial was created on the site.

So when you see the Arch on every piece of, well, everything that the University of Georgia markets in and around campus, just remember the protocol:

If you're from a different school, you can walk under it.

If you've graduated, you can walk under it.

But if you're a freshman, you have to wait a while. Unless you want to live with your parents or visit your doctor.

And it means so much more than just a 150-year-old wrought-iron design at the corner of Broad and College.

51 Kevin Butler's 60-yard Field Goal vs. Clemson

Kevin Butler continued Georgia's great kicking tradition in the early 1980s. Butler was a first-team All-State Kicker for Redan High School in 1978, and he made the team again in 1980 as an honorable mention.

Butler moved on to the University of Georgia to replace the departed Rex Robinson, who had rewritten the Bulldogs record book. Robinson had a feeling those marks were only temporary.

"The first time I saw him kick, I knew the records weren't safe," Robinson said of Butler.

Butler proceeded to better most of Robinson's numbers. He still holds the Georgia record for the longest field goal—60 yards—and that made Butler a Georgia legend.

On September 22, 1984, the Bulldogs, No. 20 in the Associated Press poll at the time, took on the No. 2 Clemson Tigers at Sanford Stadium. For the first time in five years, Georgia was not favored at home, coming in as a 3½-point underdog.

It looked like the betting line would be right as Clemson stormed out to a 20–6 halftime lead.

Georgia rallied in the third quarter. Quarterback Todd Williams connected on a touchdown pass to Herman Archie. Then Cleveland Gary ended a Georgia drive with a 1-yard touchdown run. Kevin Butler and Clemson kicker Donald Igwebuike traded field goals, and the game was tied at 23.

With 2:10 to go in the game and starting at their own 20-yard line, the Bulldogs began their final possession. After a pair of short completions and a 24-yard run by Tron Jackson, Georgia's drive stalled on the Clemson 44-yard line. Facing fourth down with only 17 seconds remaining in the game, head coach Vince Dooley ordered the field-goal unit on the field.

Butler had made a 70-yard attempt that week during practice, but this time the game was on the line. With holder Jimmy Harrell kneeling down at mid-field, Butler's field-goal attempt was 60 yards. Those listening to the game on the radio heard Larry Munson call it:

"So we'll try and kick one 100,000 miles, we hold it on our own 49½, 60 yards plus a foot and Butler kicks a long one, Butler kicks a long one, Oh my God! Oh my God! Oh my God! The stadium is worse than bonkers. Eleven seconds left and I can't believe what I saw. This is ungodly!"

Butler's 60-yard field goal was good with plenty to spare, and Georgia had pulled off a 26–23 win over Clemson.

"He busted the ball," Clemson head coach Danny Ford said after the game. "I'll bet the ball is flat now. He kicked the fool out of it."

That kick put Kevin Butler among the Georgia legends.

"People come up to me constantly and say that they were at the game when I made that kick," Butler told Loran Smith in his November 10, 2001 column for the *Athens Banner-Herald*. "Maybe they were, maybe they weren't, but I enjoy talking to them about the kick."

After his Georgia career ended, Butler was picked in the fourth round of the 1985 NFL Draft by the Chicago Bears. He was on the

Bears famed '85 team that won the Super Bowl. Butler kicked for 11 years in Chicago, then he kicked two seasons with the Arizona Cardinals.

In 2001, Butler became the first kicker inducted into the College Football Hall of Fame.

The Butler kicking tradition continues at the University of Georgia. Kevin Butler's son Drew punts for the Bulldogs, and in 2009 he won the Ray Guy award as the nation's best punter.

52 Bill Stanfill

During the late 1960s, one of the best defensive linemen in the country was Georgia's own Bill Stanfill. While growing up in the southwestern Georgia town of Cairo, Stanfill developed his football talent, leading the Syrupmakers to three regional championships, and as a senior, he was named Class AA Lineman of the Year.

Stanfill was a multi-talented athlete, winning five state championships while attending Cairo High School; but ironically, not one came in football. As a member of the Cairo Track and Field team, Stanfill won three Georgia State discus championships and a state title in the shot put. As a senior, Stanfill helped the Syrupmakers basketball team win the state championship.

Vince Dooley saw something special while recruiting Stanfill and knew it was a no-brainer that he would suit up for the Bulldogs. Stanfill would become part of Dooley's first full-fledged recruiting class at UGA.

Stanfill made an impact immediately during his first varsity season in 1966, helping the Bulldogs win an SEC Co-Championship and earning All-SEC honors as a sophomore.

1968 Was Special

The 1968 Georgia Bulldogs went through the season undefeated at 8–0 with two ties—the season opener to Tennessee 17–17, and 10–10 to Houston November 2.

Many things about the 1968 season were special for the Bulldogs. Georgia dominated its rivalry games, defeating Florida 51–0, Auburn 17–3, and Georgia Tech 47–8. The Bulldogs won their second SEC championship in three years and earned a trip to the Sugar Bowl to face the Arkansas Razorbacks from the Southwest Conference.

It was in that Sugar Bowl that Georgia faced its biggest disappointment, losing to Arkansas 16–2. The Bulldogs had the No. 1 defense, but it was no match for the Razorbacks offense. Game MVP Chuck Dicus caught 12 passes, and his second quarter touchdown catch was the only one of the game.

All was not lost as Georgia claimed a national championship from Litkenhous, which is a difference-by-score formula developed by Edward E. Litkenhous, a professor of chemical engineering at Vanderbilt, and his brother, Frank.

Ohio State is considered the 1968 consensus national champion, while the Associated Press ranked Georgia eighth in its final poll. But Georgia also claims one for that year.

In Stanfill's junior season, he again earned All-SEC honors and led the Bulldogs to the Liberty Bowl.

Saving his best for last, Stanfill enjoyed a stellar senior season, leading UGA to the 1968 SEC Championship while earning All-American honors. The recognition didn't stop there. Stanfill was named SEC Lineman of the Year and was awarded the Outland Trophy as the country's best interior lineman.

Former head coach Vince Dooley said of Stanfill, "He was everything you'd want in a defensive tackle. He combined speed, size, range, quickness, and competitiveness to make him one of the greatest linemen to ever play the game."

The Bulldogs finished 1968 with an SEC Championship and a trip to New Orleans to represent the league in the Sugar Bowl.

Though the Bulldogs lost to Arkansas in the Sugar Bowl, Stanfill's record in the red and black was 25–6–2, including three trips to bowl games and a pair of SEC titles.

Defensive statistics were not kept back then, but if they were, it would have been no surprise to have seen Bill Stanfill at or near the top of Georgia's record book. Stanfill's outstanding career at UGA led to his induction into the College Football Hall of Fame in 1998.

Stanfill joined the Miami Dolphins where he enjoyed a seven-year NFL career. As a key member of the Dolphins' famed "No Name" defense, Stanfill was part of two Super Bowl Championship teams, including the 1972 team that went 17–0, the only undefeated team in NFL history.

53 Bill Goldberg

Who's next? He's next.

If you are a fan of professional wrestling, then you probably know who Bill Goldberg is. If you are a fan of cars, you might know who Bill Goldberg is. If you are a University of Georgia football fan, you should know who Bill Goldberg is.

Bill Goldberg was a highly recruited defensive lineman out of Tulsa, Oklahoma, and he showed up in Athens to begin the 1985 season. He had an instant impact. Twice an All-SEC defensive lineman, Goldberg quickly became a fan and coach favorite. He was a three-year starter and was part of the 1987 team that won the Liberty Bowl and the 1988 Gator Bowl–winning team. Goldberg teamed with Richard Tardits to give Georgia one of the nation's best defenses in 1988. The 6'4", 290-pound bundle of energy and strength is among Georgia's all-time leaders in total tackles and quarterback sacks.

Goldberg was an 11th-round pick of the Los Angeles Rams in 1990, where he played for a season before moving on to play for the Atlanta Falcons. He spent three seasons in Atlanta as a popular defensive lineman before he suffered a severe abdominal injury. Bill attempted a comeback with the Carolina Panthers in 1995 but never fully healed from the injury. He retired from football in '95, but for him, that was only the beginning of his story

Over the next year or so, living in the Atlanta area, he became friendly with several professional wrestlers based in the area who worked for the World Championship Wrestling promotion. The wrestlers eventually convinced him to give their sport a try, not knowing what would next happen.

Goldberg shot to the top of the professional wrestling world like a rocket. After spending a couple of months at the WCW training facility near Atlanta in 1997, he hit the ground running. He got a huge push by the promotion as the undefeated phenomenon, winning 108 straight matches. By July 1998, he was headlining the company's wrestling cards.

He capitalized on his success, and by the end of 1998, he had parlayed his wrestling success into not just a movie role, but a leading role in the film *Universal Soldier: The Return*.

He remained one of most popular wrestlers in the WCW promotion for a few more years, though he slowed a bit due to some injury problems. By 2002, the WCW went out of business.

Goldberg eventually found his way to the other big wrestling promotion, World Wrestling Entertainment, where he also was immensely popular and eventually became the WWE World Champion. His stay with the promotion lasted for a year.

Not one to rest for long, Bill Goldberg turned to acting. He has appeared in eight different movies and 18 different television shows, including a hosting gig on the series *Automaniac* on The History Channel. He also hosts the show *Bull Run* on the Speed

Channel and appeared on the Spring 2010 version of *The Celebrity Apprentice* television show on NBC.

On occasion, Goldberg has come back to Athens for football games. He remains close to his coach, Vince Dooley.

Coach Dooley said of Goldberg in a story done for the University of Georgia website, "It was easy to see that Bill had it even when he was here at Georgia. He has that combination of confidence, skills, and soft-spoken nature that draws people to him. And for all his free-spiritedness, he never crosses the line of overconfidence and arrogance. He was a leader on this team, and other players rallied around him."

His name surfaces from time to time in conversations about professional wrestling, but he appears to have moved on from that part of his life.

Certainly, Bill Goldberg ended up being one of the most unique characters to ever emerge from the University of Georgia's football program. Sure, he was very successful as a player, did very well for himself, and made the NFL, but it is what he did after he ended his football career that makes him part of this list. Learning about Goldberg should be just as important to any Georgia football fan as learning about Herschel or Coach Dooley or any of the other legends associated with football in Athens.

54 Terry Hoage/Scott Woerner

The biggest question with these two defensive backs—two of the greatest in Bulldogs history—is how did these two guys get out of the state of Texas in the first place?

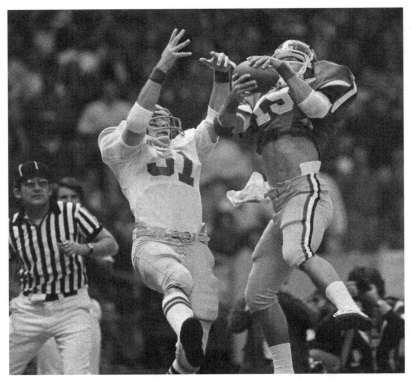

Georgia's Scott Woerner, No. 19 (right), grabs a pass intended for Notre Dame's Pete Holohan, No. 31 (left), during first-half action of the Sugar Bowl game at the Superdome in New Orleans on Thursday, January 1, 1981. (AP Photo)

Terry Hoage came out of Huntsville, and Scott Woerner came out of Baytown.

Hoage, for some strange reason, did not have one school chase after him with a scholarship when he was a high school senior. But a Georgia alumnus was teaching at Sam Houston State University and tipped off the Bulldogs about the hometown kid. One step away from pursuing a pre-med degree in Austin at the University of Texas, Hoage headed to Athens instead.

His freshman year, 1980, was spent on special teams. There was an initial thought of redshirting him, but he kept blocking kicks in practice, so Coach Dooley had to do "something" with him. That something paid off in the Sugar Bowl against Notre Dame. Hoage blocked a field goal in that game. It led to the win and the national title, and his career was off and running.

His freshman GPA was an impressive 3.75, chasing a degree in genetics.

Hoage played "roverback" in the Dawgs secondary, which meant he could wander all over the defensive backfield and head to the ball wherever it was thrown on any given play.

His sophomore year, 1981, garnered him an All-SEC honor. His junior year, he led the nation in interceptions with 12 and picked up All-American and Academic All-American recognition that led to an absolutely electric senior season.

Teams had to find ways to throw around and away from Hoage—something that's not necessarily the easiest thing to do in the world of college football. Coach Dooley once referred to Hoage as the "best defensive player I've ever coached."

In the 1983 season, Hoage's efforts against Vanderbilt personified the impact Hoage had on the Bulldogs program. Larry Munson called the win:

"They come down to the Georgia 38, with 48 seconds to go, it's 20–13. Vanderbilt comes up to the line, the Dawgs desperately trying to stay unbeaten, and I mean desperately. They're on the Georgia 38 with 48 seconds. Page, kind of a long count this time. He's back now to throw, dumps it to a running back on the 31, they hit him right away, but it was complete. They got seven yards, and the clock is running, 37, 36, 35 seconds.... Page dropping back with 16 seconds flushing out; he's gonna run to the right, he's throwing a long bomb into the corner, there he is! And somebody broke it up with a great leap! Terry Hoage got up in the air! Hoage got up with one hand and broke up a cinch touchdown down there."

Hoage finished fifth in the Heisman Trophy voting for the year and picked up All-SEC Academic honors for the third year in a row, Academic All-American honors for the second year in a row, and All-American honors also for the second year in a row.

The fifth-place finish in the Heisman voting was the highest finish at the time for a Georgia defensive player.

Hoage played 13 seasons in the NFL for a half-dozen teams, leading the pros in interceptions in 1988 and picking up a Super Bowl ring in 1992 with the Washington Redskins. He was named to the College Football, the CoSIDA Academic, and Georgia Sports Halls of Fame. Add to that the Walter Camp All-Century team from the safety position and the SEC 25-Year Team for good measure.

Hoage and his wife, Jennifer, now run Terry Hoage Vineyards in the California wine country. One of the brands he produces is named Hedge Syrah. Not bad for the last signee of his class.

* * *

Scott Allison Woerner was a four-year letterman at cornerback for the Dawgs from 1977 to 1980. He played high school ball at Jonesboro High School just south of Atlanta. He was coached by former Georgia captain Weyman Sellers, and he played quarterback and defensive back. He made All-State squads in his senior year. He was a three-sport star who lettered in wrestling and track and field—he was even able to high jump 6'6".

Georgia quarterback Buck Belue told Chip Towers of the *Atlanta Journal-Constitution* that Woerner was, "maybe the most physically gifted player on the team. I always thought he could have won the Olympic gold in the decathlon. Some of the battles he and Lindsay had on the practice field were memorable."

It showed on the field. In 1978, his sophomore year, he led the Bulldogs with four interceptions and was instrumental in the 12–0 shutout of Clemson with a fumble recovery and a pick of a Steve Fuller pass.

Fast forward to his senior year in 1980, and "Woerner the Returner" made his mark in the Clemson game with a 67-yard punt return for a score. He set the single-season mark for return yards and left campus with the career mark, as well. Damien Gary took over the top spot in that category after the 2003 season.

Everyone knows about the completion Buck Belue made to Lindsay Scott in Jacksonville to keep the season alive in 1980, but if it wasn't for Woerner's efforts against Clemson two months earlier, there may not have been a discussion about a championship.

In the 20–16 win, Woerner was responsible for 60 percent of the Bulldogs' points. He ran back a 67-yard punt for a score to give Georgia a 7–0 lead. Later in the quarter, Tigers QB Homer Jordan had driven his offense to the 11-yard line trying to even up the score, but Woerner had other ideas as he told Coach Dan McGill in his *Athens Banner-Herald* column:

"I had the tight end covered on third-and-9, but he stayed in to block. So I floated over with what I figured was a double out pattern. Instead they came back with a curl, and I was right with it. As I caught the ball, the momentum carried me into the end zone. I looked up the sideline and saw Chris Welton throw a real good block on a big tackle, and after that it was just me and the goal line. I was running out of gas when Clemson's tailback [Chuck] McSwain caught me."

The 98-yard interception return set up the Bulldogs with a first-and-goal at the Clemson 2-yard line. Belue scored two plays later for the 14–0 advantage.

Sports Illustrated named Woerner their Defensive Player of the Week.

Woerner came up big again in the Sugar Bowl against Notre Dame with a pass break-up of a sure Blair Kiel touchdown pass to

Pete Holohan, and an interception in the fourth quarter to seal the win over the Irish.

When that senior season was over, Woerner was named first-team All-SEC at safety by the Associated Press and UPI. He was also named first-team All-America at corner by the *Football News*, UPI, Kodak, and Walter Camp publications. His place in the Circle of Honor was secured in Athens.

He was drafted by the Atlanta Falcons but transferred to the fledgling United States Football League to pick up two titles with the Philadelphia Stars before his playing career was through. He now spends his time as a physical education instructor in the Rabun County, Georgia, school system.

55 David Pollack

If you look up "Guy Who Gave It Everything He Had To Give" in a book of football terms, there is a really good chance that you'll find a picture of David Pollack. There is a reason that he was recently voted one of the College Football Players of the Decade by *Sports Illustrated*.

The University of Georgia has been lucky enough over the years to produce some great defensive football players, such as Bill Stanfill, Charles Grant, Richard Seymour, Bill Goldberg, and Freddie Gilbert among many others, but none have been as recognized as David Pollack.

Pollack was a three-time All-American football player. The only other Bulldog to accomplish that was Herschel Walker. Twice, Pollack won the Ted Hendricks Award for the best Collegiate

Defensive End. He was not just the 2004 SEC Defensive Player of the Year; he was also the 2002 SEC Player of the Year—the season that the Bulldogs won the SEC title and beat Florida State in the Sugar Bowl.

He came to Georgia via Shiloh High School in Snellville, Georgia. An All-State player as a senior, he was a defensive end and played fullback—a position he was originally recruited to play in Athens. He went to Georgia with his best friend, David Greene, a quarterback. The stretch where the two Davids were team leaders, from 2001–04, is among the most successful in Georgia history. Pollack was one of the captains on the 2004 team that went 10–2 and finished with a win in the Outback Bowl over Wisconsin.

David Pollack holds the Chuck Bednarik Trophy for best defensive player after winning it at the Home Depot College Football Awards on Thursday, December 9, 2004, in Lake Buena Vista, Florida.
(AP Photo/Scott Audette)

Perhaps the single biggest play that Pollack will be remembered for happened during 2002, his best year in college. In the game against the University of South Carolina, Pollack basically grabbed the ball out of South Carolina quarterback Corey Jenkins' hand while he was attempting to pass. The play was ruled an interception, one that was returned for a touchdown. It's a play viewed over and over in Athens. It's part of the pregame highlight video shown before the team comes onto the field in Sanford Stadium—a video that whips the Bulldogs crowd into a frenzy.

Pollack scored another touchdown in the first game of the 2003 season on an interception against Clemson—a play were he just jumped as high as he could and the ball landed in his hands—and he returned it for a touchdown to trigger a Georgia 30–0 victory.

He established a Georgia record with 36 sacks and even blocked a couple of field goals on special teams. But he was most known for his fiery enthusiasm on the field. It was not unusual to see him chatting up opposing players, laughing and smiling the whole time. He was often the player most trying to excite the home fans, frantically waving his arms and jumping up and down, getting people as excited as he was.

His own teammates called Pollack one of the most competitive people they had ever been around.

In 2005, Pollack was a first-round draft pick of the Cincinnati Bengals, but his NFL career did not last very long. He was injured in a 2006 game against the Cleveland Browns, breaking a vertebra in his back trying to make a tackle. It was the last football play he would ever make. He retired some 18 months later unsure if he would be able to remain healthy and play football.

Since his retirement, Pollack has been very visible around the Atlanta area. In 2008, he became the co-host of the afternoon drive-time radio program at 790 "The Zone" sports radio. He also does some college football analyst work for ESPNU.

If you have the opportunity to meet Pollack, he is a great resource on Georgia football. Having created part of its rich history as one of the school's most successful players, he can often be seen on the sidelines in Athens.

56 David Greene

At the turn of the 21st century, the Georgia Bulldogs returned to a championship level. Mark Richt took over as head coach in 2001, and before the season began, he named redshirt freshman David Greene as the starting quarterback.

Greene had a highly successful high school career at South Gwinnett High School in Snellville, Georgia. Greene led South Gwinnett to two consecutive state playoff appearances, but he really took off his senior year. Greene threw for 2,102 yards and 19 touchdowns his final high school season. Then the honors poured in. Greene was named to the Class AAA All-State team by the Georgia Sports Writers Association, plus he was named Gwinnett County Co-Offensive Player of the Year and Quarterback of the Year by the Atlanta Touchdown Club.

After Greene's high school career, he was recruited by former head coach Jim Donnan and came to the University of Georgia.

In Tony Barnhart's book *What It Means To Be A Bulldog,* Greene shared that he wasn't all that highly recruited, "…but coach Donnan seemed to see something in me that I really didn't see in myself. In my dealings with him, he gave me the confidence that I could be a good player if I worked at it."

With Quincy Carter entrenched as the starting quarterback, plus some maturing to do, David Greene redshirted for the 2000

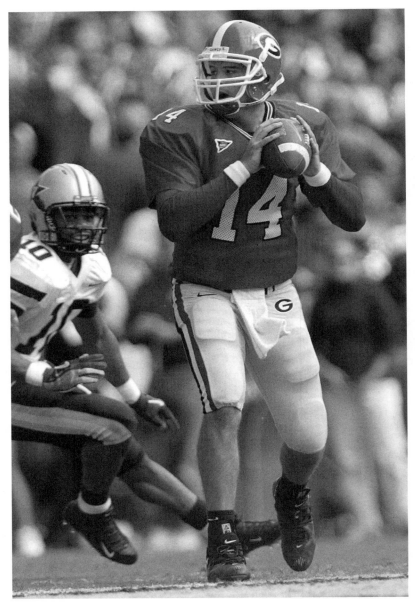

Georgia quarterback David Greene looks for an open receiver as Vanderbilt's Dominique Morris defends in a game on Saturday, October 16, 2004, in Athens, Georgia. (AP Photo/John Bazemore)

SEC Top 10 Career Passing Yards

1. 11,528 David Greene, Georgia (849-of-1,440) 2001–04
2. 11,213 Chris Leak, Florida (895-of-1,458) 2003–06
3. 11,201 Peyton Manning, Tennessee (863-of-1,381) 1994–97
4. 11,153 Eric Zeier, Georgia (838-of-1,402) 1991–94
5. 10,875 Danny Wuerffel, Florida (708-of-1,170) 1993–96
6. 10,354 Jared Lorenzen, Kentucky (862-of-1,514) 2000–03
7. 10,119 Eli Manning, Ole Miss (829-of-1,363) 2000–03
8. 9,707 Casey Clausen, Tennessee (774-of-1,269) 2000–03
9. 9,360 André Woodson, Kentucky (791-of-1,278) 2004–07
10. 9,287 Shane Matthews, Florida (722-of-1,202) 1989–92

season. Following that season, Jim Donnan was relieved of his head coaching duties, and Mark Richt was hired. Greene had a new offensive system to learn and a new head coach to impress.

Greene and Cory Phillips battled for the starting quarterback position. They were named co-No. 1 quarterbacks heading into preseason practice. Before the Bulldogs opened the 2001 season against Arkansas State, Greene was named the starter.

It was a successful first year for Greene as the Georgia starting quarterback. Greene led the team to an 8–4 record and a berth in the Music City Bowl. He also threw for 2,789 yards and 17 touchdowns and was named the Southeastern Conference's Offensive Freshman of the Year.

In 2002, Greene solidified the Bulldogs return to glory, leading Georgia to the SEC Championship Game against Arkansas. Against the Razorbacks, Greene threw for 237 yards and was named the game's Most Valuable Player as Georgia routed Arkansas 30–3. It was the Bulldogs' first SEC Championship since 1982.

The next season, Georgia posted a 10–2 regular season and an SEC Eastern Division championship. David Greene threw a career high 3,307 yards, leading the Bulldogs back to Atlanta for the SEC Championship Game.

Hobnailed Boot

David Greene arrived as a Georgia quarterback legend on the afternoon of October 6, 2001, in from of 107,592 at Neyland Stadium in Knoxville, Tennessee.

The Bulldogs faced the No. 6 Tennessee Volunteers. Georgia had not beaten the Vols in Knoxville since 1980, the game where Herschel Walker ran over Bill Bates. That game was a Bulldogs classic, and this one would also prove to be legendary.

The game came down to a first down at the Tennessee 6-yard line with 10 seconds left to play. The Georgia coaching staff called for a P-44, which was a play-action fake to the tailback designed to stall the blitzing linebacker, leaving the middle open for the fullback. Greene knew this play would only work if Tennessee had two safeties on the field, and they did.

When the ball was snapped, here's how Munson described it:

> "Ten seconds, we're on their 6. Michael Johnson turned around, asked the bench something. And now, Greene makes him lineup on the right in the slot, we have three receivers. Tennessee playing what amounts to a 4-4. Fake, and there's somebody—touchdown! My God, a touchdown! We threw it to Haynes. We just stuffed them with five seconds left! My God almighty, did you see what he did? David Greene just straightened up, and we snuck the fullback over! Haynes is keeping the ball? Haynes is come running all the way across to the bench. We just dumped it over 26–24. We just stepped on their face with a hobnailed boot and broke their nose. We just crushed their faces!"

And from then on, the 26–24 win over Tennessee would be forever known as the "Hobnailed Boot" game.

"I knew when I saw two safeties it would be there if Verron could slip past that linebacker," David Greene said after the game. "It was a great call."

"By the grace of god I caught the ball," Verron Haynes said.

It's a game that began the quarterbacking legacy of David Greene, jumpstarted the Mark Richt era at Georgia, and gave Munson another call for the ages.

This time the Bulldogs ran into an LSU team on a national championship run that featured the top defense in the country, which overwhelmed David Greene. He ended up with three interceptions in the game, and LSU defeated Georgia 34–13.

Greene rebounded with an MVP performance in the Capital One Bowl against Purdue, throwing for 327 yards as the Bulldogs defeated the Boilermakers 34–27 to end the 2003 season on a high note.

By the time David Greene's senior year arrived, he was approaching some record-setting milestones. Although the 2004 season ended without an SEC championship, Greene ended his Georgia career leading the Bulldogs to a 24–21 win over Wisconsin. The numbers Greene totaled put him in the company of Bulldogs' legends.

Greene became only the second quarterback in Georgia history to start all four years. John Rauch accomplished it first when he was Georgia's starting quarterback from 1944–48. Greene's 42 wins as Georgia's starting quarterback set an NCAA record since broken by Texas' Colt McCoy in 2009. His 214 consecutive pass completions in 2004 is an SEC record, and David Greene ended his college career as the Southeastern Conference's all-time career leader in yards gained with 11,270.

57 John Rauch

At the age of 14, a doctor diagnosed John Rauch with a heart murmur and told him not to participate in any athletics. Rauch's family got a second opinion, and after being noticed in a flag football game on the University of Georgia campus, head coach Wally Butts made Rauch his starting quarterback.

By the time Rauch graduated in 1948, he was the first quarterback to start in four consecutive bowl games. He set the record for passing yards in the NCAA with 4,044 and finished with a record of 36–8–1 as a starter. He also led the Bulldogs to two SEC titles and was named All-America and the SEC Player of the Year in his senior season. He didn't just play quarterback, though. He played the other two phases of the game and returned punts, as well.

"The thing that I remember the most about him would be he was a winner," Charley Trippi said in an interview with Travis Fain of the *Macon Telegraph*. "He knew how to win. And he utilized his personnel that played behind him. He had a good football mind.... Anybody that's ever coached with him or played with him would have high praise for him."

Rauch was the second overall selection in the 1949 NFL draft, but the Detroit Lions traded him to the New York Bulldogs for the No. 3 overall pick, SMU running back Doak Walker. Rauch played three seasons before turning to a career as a college coach that included a four-year stint in Athens from 1955–58.

He moved on to the pro ranks in the early 1960s where he worked for the Oakland Raiders among others and was named head coach by Al Davis in 1966. Rauch's two assistants were John Madden, a 31-year-old assistant from San Diego State who worked the line, and Bill Walsh, who worked with the backs.

Bill Walsh, when asked about his West Coast Offense that he later ran as head coach for the San Francisco 49ers, admitted that its origins came from what he learned from Rauch. Rauch learned that same offense from Coach Butts as his quarterback.

Rauch was interviewed by Loran Smith for his statewide newspaper column about his formative years as a quarterback:

"We never had a playbook, but those long sessions with him, Coach Butts talking and me making notes in a stenographer's

Did You Know?

While it is widely regarded that George Allen was the first coach to hire a special teams coach for his staff, Rauch admitted in an interview that he brought along Lewis "Bugsy" Engelberg for that same purpose in 1966 for his Raiders staff—two seasons before Allen hired Dick Vermeil for the same job with the Los Angeles Rams.

notebook, became my playbook. At home at night, I would study those notes and diagrams, and that was my basic education in football."

Rauch coached the Raiders to their appearance in Super Bowl II, where they lost to the Green Bay Packers 33–14. He was also named AFL Coach of the Year in 1967. He left the silver and black two years later after clashing with Al Davis and coached in Buffalo and Tampa Bay among other teams in the NFL through the late 1970s. His last coaching stop was with the Tampa Bay Bandits of the United States Football League where he was Steve Spurrier's director of football operations.

Rauch was inducted into the Georgia-Florida Hall of Fame in 2000, Georgia's Circle of Honor in 2001, and the College Football Hall of Fame in 2004 alongside Barry Sanders and Joe Theismann.

Rauch died in his sleep at the age of 80 in June 2008 at his Florida home.

58 Hines Ward

Mike Parris was a 27-year-old first-year head coach at Forest Park High School when Hines Ward was going through his junior year at the school. Parris witnessed the maturation of a future Super Bowl MVP up close.

Georgia scat back Hines Ward, No. 19, heads for the end zone on this 35-yard touchdown run while Conrad Clarks, No. 2, looks on in first-quarter game action in Athens, Georgia, on September 17, 1994. (AP Photo/Andrew Innerarity)

"Hines was unbelievable," Parris admitted. "I would have Bobby Bowden in my office with Philip Fulmer outside waiting. Steve Spurrier would be on his way from Florida. Georgia wanted to bring their entire offensive staff when they recruited him. We ended up meeting at my house to talk."

It didn't stop there. Tom Osborne was interested. Notre Dame was interested. But Hines always wanted Coach Parris with him for all of these recruiting visits, and the schools had to survive a question-and-answer period from Hines himself—and he wrote every answer down.

Florida didn't survive Hines' interview process. When Hines asked specific questions about the university, Coach Spurrier gave some canned answers. And that didn't fly with Ward.

Clemson wanted Ward to be a backup quarterback, and he was close to going to Lincoln to play for Osborne. But the issue of quarterback was one of Hines' questions in the book of notes.

His courting by the University of Tennessee was interesting, "David Cutcliffe had come down to talk to the two of us," Parris remembered. "He wanted him to play quarterback at UT and even told us in the meeting that he would call Peyton Manning right then and there and tell him that they would take Hines and not Peyton. Hines and Peyton were really close to each other and would even call each other every once in a while about things like that."

Recruiting got so out of control at times that Ward would go babysit Parris' kids just to get away from all the calls at his house. Ward ended his high school career as a two-time Clayton County Offensive Player of the Year. He earned All-American, All-State, and Super Southern Top 100 honors, as well.

Ward selected Athens, but his time under Coach Ray Goff frustrated him. Eric Zeier was the senior QB, and Hines was moved to receiver. Parris heard about that, too.

"Hines' mom called me and was saying, 'You made him go! You made him go! Junior is upset, and he's ready to transfer!' Believe me, she didn't want Junior upset."

As a wide receiver during the 1995–98 seasons, Ward's 149 catches and 1,965 yards placed him second in team history at the time. He also played tailback and quarterback, and his 3,870 all-purpose yards is still second only to Herschel Walker. In 1997, Hines was named an All-SEC performer.

Ward received his bachelor's degree in consumer economics from UGA, but his thoughts of going pro and being drafted in the early rounds took a step back when it was discovered that he was playing without an ACL in his left knee—the result of a childhood bike accident. The Pittsburgh Steelers took Ward in the third round, and he has been showing the other NFL teams what they missed out on ever since. He became the first American of Korean descent to win the MVP award at the Super Bowl, earning the honor in Super Bowl XL.

"I may not be the flashiest, most flamboyant wide receiver out there," Ward told *USA Today*'s Daniel Powers after the win. "But I get the job done for my team."

He also gets it done in the community. And that dates back to when he signed his first contract. Ward told his friend, Andy Rees, to seek out Pennsylvania-based charities focused on needy children and single-parent homes. After the Super Bowl win, Rees' next job was to figure out a way to expose the plight of mixed-race children in Korea.

"I have always wondered what my purpose was here on Earth," Ward told Rob Rossi of the *Pittsburgh Journal-Review*. "It wasn't just to play football. It was to do bigger things."

Ward was born in Seoul, South Korea, to a black father, Hines Ward Sr., and a Korean mother, Kim Young-he. The family moved to Georgia when Hines was barely a year old. After his parents broke up, courts ruled that his mother was not financially fit to raise him, but Hines eventually ended up living with his mother.

That's what has driven Ward to make a difference. Hines never had a father figure, and Parris stepped into that role. They would talk about "little" things and "big" things, and Parris is very proud of what Ward has been able to accomplish as a collegiate and professional receiver.

"He's true to his friends and true to what he believes in," Parris said. "What you see is what you get. He always takes care of his mom. He's more than willing to give a hand to people he's close to, and it's not a put-on. I'll give you an example. About eight years ago, he cut a check to get new football uniforms for the kids I was coaching then—kids I didn't even know."

In the same interview with Rossi, Ward summed up his place and his mission. "My mom always said, 'Never forget where you came from.' When you look at the different perspectives some people have in life, you cannot get caught up in playing football. I am never going to think I am better than anybody else. I am blessed to be doing what I love to do. Not everybody is so blessed."

Bulldogs fans are thankful for Ward's place in Athens.

59 The Countdown Game vs. Auburn, 1992

Garrison Hearst had a decent game rushing for the Bulldogs on November 14, 1992, with 35 carries for 105 yards, but it's the game's ending that everyone remembers on both sides of the ball in the 14–10 Georgia win.

Auburn fans maintain that the Georgia players sat on Auburn players and refused to get up. Georgia fans maintain that the Bulldogs were just doing their own version of clock watching and clock management. Larry Munson, was again, at his emotional best:

"Now Auburn's stadium roars as its offense runs out on the field. Stan White waving at the crowd to make a lot of noise and he says something to an official, and he bumps one of his tight ends. Here they are in that old fashioned T again."

Georgia's No. 12 ranking was threatened by a 5–3–1 Tigers team as James Bostic took the handoff with 19 seconds to go in the game. He hit the line just off left tackle, was stopped short of the goal line, and fumbled into the mass of bodies. Auburn, apparently, recovered:

"Three backs, they only need 8 or 9 inches, and White tries to keep it and sneak late, he didn't do it there. He tried to keep it, they ran the fullback.... White tried to step in.

"Watch the clock, 9, 8, 7, 6, 5, 4, we're not lined up, 3, they have no time-outs. 2, 1. I think it's over, they can't get a play off. We saved ourselves, I don't know how, they couldn't get a play off."

It was at this point where Auburn quarterback Stan White was chasing after officials trying to get one more play for the game, claiming the Bulldogs were taking their own sweet time getting up before time expired.

"White tried to fake it, they ran to the full, and then he tried to sneak in. Auburn wound up, Auburn messed up with the clock. Auburn couldn't get a play off; the Dawgs stop White trying to sneak in. We saved ourselves. No we didn't. Old Lady Luck saved us. Old Lady Luck has defeated them. The defense won the ballgame, make no mistake about that. 14–10. The defense saved our whatchamacallits."

Approximately 85,214 screaming Jordan-Hare Stadium ticket holders littered the field with anything they could get their hands on to make sure the zebras knew 5–4–1 was unacceptable on the Plains, but the top-15 ranking for Georgia was still intact with their 8–2 record, 6–2 in the SEC.

The Bulldogs finished the season 10–2 under Ray Goff, who is seen on all the television cameras at the game, motioning frantically to keep everything and everyone down on the ground.

Munson, before it was all said and done, went 69 seconds describing the frantic last 19 seconds of the game. Pat Dye finished his last season as Auburn head coach at 5–5–1, 2–5–1 and fifth in the SEC West, yielding to the Terry Bowden administration.

Stan White, the quarterback of that particular Auburn squad, recalled the events as Larry Munson called both teams to the line of scrimmage through the end of the game:

"To my recollection, there were 19 seconds left on the clock. It was second down on the 1-foot line, and we were in our last time out. On the sideline, our offense was discussing a QB sneak or a quick hitting handoff to our tailback, James Bostic, over left guard. The coaches decided to go with a quick handoff over left guard to Bostic.

"From the old T formation, the lead blocking back on the play collided with Bostic on the handoff, forcing a bobble of the ball. But James recovered the ball at the bottom of the pile actually closer to the goal line. Knowing we had no timeouts, I and other players were scurrying to get off the ground to get lined up to spike the ball on third down. Upon lining up and getting everyone set, I glanced at the clock and noticed approximately 10 seconds left.

"Then after the referee spotted the ball, a Georgia defensive lineman kicked the ball from the spot out to around the 10-yard line. Instead of stopping the clock for a delay of game or flagging a defensive player for impeding the spot of the ball, the head referee just jogged over and picked up the ball and went and spotted the ball again as the clock ran down to double zero.

"Afterwards, I chased down the head referee and would not allow him to leave the field, and I demanded he put more time on the clock. Obviously, I lost that battle, but he knew that a mistake had been made by the officiating crew—which in the end was very costly to us. The very next year, the NCAA passed a rule because of that game. If a defensive player impedes on the spot of the ball after it's put into ready for play, then it's an automatic defensive delay of game penalty and the clock will be stopped.

"Too little, too late for the 1992 Auburn team."

60 The Butts-Mehre Building

Go ahead, everyone else has heard the joke before.

We've already discussed what Wally Butts meant to the Bulldogs. Harry Mehre, who coached the team from 1928 to 1937, was SEC Coach of the Year twice, and was even named runner-up for National Coach of the Year honors.

Coach Dooley wanted a place that resembled a Hall of Fame on the campus, and the Stegeman Coliseum was running out of room itself. So in 1987, $12 million was spent on the initial version of the structure that houses the football offices, weight room, sports information, and sports medicine facilities.

The turn around in front of the building, Selig Circle, was named after Simon Selig Jr.—the largest single contributor toward the construction.

"They had to blast out 3,700 square yards of solid granite, so that building is sitting on solid granite," Dooley told the *Red and Black's* Angela Jett in 2002. "Nothing has a foundation like that."

What draws people there on football weekends is the Heritage Museum on the third floor. It hosts memorabilia from all the sports on campus and is a living, breathing, historical representation of everything you always wanted to know about Bulldogs athletics. The Heisman Trophies that were awarded to Frank Sinkwich and Herschel Walker are also there for viewing.

"Fridays before the football game, it is exciting to see how many fans stop by early…to see the new exhibits and get posters," John Bateman, associate promotions director for the Athletics Association, also told Jett during the 15th anniversary celebration. Each sport has its own space that gets updated at the beginning of every fall season.

The museum was even instrumental in bringing an athlete to Athens—Terrell Davis. In an interview Davis did with Austin Murphy of *Sports Illustrated* in 1996, "Boss Hog" talked about how one building swayed his opinion of the school:

"They took me through this big old museum-looking building with all these trophies and video screens. When you touched the screens, they showed famous plays. Downstairs, in the locker room, it's all red and pretty. They give you cleats and gloves—at Long Beach we had to pay for those things. You get a game helmet and a practice helmet. They had my jersey with my name already on it. I was like, 'I'm here!'"

Coach Dooley always thought a building like the Butts-Mehre was needed for recruiting—Davis is one example of how Dooley was right.

Like most buildings, Butts-Mehre has required some upgrading and updating. In 1999, there was a $2 million expansion of the weight room and the training room.

If you've wandered by campus in early 2010, there's a big change happening that you're seeing first-hand. An increase in the building by 53,000 square feet is underway that is scheduled to be completed within the next year and a half. There's also a renovation planned of 23,000 square feet of existing space.

The cost is $40 million—half of that sum has already been pledged by private donors.

The strength and conditioning areas are being expanded, the training room is receiving an overhaul, and a synthetic turf field is being installed so the team can work walk-throughs if needed. The space can also be converted to party space if anyone is inclined to have an official gathering on the same field that the Bulldogs call home.

New team meeting rooms and renovated coach's offices are also in the offing. And for those of you used to the original configuration of the practice fields, expect them to be rotated to be more in line with the new look of the building.

Got all that?

"We've got to still move forward as an entity [and] position ourselves to have success in the future," athletic director Damon Evans told Marc Weizser of the *Athens Banner-Herald*. "I want people to know we have been fiscally prudent over the last 10–11 years, and it has gotten us in a position where we can move forward right now."

The Butts-Mehre Building is certainly an example of that.

61 Richard Tardits, "Le Sack"

Biarritz, France, is known for its place alongside the Beach of Kings, the Museum of Chocolate, the lighthouse on Cape Hainaut, having one of the top five museums displaying Asian art in Europe, and something called thalassotherapy—the idea of using sea-based cures in a spa setting to get your mind and body right.

But Georgia Bulldogs fans know it more for being the home-town of one of the best linebackers in the history of the program, Richard Tardits.

In 1984, when Tardits was 19, he was staying in Augusta with a friend's family. He enjoyed the idea of staying on this side of the Atlantic and decided to enroll at the University of Georgia. When he found out that colleges and universities can pay their own student-athlete's way with something called "scholarships," he put on a pair of rugby shorts and knee-high socks and wanted to get a try out with Coach Dooley's Dogs.

First time out, Coach Dooley lined up Tardits at tight end and instructed him to block the defensive end across from him. Tardits tackled the guy instead, given his background with the French junior national rugby team.

As the story goes, Dooley then said, "So we figured we better put him on defense pretty quick." Dooley put Tardits on scout team defense, and the offensive linemen he was up against had a really hard time catching him and keeping him away from the quarterback. His freshman season was spent mainly on special teams.

In his sophomore year, just before his father was going to have him return home to France, Tardits was given his scholarship right on the practice field in front of all of his teammates.

He went on to set the Bulldogs record for sacks in a career with 29 in just three seasons of work—only one of them in which he was a starter. He broke Jimmy Payne's record of 28 sacks, and the record held until David Pollack came along and took it for himself 16 years later.

Tardits' adjustment on the field wasn't without its growing pains. Bill Lewis, the Bulldogs defensive coordinator, told *Sports Illustrated's* Hank Hersch that Richard was incredibly talented, "But when he first came here, it was almost—almost—a joke."

There was the one game where, as he was racing off the field so the defense wouldn't get a penalty for 12 men on the field, he ran to the other sideline to wait out the play. And then there was the game against LSU where he thought he got cheapshotted and started cussing in French at the guy who he thought pulled the stunt. The LSU player cussed back in French—that took a little getting used to.

Tardits became the eleventh player in Bulldogs history to earn a postgraduate scholarship, but he also put in a few years in the NFL with the Patriots and the Cardinals. A chronic ankle problem caused an early retirement, but Tardits enjoyed a bit of a cult following back home. Interest in American football skyrocketed to the point where the number of players in France doubled and the number of organized teams increased by 35 percent.

He's now in golf course development and management back home in France and is another great example in Bulldogs history that you can do anything you put your mind to if the drive, dedication, and teachability are there.

Tardits' linebacking prowess and ability to learn were, of course, *c'est magnifique!*

62 Bill Hartman

William C. Hartman Jr. played football in Athens in the 1930s and played professionally after graduation for the Redskins. Dawg fans may not know that he coached the backfield under Wally Butts from 1939 to 1956—after he played for Harry Mehre during his undergrad days.

Wally Butts convinced Hartman to come back to Athens. His son Bill remembered, "Daddy quit the NFL because he could make more money there [Georgia] than playing in the pros."

If Butts was the bad cop on the field, Coach Hartman was the good cop.

After leaving in 1956 to sell life insurance, a rule change by the NCAA brought Hartman back one more time. In the early 1970s, "volunteer coaches" were allowed on staffs. Hartman had to pay his own way to stay a coach, but he did so—in some form or fashion—until 1993. The NCAA abolished the idea of the volunteer coach, but Ray Goff and Vince Dooley convinced Hartman to become a graduate assistant, a position he held for another three seasons before his retirement.

It was during those tours of duty that he became nationally known as the school's volunteer kicking coach. At age 81, he eventually ran out of options inside the NCAA rule book. But he had plenty of memories to share with his son about how the program used to be in the early days:

"In the 1980 season, we went to New Orleans for the Sugar Bowl," son Bill said. "He was coaching the kickers at the time. We were eating lunch the day before, and he would tell me that in 1946, 'We came here and had dinner.' Things like that.... He got to show me where he had been in his heyday.

"In 1995, we were at the pregame warm-ups between Georgia and Georgia Tech at Grant Field. He showed me what he did during his 93-yard TD kickoff return in 1937—where he caught the ball—where he moved this move and moved that move.

"Almost 60 years later, he's showing me where he'd done that on the same field."

Hartman spent seventy years of his life associated with the same school, the same football program, in one function or another.

Here are a few of his achievements:
- President of the Georgia Student Education Fund for 50 years
- President of the Bulldog Club, the money collected for athletic scholarships is now donated to what is referred to as the Hartman Fund
- President of the Boys and Girls Clubs for the Athens YMCA
- Sat on the Athens City Council, ran for mayor of Athens, and ran for a seat in the state legislature

He died just one day shy of his 91st birthday in March 2006.

Hartman's funeral gave Dawgs' fans chills. It all started at First United Methodist Church before the burial. Oconee Hill Cemetery is outside the horseshoe end of Sanford Stadium. Bill Hartman's mother, father, and even the founders of the city of Athens are buried there. But it's also within earshot of Sanford Stadium.

As the casket was lowered, those who were there witnessed a very special send-off.

"I had some of dad's best football moments made into a play-by-play tape that Larry Munson cut in a studio," Bill said. "Only Larry, my wife, Glee, and I knew about it. My sisters didn't even know.

"[Longtime Atlanta sports anchor and family friend] Chuck Dowdle is looking at his watch saying, 'I gotta go back to Atlanta.' I told him not to leave yet. Something special was about to happen. At a point in the graveside service where the preacher talked about 'listening to the trees,' Claude Felton called the press box. He and Loran orchestrated the whole thing. They played Munson's calls over the Sanford Stadium PA.

"Now that was cool."

Munson had done a thoughtful, ad-libbed call on the 93-yard runback of the second-half kickoff of that Georgia–Georgia Tech game in 1937 and an 82-yard punt against Tulane—a record that held for years. It became the genesis of the Letterman's Club idea of purchasing plots at Oconee Hill where, as Hartman says, you can "hear the cheers as greatness drifts into Oconee Hill Cemetery."

Now that is cool.

What some people may not know is that Hartman was probably responsible for the most money ever donated to UGA. Alum Bernard Ramsey, the one-time CEO of American Express, donated an impressive $10 million in 1993. The single largest cash gift in university history was supplemented handsomely in 1996. Upon Ramsey's death, the bulk of his estate went to the school. If you count the cash gift, the total donation runs just less than $45 million. The money went to the Ramsey Center, the Terry College of Business, the Performing and Visual Arts Center, a pair of Georgia Research Alliance professorships, athletics, and the library.

It all coame about after Hartman invited Ramsey down for a football game in 1980.

63 Rex Robinson's Game-Winning Field Goal vs. Kentucky

"He puts it up. It looks good. Watch it. Watch it. Yeah! Yeah! Yeah! Yeah! Three seconds left. Rex Robinson put them ahead, 17–16. The bench is unconscious."

Rex Robinson missed his first PAT when he was kicker for the Bulldogs in 1977. It was the only one he missed as he went 101-for-102 during his career. His record for accuracy lasted until Brandon Coutu was a perfect 114-for-114 from 2004–07.

Robinson's field-goal numbers still have their place in the Georgia record book. He's still top five in career field goals, career field goal attempts, percentage made in a season, most points in a career, and field goals made over 50 yards in length.

One field goal in Lexington gave Larry Munson cause for another memorable moment.

The Bulldogs were 5–1 heading into their game against the 2–3–1 Wildcats in 1978. Commonwealth Stadium has traditionally been a tough place to play for UGA no matter the record of the home team going in. This game was no different as Kentucky had a 16–0 lead in the third quarter and Georgia had to battle back. The Bulldogs scored twice to cut the lead to 16–14 in the final 15 minutes. Robinson had the last chance to get the win with a 29-yard field goal with three seconds left on the clock. But there was one problem.

Coach Dan Magill tells the story this way:

"Coach Dooley, on the sidelines, yelled to his right tackle Tim Morrison, 'What are you doing here?'

"Morrison replied, 'I'm praying that Rex will make that field goal, Coach.'

Nine Bulldogs Kickers Have Earned the Honor of All-SEC

Jim McCullough, 1968
Kim Braswell, 1970
Allan Leavitt, 1976 (All-America)
Rex Robinson, 1978–80 (All-America 1979, 1980)
Kevin Butler, 1981–84 (All-America 1983, 1984)
John Kasay, 1990
Billy Bennett, 2002–03
Brandon Coutu, 2005
Blair Walsh, 2009 (Second Team)

"To which Coach Dooley exclaimed, 'My God, you're supposed to be in there right now blocking for Robinson. We only have 10 men on the field.'

"Fortunately, Coach [Fran] Curci of Kentucky called a timeout to put some added pressure on Robinson, which enabled Morrison to rush back on to the field."

Suffice it to say Robinson made the kick. Georgia finished the year 9–2–1, losing to Stanford in the Bluebonnet Bowl 25–22.

Fran Curci had three more chances to beat Georgia but finished his career 2–7 against the Bulldogs before Jerry Claiborne took over as head coach in 1982.

64 The Bookstore

You might be asking yourself, "Why include a bookstore in this list?" That's a very good question and yet another reason why there are oh-so-many interesting places and things to check out in Athens on a Georgia football game day.

The quick and easy reason to find the Bookstore is that it's located right near the stadium. Actually, it's across Sanford Drive from the stadium, attached by a courtyard to the Tate Student Center. It's a pretty large store with two floors that have pretty much everything you can think of that is related to the university and Georgia football.

If you find your way to the Bookstore on a game day and stand outside and watch, you will see that an awful lot of people come in and out of the place over the course of the day. There is no telling who you might run into inside. A couple of seasons ago, they had a rotating group of guest authors who came to sign their most recent book.

If it is a big name like a Vince Dooley, you can expect that the store will be packed.

The day a couple of years ago that Larry Munson, the legendary voice of the Bulldogs, appeared to sign his book, the line began forming about 4:00 AM. By the time Munson appeared to start signing, the line ran through most of the second floor, down the stairway, and wound through the better part of the first floor, as well. Munson stayed as long as he could, signing and posing for pictures with everyone.

The man considered the most famous Bulldog, Herschel Walker, received the same treatment when he showed up to sign his latest book. The line wound through the entire building. He also stayed a good hour after he was scheduled to leave.

Days like these give the Bookstore a place in the game-day lore. Aside from the size, it isn't really much different from any other campus bookstore. Sure, it carries textbooks. It also has plenty of Georgia football and athletics gear, as well. There is a nice selection of books on both the school and the athletic program, and there is even a snack section—if you're into that sort of thing.

A trip to the Bookstore should be part of every fan's game-day experience. Much like the Bridge, the Tate Student Center, the Dawg Walk, and other campus atmosphere activities, you and 50,000 other people can make the lap. Meaning you can start at the Tate and walk over to the Bookstore to browse or buy yourself a jersey or T-shirt and a book. Once you leave the Bookstore, look up and you are right in front of Sanford Stadium. If you look across the street, you can walk through a gate into the stadium if it is open. If it isn't, you can make your way down Sanford Drive and peer over the side and watch the Dog Walk. Or go to the other side and check out what is going on inside the stadium.

Chances are you will see the teams doing pregame warm-ups and fans making their way into the stadium.

65 The Tate Student Center

Of course it's perfectly normal for a university to put its Student Center right across the street from the football stadium. Or so you would think if you were walking down the middle of Sanford Drive or driving down Lumpkin Street right through the heart of the campus.

The Tate Student Center is a large building that borders on either end of the two most popular routes through the campus. It houses a multitude of dining areas, movie theaters, TV and study lounges, meeting and conference rooms, a post office, a business office, student organization offices, and the student radio station.

The Center was named for William Tate, a former Dean of Men at the university, and it opened in 1983. Along with all of the amenities that it provides for the students, it quickly became a popular place for people to visit before football games. The location was a dead giveaway. Though you could enter from the ground level on Baxter Street, if you go to the top level—level three—and exit at the rear of the building, you're right across the street from Sanford Stadium.

On a game day, it's not uncommon to see thousands of fans milling in and out of the center. You will often find them parked in front of one of the televisions scattered throughout the building, possibly watching one of the earlier football games. Or if the Bulldogs are playing a night game, quite often the movie theater will play the "SEC on CBS Game of the Week" on the theater's screen. Be aware though, the crowd picks up in there very quickly.

Remember, for those who haven't been, it's a college football Saturday in the South. Everyone, be it the tailgaters or the folks wandering around the area before the game, follows all the other teams and games. They know what's going on.

Another reason that people find their way to the Tate is the food court. If you walk in from the courtyard or from the Student Bookstore on the top floor, you can find the Bulldog Cafe with a Chick-fil-A Express right there. You'll also find one heck of a long line of people waiting for a chicken sandwich.

The new addition to the Tate, affectionately called Tate 2, opened in June 2009. It is a 100,000-sq.-ft. expansion that doubled the size of the student center. It was built on top of a two-story parking deck. Among the highlights of the New Tate Center are a 12,000-square-foot ballroom that can be broken up into smaller rooms if needed, six more conference rooms, a small amphitheater with a projection system, the new Print and Copy Services office, and a sports lounge named The Dawg Pen. They also went all out on the food court, bringing in several local chains and a restaurant that was developed by the school's Food Services.

Another highlight of the building is a 15-foot tile UGA Arch embedded within the floor that greets visitors as they pass through the main entrance to the building. This Arch apparently can be passed through if you're a freshman. But freshmen don't really press their luck with the indoor version, either.

The two buildings combined make for a big comfortable space for both the university and its students to relax and enjoy campus life and for alumni and others to gather and get fired up for football. The new addition doubles the capacity for fans looking to sit down, maybe grab a bite to eat, watch a little football, and catch up before the Bulldogs play.

From there you can either go up to Sanford Drive and make your way into the stadium, or you can head over to Baxter Street and work your way in at ground level. Either way, it's an opportunity to take in Georgia football in a way that not every school is able to provide. Most stadiums are somewhat isolated from other parts of campus.

Not at Georgia—where the Student Center, a big part of daily campus life, is also a big part of the game-day activities.

66 Knowshon Moreno

In the University of Georgia's colorful history of great tailbacks, one of the wildest stories is Knowshon Moreno's journey from New Jersey to Athens.

Moreno put impressive numbers on the board in just a few short years of taking handoffs from Matthew Stafford, and the program reached new heights the with him seven yards deep in the backfield. For all that effort, you can thank Moreno's high school SAT prep tutor.

Jean D'Arcy Maculaitis taught a class for high school athletes who were likely to head to college and play football. She had Moreno and Kade Weston, another New Jersey kid looking to play in a warmer climate than he enjoyed in high school, in her class. "Doctor Mac" just had a daughter graduate from UGA, and recommended the school to both Weston and later on Moreno.

Moreno wanted to attend a football camp in Athens between his junior and senior seasons, but there was an issue. Moreno was only 17, and he couldn't fly down to Athens by himself to attend the camp. So he traveled 16 hours on a train from New Jersey to attend the camp and piqued the interest of the Bulldogs and the coaching staff heading into his senior season.

His Middletown South High School team won its third straight state title that year, and he finished with the second-most rushing yards in New Jersey state high school history. The decision came down to Georgia, Virginia Tech, and Florida. All this for a kid who, if you asked him, thought he really couldn't play college football until his senior year at Middletown. Knowshon Moreno ultimately selected Georgia.

After redshirting his freshman year in 2006, Moreno was unleashed onto the unsuspecting SEC halfway through the 2007 season in the game against Vanderbilt. Five straight 100-yard-plus rushing performances later, his 1,334 yards were good enough for second all-time in UGA history for yards gained by a freshman—second only to Herschel Walker.

Knowshon picked up All-SEC freshman team honors in three separate polls, and he was even named freshman Offensive Player of the Year by *The Sporting News.* He was also the first freshman since Herschel Walker to gain 100 yards or more in five straight games.

His redshirt sophomore year was more of the same. Moreno was named to seven preseason All-America teams and preseason All-SEC by seven more groups. There was even some Heisman Trophy buzz surrounding No. 24. The signature move that every Bulldogs fan associates with Moreno in that season came in Week 2 against

Georgia running back Knowshon Moreno, No. 24, makes a third-quarter leap over Central Michigan's Vince Agnew, No. 22, during a game at Sanford Stadium in Athens, Georgia, on September 6, 2008. (AP Photo/*Atlanta Journal-Constitution*, Ben Gray)

Central Michigan.

Late in the third quarter with Georgia up comfortably 42–17, the Bulldogs ran a simple "student body right" play. Moreno found a huge hole off the right side, cut upfield, and was untouched for 23 yards. Chippewas defensive back Vince Agnew thought he was going to get Moreno around the waist, but Knowshon had other ideas.

He jumped over Agnew, using him as a leapfrog partner, and gained another four yards before he couldn't maintain his balance any longer. The play call by Fox Sports Net's Bob Rathbun was simply, "Look at him jump the defender!" followed by 12 seconds of laughter and a Sanford Stadium crowd going insane.

The clip has become a YouTube staple to this day, registering more than 526,000 views. Coach Richt can trace that particular move to a spring practice in 2007. While it may have been new to Bulldogs fans, Moreno's teammates had seen it and been victim to it before.

Moreno went airborne two weeks later in the Arizona State game, but it was more of a nosedive than a hurdle. The result on the scoreboard was better in Tempe, however, with the game's first touchdown in the Bulldogs' win a result of that toss play.

After being held in the Alabama game to only 34 yards, Knowshon really had to turn on the jets to get back in the national spotlight. Five of his next six games were 100-yard-plus performances, and he wrapped up the year with an even 1,400 yards and 16 rushing touchdowns. He became the second Bulldogs rusher to exceed 1,000 yards in back-to-back seasons—second to Herschel Walker again who did it all three years on campus. The 1,400 yards were good enough for a top five in the Georgia record book, as well.

After being named a semi-finalist for the Maxwell Award and a finalist for the Doak Walker award and having his name attached to either first- or second-team All American lists, Moreno had a tough decision to make: would he come back to Athens for his junior year in 2009?

The decision wasn't all that tough. It was time to go.

The Denver Broncos selected Moreno 12th overall in the 2009 NFL Draft. He finished his rookie year with a combined 1,162 yards for the Broncos offense, playing in all 16 games for head coach Josh McDaniels. Knowshon finished third in the Associated Press version of the Offensive Rookie of the Year voting.

The speedy tailback named for his father, Knowledge, and his mother, Varashon, will always have a place in the record books and the "best of" conversations regarding Bulldogs runners.

67 2005 Sugar Bowl Played in Atlanta

The Georgia Bulldogs ended the 2005 football season with a 9–2 record and an SEC Eastern Division Championship, the team's third in four years. Georgia closed that season by heading down State Highway 316, going south on I-85, and turning right onto North Avenue to arch rival Georgia Tech's Bobby Dodd Stadium where they defeated the Yellow Jackets 14–7.

The next week the Bulldogs again made the trip to Atlanta. This time, the Bulldogs went downtown to the Georgia Dome where Georgia faced LSU in the SEC Championship Game. The determined Georgia team took care of business, defeating LSU 34–14, winning its second SEC championship in four years, and earning a BCS bowl bid.

That bid was for the Sugar Bowl, but circumstances would be different.

Normally that bowl bid would mean a trip to New Orleans, Louisiana. However, months earlier, the city was nearly destroyed by Hurricane Katrina. The Superdome, which hosts the game annually, was severely damaged by the storm and virtually gutted by inhabitants who used the facility as a shelter.

With New Orleans in peril and the Superdome out of commission, the Sugar Bowl found refuge in Atlanta, which agreed to host the game on January 2, 2006.

For the third time in a month, the Georgia Bulldogs trekked to Atlanta. It marked the first time the Bulldogs would play in a major bowl in the state of Georgia. While not truly their home field, the Bulldogs would have an advantage, especially with their fan base staying in-state to attend the game.

The opponent was the West Virginia Mountaineers, who had won the Big East Conference championship. The Mountaineers were a young but very talented team loaded with speed at the skill positions. West Virginia also had an advantage—the element of surprise.

With three-quarters of the crowd of 70,000-plus in the Georgia Dome wearing Bulldogs colors and making all kinds of noise, the Mountaineers, and Steve Slaton in particular, dropped the jaws of the Bulldog fateful, who quickly fell silent.

On West Virginia's first possession of the game, Slaton took the ball and went 52 yards for a touchdown. After that, Georgia fans couldn't believe what was happening.

West Virginia scored three touchdowns in the first quarter and added another score at the beginning of the second quarter. The Mountaineers were up 28–0 before Georgia fans were even comfortable in their seats.

Georgia's Will Thompson, No. 58, drops West Virginia quarterback Pat White for a loss in the second quarter of the Sugar Bowl held at the Georgia Dome in Atlanta on Monday, January 2, 2006. (AP Photo/Bill Haber)

West Virginia's fourth touchdown came from a Bulldogs turnover by their senior quarterback. West Virginia's Mike Lorello sacked Georgia quarterback D.J. Shockley, forcing a fumble with the Mountaineers Marc Magro recovering.

The 2005 Bulldogs were D.J. Shockley's team. He had waited three years as David Greene's backup for his one year as Georgia's starting quarterback. While Shockley led the Bulldogs to an SEC Championship, this wasn't exactly the ending he wanted.

Following West Virginia's fourth touchdown of the game, Georgia began using the short passing game to spark the comeback. Shockley completed three straight passes—a 15-yard completion to Leonard Pope followed by a 14-yard catch by Kregg Lumpkin, then a 17-yard pass to Bryan McClendon. On the next play, Lumpkin took off on a 34-yard touchdown run that gave the Bulldogs a much-needed lift.

On Georgia's next possession, the offense followed the same script. Shockley completed three short passes, then Thomas Brown broke out a long touchdown run. Brown's 52-yard run to the end zone cut West Virginia's lead in half, 28–14.

West Virginia added a field goal before Georgia scored once again before the half. This time Shockley completed a 4-yard touchdown pass to Leonard Pope, and the Bulldogs were down by 10 at 31–21.

In the second half, D.J. Shockley hit two long passes that led to Georgia scores—a 34-yard touchdown pass to A.J. Bryant late in the third quarter, and a 43-yard scoring strike to McClendon again late in the fourth quarter. Shockley finished the game with 277 yards passing and three touchdowns.

While D.J. Shockley had a tremendous game to close his Georgia career, West Virginia freshman Steve Slaton was the star of the show. Slaton's 52-yard touchdown run before Georgia's final score was too much to overcome, and the Mountaineers prevailed, winning the 2006 Sugar Bowl 38–35. Slaton rushed for 204 yards to earn Sugar Bowl MVP honors.

It was a tremendously disappointing loss for the Bulldogs, who finally had the opportunity to play in a BCS bowl within the state borders and couldn't get the win. The next year, the Sugar Bowl returned home to the Louisiana Superdome.

Georgia returned to a postseason game at the Georgia Dome, facing Virginia Tech in the Chick-Fil-A bowl. The Bulldogs defeated the Hokies 31–24.

68 Get a Picture Taken with "Big Dawg"

If you've been to a Georgia home game or have seen one on television, you've seen a guy right up against the hedge-line who has sacrificed his bald head for the sake of artwork. His head sports a very well-detailed version of the Georgia Bulldogs mascot in all its red, white, and black glory. He's usually wearing a pair of overalls ordained with all kinds of Bulldogs paraphernalia and patches covering a red polka-dotted undershirt. His name is Mike Woods.

The routine goes a little something like this. He is spotted by the television camera. He nods slightly, raises an index finger in a "No. 1" fashion, barking follows as he bows his head, and the artwork is seen across the country.

"They bring all their babies and their little kids over to have their pictures made," Mike Woods revealed in an interview with CBS College Sports Television. "I bet you I've taken 50,000 pictures of babies and kids and fans. It's just unreal! I mean, I've never seen anything like it."

Although his name is Mike Woods, the Bulldog Nation knows him by another name—Big Dawg.

And here's how Big Dawg and his unique place in Bulldogs lore came to be. Mike Woods' father, Lonnie, was a volunteer Bulldogs bus driver for a number of years and was responsible for making sure the Bulldogs defense was driven around the region in one piece on game days.

Erk Russell was the defensive coordinator during the elder Woods' years as driver. Russell's players, as Woods tells the story, constantly tried to get his father to shave his full head of hair to resemble Russell's bald head.

The first game that Lonnie Woods shaved his head for was the 1980 National Championship Game at the Sugar Bowl against Notre Dame. A family tradition was born. He kept the bald look until his passing in 1987, and that was when Mike took over.

Obviously, Mike can't do the paint job himself. That duty and imagination falls to his wife of almost 40 years, Dianna. It takes her about 45 minutes, at last check, to paint her husband's head, and he hasn't missed a home game in Sanford Stadium in almost 50 years.

"I'm really thrilled that he's doing this," Dianna said in the same television interview. "Because his daddy was a really nice man, people loved him. The students fell in love with him. He had a great personality."

Dianna says she modified the look on her husband's head a few times, but they both agree that the hat atop the bulldog's head takes the longest to paint. The rest of the look is pretty quick to put in place. But there are times that she forgets to put both ears on Uga, and she admits that there are probably no two paintings that have looked the same during all this time.

Woods also attends other sporting events on campus with his unmistakable look, and he was even named a Super Fan in 2006 during a contest held by Lincoln Financial Services (the former Raycom people who broadcast a Saturday SEC Game of the Week).

Woods already has his tombstone constructed—black granite with a simple "Woods" nameplate and a bulldog adorned above. He hopes his sons will continue the painted tradition long after the Big Dawg has headed for the Dawghouse in the sky.

There's a pretty good feeling that's one of the safer bets around Athens. As is the idea that Big Dawg's Facebook page will continue to grow.

69 Hairy Dawg

There's the real-life, breathing, ice-sitting, dawg-house-living, snapping-at-Auburn receivers mascot, and then there's the walking-upright version with the rock-solid jawline.

Sonny Seiler is in charge of the former. The university is in charge of the latter.

What's it like to be the one on two legs? What does it take, and how could you get the spot?

Allen Kinzly talked about the experience, what it takes to get to wear the suit, and what it's like wearing the suit in front of so many people on Saturdays. Kinzly is now a television sports anchor.

Kinzly spent two years as "Spike," the inflatable mascot that's seen at other campus sporting events. He "graduated" to a year as Hairy Dawg. Usually, tryouts are through word-of-mouth or through the odd advertisement placed by the head cheerleading coach on campus.

"If you're interested, you figure it out," Kinzly admitted.

The year he tried out, Kinzly had nine opponents. And it's a three-day process. There's a fitness test as the cheerleaders record how fast you can run the mile and how many push-ups you can do in a given amount of time. The next day, you interview with judges. You show them your personality. They ask why you want the position, what you think Hairy Dawg brings to the school, and how you would handle a kid who's crying in front of you.

"Maybe you act shy yourself, play a game of Peek-a-boo, or hide behind the dad to try and stop the child from crying," Kinzly said. "You show the judges how you take a situation like that and turn it around."

You then put on the suit and dance to a piece of music for 30 or 45 seconds.

"You show the judges how you groove to the beat," he continued. "You have to make big motions and stay active. You carry the attitude that someone is always watching. You can't just sit there."

Day two ends with random props (Kinzly got a toy electric guitar and a beach ball to play with) and a scenario painted by the judges to show enthusiasm to a crowd in a random game-day situation.

Day three starts with a three-minute skit. You make your own props, have your own soundtrack, and develop your own storyline. It's the candidate's opportunity to convey Hairy Dawg's personality. Kinzly had a plastic television displaying different channels and commercial products.

"The biggest rule of mascots is you can't talk," Kinzly reveals. "You might have 30 seconds to ask a question to someone you're working with, but that's about it. And you can never take the head or any part of the costume off in public."

His workouts were the same as the cheerleaders in the mornings. There's running, lifting weights, practices, meetings, appearances, community events, birthdays, and weddings that all get thrown into the mix. Hairy Dawg makes anywhere from five to 10 appearances in Bulldog Nation during game weeks.

An average game-day schedule is busy. "At 8:00 AM, you're at tailgating," Kinzly said. "Then there's the Dog Walk, pregame stuff before the game itself. And then there might be a birthday party afterward.

"You wear everything the players wear—plus fur. You do lose a couple of pounds of water weight during the game, and you start seeing double by halftime some games. You start looking out of one eye because you get a little cross-eyed. But you can hide underneath the cheerleading platform to catch your breath."

It may seem a little odd to ask a mascot for career highlights, but Kinzly has them just like the guys on the field. "It was the best three years of my life. The 2005 SEC Championship Game—the players are going crazy. You're trying to grab a hat or a T-shirt. I got to touch the SEC trophy and leap into the crowd. I got a free trip to the NCAA Final Four in St. Louis to be with the other mascots selected to represent the NCAA. When I was 'Spike' the inflatable mascot, I ended up going to New York and appearing on CBS' *Early Show* and *The Tony Danza Show*."

Kinzly also notes that Hairy Dawg finally got to start wearing different wardrobes during his time in uniform. For homecoming, he broke out the tuxedo look—gotta look smooth for the camera.

"Biggest idea is that you've got to have fun with it," the guy whose license plate says "Hairy '05" admitted. "If you're not having a good time, no one's having a good time watching you.

"You wanna know who 'that guy' is? I was 'that guy.' The best part and the worst part of being Hairy Dawg is that no one knows who you are."

70 College Avenue and the Party District

From the perspective of many students at the University of Georgia, Athens by itself can be identified as a "party district." Recommendations about where to go and what to do are plentiful.

Hannah Smith is the communications manager for the Athens Convention and Visitor's Bureau and she offered an eclectic mix of sights and activities for visitors.

"I would take enough time to explore every nook and cranny of Agora, on Clayton Street, for all things funky and vintage," she said. "Bead my own necklace at Native America Gallery. Thumb through the vinyl at Wuxtry records, and imagine Peter Buck and Michael Stipe meeting up as college students in that very spot. Get my picture made with the Caesar Dawgustus statue. Kick back with good tunes and food on the patio at Farm 255 or The Melting Point. Stay out late and get one last huge burger from Clocked. Make sure I was downtown with throngs of people during the Twilight Criterium, Athens Human Rights Festival, and AthFest.

"If you're in need of a sentimental angle, I once happened to be on a press visit the morning after UGA graduation, and saw numerous proud parents taking photos of their graduate in cap and gown, huge smiles, finally *underneath* the arch. Great people-watching moment."

The Caesar Dawgustus statue at the corner of College and Broad is part of a series of fiberglass "dawg" statues in the Who Let the Dawgs Out statue series. There about forty of these statues, normally outside buildings in and around town, that the Athens-Oconee County Junior Woman's Club started in 2003 to raise money for local charities.

Zurich, Switzerland, is thought of as the origin of the statues-on-display idea with their 800 cows throughout the town. The idea spread to New York for their CowParade. And that was where Woman's Club members Linda Ford and Julie Walters got the idea of the Athens version. The woman's club is starting to offer miniature replicas of the statues to raise funds from a different angle.

Farm 255 is part of the "slow-food movement," planting and reaping their own seeds and food for a return to the days before microwaves and take-out. They even have their own organic farm for that purpose and take pride in the idea that they don't use any chemicals as part of their production. Local farmers are also part of the dynamic, providing food for sale for anyone who walks in the door.

The Twilight Criterium is the initial stage of a bike race that turns 30 in 2010. It's part of a two-day festival that celebrates Athens, biking, and it is the second-largest event in town. There are eight different classes to choose from, and the event is regarded by *VeloNews* magazine as the "Criterium Not To Miss" if you're a competitor. It also holds the largest and oldest hand-cycling race in the country.

AthFest happens every June and is a four-day celebration of music, the arts, and film. There are outdoor stages and indoor concerts. Bands have reunited to perform at AthFest over the years to recapture their sound and re-launch their careers. And the Southeast Tourism Society has named AthFest one of the "Top 20 Events for June" five times in the last decade.

For more than 30 years every April, the Human Rights Festival has been a gathering to speak, sing, and compare notes on the issue of human rights in a town-square setting. Every point of view is represented, and all speakers and musicians have one message and goal—world peace and the discussion of the topic.

Kathryn Lookofsky, the director and CEO of the Athens Downtown Development Authority, offered her own recommendations with some ideas ranging from music and clothing to off-the-beaten-path material.

"Heery's Clothes Closet carries high-end designer fashions that rival the best boutiques in the Southeast," she said. "George Dean's Menswear is a step back in time. They carry classically tailored menswear, game day pants, seersucker suits, and where else can you still purchase a properly fitted men's hat? Aurum Studios features local art and beautiful custom jewelry as unique as you are. Helix has great quirky gifts and homegoods. Toula's has an incredible candle selection and R. Wood pottery. Jackson Street Books has a huge selection of rare and used books. School Kids and Wuxtry Records are great places to purchase tunes from the hottest local bands.

"I once heard downtown Athens described as a 'Southern Belle with a nose ring.' You really can't get a much more accurate description. The downtown district has all of the charm and beauty of an iconic small Southern town with an über-cool, bold rock edge. There truly is something for everyone here.

"You can sit on College Square on any given fall day and you might see a punk kid with a blue Mohawk eating lunch two seats down from a banker in blue pinstripes sipping coffee a few feet away from a couple of sweet elderly 'blue-haired' ladies. It's just that kind of place. Every semester we have a few more thousand students fall in love with Athens all over again, and they never want to leave."

It's easy to see the district has something for everyone, and you don't have to look very far to leave town with more than what you had when you first arrived.

71 The Varsity

Frank Gordy didn't play football at the University of Georgia. Nor is Frank Gordy from Athens. In fact, you can trace his history back to arch rival Georgia Tech. But Frank Gordy and his creation, The Varsity, is one of the most famous landmarks and popular restaurant stops in Athens.

The Athens version of The Varsity opened up in 1932 in downtown at the corner of Milledge and Broad Streets, right across from the UGA campus. In 1963, Gordy closed that location to concentrate on the current one further down Broad Street.

A look at its history explains why The Varsity is held in such high esteem. Gordy opened the original Varsity in 1928 across from the Georgia Tech campus. It was a wild success. It was only logical that he take that creation and try to establish it in Georgia's other significant college town, Athens.

Moving to the second location in Athens gave the restaurant a similar feel to the successful one in Atlanta. From the drive-in format complete with carhops to the hot dogs and fried pies, the two restaurants are one and the same.

When you make a trip to Athens, The Varsity is a must do. One of the first things that you will notice is the hectic pace. The place is always busy, and the cashiers are constantly hollering out their orders. Not only do they holler, they holler in a language all its own.

The first thing that you will hear when you walk to the register is always, "What'll ya have? What'll ya have?"

From a Heavy Weight (hot dog with extra chili), to a Yellow Dog (naked dog with mustard), or a Squirt One or an F.O. (Varsity Orange), and a Ring One (order of onion rings), it is a sport all unto itself to try to figure to what the cacophony of terms actually means.

Don't forget the chili! If you try it, you will know why I say that. It is present on a hot dog (the standard is a hot dog with chili and mustard) or a hamburger (chili steak). In fact, on the hot dogs, you'll be getting it unless you ask for one without it.

Really, you wouldn't think about this, but the food itself isn't as unhealthy as it sounds. The highest calorie item on the menu is the Frosted Orange. Not what you would think for a fast food place, but one of the things Frank Gordy set out to do when he started the restaurants was to make sure that he served "Good Food, Fast."

On a game day, it will be crowded. There will be plenty of students—after all, the food is cheap, and what is more appealing to a college kid than that? But there will also be alumni and townsfolk and people passing through. To the people in the area, The Varsity is someplace you go. Not every day, mind you, but for special occasions, maybe to get some tailgating food, or just to say that you went.

Really, there isn't one particular thing that makes The Varsity a required stop on any tour. It is a combination of history and nostalgia with an old school kind of feel. Walking into the place feels like you stepped into something from the 1950s or '60s.

It is not a to-die-for kind of food, but in the era of McDonald's, Burger King, and Wendy's, it is something different. Much like football in the South, it may not be something that you would understand unless you were part of it. Southern football and the University of Georgia have unique traditions and an interesting variety of historical people, places, and things.

72 Ray Goff

Bulldogs red and black runs through the veins of Ray Goff, who had a lasting impact as a quarterback for Georgia, then he went on to become head coach of the Bulldogs.

Goff grew up in the South Georgia town of Moultrie in Colquitt County where he was a quarterback for the Packers. In 1971, Goff led Moultrie High School to an 8–2 record and received honorable mention All-State honors.

In 1972, Goff quarterbacked the Packers to an undefeated regular season and a 1-AAA Region championship, only the second in school history. Moultrie ended the 1972 regular season No. 1 in the *Atlanta Journal-Constitution* poll. In the Georgia state playoffs, Moultrie High defeated Glynn Academy 26–8 in the quarterfinal round, but the Packers' season ended in the semi-final round as they lost to Central (Macon) 16–15.

Goff led the 1972 Moultrie Packers to an 11–1 season while earning first-team All-State honors.

With his career at Moultrie High School complete, Goff took his talents up to Athens to play for the Bulldogs.

Goff had to wait for his turn as the Georgia quarterback. By 1974, he was competing against Dicky Clark and Matt Robinson. Clark won initially, but Robinson proved to be the more efficient passer and started the rest of the '74 season.

By the time the 1975 season arrived, Georgia's offensive line was developing into a well-oiled machine and the Junkyard Dog (or "Dawg" depending on your perspective) defense was beginning to make stops. Georgia's offense committed to running the football. Vince Dooley and his staff realized that they had the best of both worlds at quarterback—Matt Robinson could make things happen with his passing skills, and Ray Goff could run the option.

Robinson remained Georgia's starting quarterback for the 1975 opener against Pittsburgh, but he broke a rib before preseason camp started. Goff started against the Panthers, and the job was his from then on.

One of the most memorable moments in Goff's Bulldogs career occurred at Vanderbilt on October 18, 1975, thanks to some trickery from head coach Vince Dooley.

Down 7–3 to the Commodores late in the second quarter, the Bulldogs faced second down at the Vanderbilt 26-yard line. Needing a big play to capture some momentum heading into half-time, Dooley decided to run a shoestring play that the Bulldogs practiced the Thursday before the game.

Georgia offensive line coach Jimmy Vickers thought the play would work. After viewing film, Vickers noticed the Vanderbilt's defense tended to lose focus in between plays. So the shoestring play was called.

The football was placed on the right hash mark, so Goff approached the ball while Vanderbilt was huddled and pretended to tie his shoe. The rest of the Bulldogs offense stood around the left harsh mark. Like a center, Goff flipped the football to flanker Gene Washington who had a nine-player escort down the left sideline. The Vanderbilt defense was caught off guard, and Washington had an easy 36-yard touchdown run.

"The more I thought about it, the less I thought it would work," Goff said.

The next year, Goff put on one of the best all-around performances by a Georgia quarterback against Florida at the Gator Bowl. Down 27–13 to the Gators at halftime, Goff lead Georgia to 27 unanswered points and a 41–27 win.

Matt Robinson

Back in the mid-1970s, Ray Goff was the running quarterback and Matt Robinson was the passing specialist.

As the full-time starter in 1974, Robinson threw for 1,317 yards for a Bulldogs team that finished 6–6. The next two seasons as Georgia put greater emphasis on the run and Robinson split playing time with Goff, his passing numbers fell considerably. In 1975, Matt Robinson threw for 369 yards and tossed for 609 yards in 1976 to lead Georgia in passing. During the 1975 and 1976 seasons, it became obvious that Georgia was going to throw the ball when Robinson entered the game.

Matt Robinson's name is still very prominent in the Georgia record book. He still tops the record book in four categories. He's still the Bulldogs record holder in average gain per pass attempt in a career (8.38) and in a single season (10.88 in 1974) and remains the Georgia record holder in average gain per pass completion in a career (18.36) and in a single season (21.95 in 1974).

Goff's performance against Florida was one for the ages. He rushed for 184 yards and three touchdowns and was a perfect 5-for-5 passing and two touchdowns. During Goff's playing career, he was a perfect 3–0 against Florida, and the 1976 win over the Gators was the momentum the Bulldogs needed toward the SEC championship. Goff was named SEC Player of the Year.

Ray Goff's ties to Georgia were very strong, and after three years coaching at the University of South Carolina, Goff returned to Athens to join Vince Dooley's staff. His responsibilities included coaching the tight ends, running backs, and working as recruiting coordinator from 1981–88. Goff assembled some outstanding talent for the Bulldogs that lead to their success during the 1980s.

In 1988, Vince Dooley retired as head coach of the Bulldogs and the search began for his replacement. Former defensive coordinator Erk Russell was offered the job but turned it down to stay at Georgia Southern. Then Dick Sheridan, who was the head coach at North Carolina State, was offered the position, and he turned it down.

When the search began, Ray Goff wasn't on the radar screen. But after Russell and Sheridan decided to turn down the job, the University began to look internally.

"They were in a scramble," Goff told Dawgpost.com and Scout.com in 2007. "There were a couple of assistant coaches at Georgia that put in for the job."

One was George Haffner, who was the consensus choice within the coaching staff to get the job, but for one reason or another it wasn't going to happen. That's when Goff decided to throw his hat in the ring. With no head coaching experience, Goff was offered and accepted the job.

"They've gone out on a limb, there's no doubt about it," Goff told the Associated Press after the announcement of his promotion to head coach. Not since W.S. Whitney was hired had the

University of Georgia offered the head coaching job to someone with no prior experience at that level.

"Ultimately I felt that Ray Goff, a Georgia man, deserved a chance [to be head coach]," DawgPost.com and Scout.com added. "The Georgia people liked him, and it would obviously be a very popular choice,"

Goff's first Bulldogs team in 1989 finishing a mediocre 6–6, but to the satisfaction of the Georgia fans it defeated Florida 17–10. It would prove to be the only success a Goff-coached Bulldogs team would have against the Gators.

The next season the Bulldogs won only four games, including double-digit losses to traditional rivals Florida (38–7), Auburn (33–10), and Georgia Tech (40–23). Goff's record his first two years as head coach was 10–13. It was not a good start, and when you couple that with hated rival Georgia Tech claiming a share of the 1990 national championship, the Georgia fans were becoming very restless.

Things had to turn around in 1991, and they did. With Eric Zeier taking over as quarterback midway through the season, the Bulldogs finished 9–3, defeating Arkansas 24–15 at the Independence Bowl in Shreveport, Louisiana. Georgia had some momentum heading into the 1992 season.

Georgia started the 1992 season 7–1 before losing to Florida 26–24. The Bulldogs did defeat their other rivals Auburn and Georgia Tech, defeated Ohio State in the Citrus Bowl and went into 1993 feeling pretty good about the direction of the program.

That changed when the Bulldogs got off to a 4–4 start heading into the Florida showdown. It appeared Georgia had tied the game against the Gators when Eric Zeier hit Jerry Jerman on a 12-yard touchdown pass, and the celebration ensued. No one noticed that Florida's Anthone Lott had called a timeout right before the ball was snapped.

Georgia had two more shots at the end zone very deep in Florida territory but couldn't score. The Gators prevailed 33–26.

After the Florida loss, Georgia lost to Auburn 42–28 and was thrashed by Georgia Tech 43–10 to finish 5–6 on the year. Support for Goff was beginning to erode.

In 1994, it got worse. Georgia finished with a 6–4–1 record, but a bad loss to Vanderbilt in Athens 43–30 soured Bulldogs fans. Losing to Florida 52–14 in Gainesville cast serious doubt, and Ray Goff was officially on the hot seat.

The next season was Ray Goff's last at Georgia. A series of bad losses in 1995 in front of the Bulldogs fans in Athens did Goff in. Alabama shut out Georgia 31–0, Florida put up 52 points on Georgia at Sanford Stadium, and Auburn won there too, 37–31. After the Auburn loss, Vince Dooley made a very difficult choice. Dooley pulled the trigger and fired Ray Goff as head coach.

Goff moved away from football into the business world where he has found success. He became part owner of the Zaxby's restaurant franchise that has expanded throughout the Southeast.

As for his days as Georgia head coach, he has no regrets. "I am proud of what we accomplished at Georgia," Goff told DawgPost.com and Scout.com in 1997. "We didn't win every game, but he had good kids."

73 5 and 10 Restaurant

In Athens, there are certain restaurant types that you will find much like any other city. You'll find your fast-food hamburger joints, pizza delivery, chicken-finger restaurants, and sports bars. If you look hard enough, you'll find some fine dining as well—nationally known fine dining.

Imagine being in a small college town and having a restaurant with an accomplished chef, Hugh Acheson, who has been nominated for The James Beard Foundation's Best Chef Award. Acheson is the same chef who has been recognized in local newspapers, *Food and Wine* magazine, *Bon Appetit* magazine, and StarChefs.com.

Top-flight food and a small Southern town, a combination that would have seemed unlikely not so long ago, is certainly working in Athens. Acheson, originally from Canada, settled in Athens. A self-taught cook, he spent time working for some of the great chefs all over the United States before he decided in 2000 that it was time to go it on his own. He had spent time in Athens, working as chef and general manager at the Last Resort Grill, and he decided he wanted to return to the area.

If you spend time in the Atlanta-Athens area and know your food, the style of choice for serious foodies is "homegrown natural." Those words are the key to Acheson's cooking techniques and what his restaurant was built on. He draws from a wealth of experience with Southern cooking and presents it with unique French and Italian twists. The restaurant not only has a local clientele, it draws a steady stream of fans from the Atlanta area more than an hour away.

The 5 and 10, situated right near downtown on Lumpkin Street, stands as the benchmark for the Athens food scene. It is also the beginning of the chef's empire. The National restaurant, another creation, opened in 2007. He also opened a wine store and has his own channel where he talks about cooking on YouTube.

So if you're not just a football fan but a foodie as well, fear not. There is fine dining for you along with the endless line of restaurants that cater to the fast-food fans. There is more to Athens than just football and music. There is also some very good food out there. You just need to know where to look for it.

74 The Charlton County Baileys

The good folks in the South Georgia town of Folkston can tell you all about the Bailey boys—Roland Jr. and Rodney. The Bailey brothers are more commonly known as Champ and Boss, respectively.

Champ Bailey was an energetic child growing up, so his mother, Elaine Bailey, nicknamed Roland Jr. "Champ" about the time he was two years old. The name proved appropriate as Champ excelled in the classroom and was placed in Charlton County's gifted program in the fifth grade.

Champ's high school career was one for the ages. From the quarterback position, Champ rushed for 3,572 yards with 58 touchdowns and threw for 1,211 yards and 10 touchdowns. On defense, Champ totaled 79½ tackles and eight interceptions during his high school career. After his senior year, Champ was named to *Parade* magazine's High School All-American team.

Champ Bailey's older brother, Ronald Bailey, was a standout quarterback, defensive back, and kicker for Charlton County High School and was the first of the Bailey boys to play for the Georgia Bulldogs. As the big brother, Ronald's influence on Champ was tremendous.

"I'm a big believer in leading by example, and Ron is who I learned that from," Champ Bailey told the *Denver Post* back in July 2008.

Having his big brother already in Athens made the transition from high school to college much easier for Champ, who in Tony Barnhart's book, *What It Means To Be A Bulldog*, said, "It helped me to have my older brother, Ronald, already there. He was a starter, and he just kind of showed me what to do."

Once in Athens, Champ Bailey was perhaps the most versatile player to ever suit up for Georgia since two platoon football started.

For his freshman season in 1996, Champ Bailey stayed on the defensive side of the ball at cornerback, making 47 total tackles and two interceptions.

In 1997, head coach Jim Donnan decided to take advantage of Champ Bailey's versatility, letting him play offense and special teams. As Champ said in that same Barnhart book, "In high school, I had played a lot of offense, and once coach Donnan gave me a taste of it, I didn't want to go back."

Champ Bailey's offensive participation came mainly when the Bulldogs were in passing situations, and he caught 12 balls for 234 yards his sophomore season. Against arch rival Georgia Tech, Bailey made two key catches with less than a minute left in the game to set up the Bulldogs winning touchdown in their 27–24 win over the Yellow Jackets.

In 1998, Champ's brother, Boss, joined the team after a stellar high school career at Charlton County. Like his brothers before him, Boss Bailey played quarterback, defense, and even punted the ball in high school. He felt no pressure from his older brothers to go to Georgia, but Athens seemed like a second home, so Boss Bailey followed suit.

While Boss Bailey saw limited action in 1998, big brother Champ Bailey never got off the field. Boss started on defense, offense, and special teams, participating in more than 100 plays in six different games that season.

The high-water mark for Champ Bailey came in the Bulldogs 28–17 win over Auburn. Champ totaled 119 plays against the Tigers, 62 on defense, 49 on offense, and eight in special teams.

"I was just doing my job, whatever I could to help the team," Champ Bailey told the *Athens Banner-Herald*. "To me it wasn't that big of a thing."

Champ Bailey ended his junior season with 52 tackles and three interceptions. That earned him first-team Associated Press All-American honors and won him the Bronko Nagurski Award as the nation's best defensive player from the Football Writers Association of America.

Although his younger brother, Boss, was in the mix at Georgia and he wanted to look after him, Champ Bailey was feeling the pull of the NFL and decided at the end of his junior season that it was time to move on. The Washington Redskins selected Champ Bailey in the first round, and he played five seasons in the nation's capital before a trade to Denver.

In 1999, Boss Bailey moved into Georgia's starting lineup on defense. While Champ weighed in at just less than 200 pounds, Boss filled out to 230 pounds but was blessed with speed. Boss Bailey was timed at 4.31 in the 40-yard dash, the third-fastest time in school history and a hundredth of a second behind Champ.

Boss Bailey tore a ligament in his left knee in high school and recovered. On the opening kickoff of the 2000 season playing special teams, Bailey tore a ligament in his right knee.

"As soon as it happened, I knew the knee was gone because I had hurt the other knee like that in high school. I knew I was done for the season," Boss Bailey told Barnhart.

Boss returned for the 2001 season and then had a breakout senior season in 2002, leading the Bulldogs in tackles with 114 and six quarterback sacks. Boss was a big part of a Georgia squad that led the SEC in total defense and was fourth in the nation. Boss Bailey's final year at Georgia ended with first-team All-SEC honors, and he was named to the Walter Camp and AFCA All-American teams.

That season was special for Boss Bailey because he was part of an SEC championship team. Neither Ronald nor Champ experienced that.

Boss Bailey was off to the NFL where the Detroit Lions selected him in the second round. After five seasons in Detroit, Boss signed a contract with the Denver Broncos and joined his big brother, Champ. Boss was released by Denver before the 2009 season.

75 Matthew Stafford

Matt Stafford had stellar credentials when he stepped onto the University of Georgia campus. Stafford came from one of the most prominent high school football programs in the country, Highland Park High School in Dallas, Texas. One of the greatest quarterbacks in football history, Bobby Layne, graduated from Highland Park and went on to a legendary career at the University of Texas, then he guided the Detroit Lions to back-to-back NFL championships in 1952 and 1953.

Stafford's high school career was outstanding. As a senior, Stafford threw for 4,018 yards and 38 touchdowns, leading the Scots to the Texas Class AAAA state championship—the school's first state title since 1957.

Many high school awards and accolades were showered on Stafford. He earned EA Sports National High School Player of the Year recognition while taking Texas Player of the Year honors, as well. Stafford earned "five star" status from many recruiting services and was dubbed the nation's No. 1 quarterback by Rivals.com.

Stafford arrived at Georgia much ballyhooed, but he had to earn the opportunity to start. Georgia head coach Mark Richt rotated among three quarterbacks for the first half of the season. Senior Joe Tereshinski III started the first two games with redshirt freshman Joe Cox and Stafford getting limited playing time.

Quarterback Matt Stafford sets the offense during the first half of a game against Georgia Southern on Saturday, August 30, 2008, in Athens, Georgia.
(AP Photo/John Bazemore)

In Georgia's third game of the 2006 season, Stafford had his first career start against the University of Alabama-Birmingham. He completed 10-of-17 passes for 107 yards as the Bulldogs won 34–0.

For the next four games of his freshman season, Stafford was struggling to establish himself in the SEC with subpar performances. Stafford was splitting playing time with Joe Cox.

Stafford got the start against Mississippi State and had a breakout performance, throwing for 267 yards and two touchdowns as Georgia won 27–24. His confidence was beginning to grow, but in the next two games against Florida and Kentucky, Stafford struggled again as he threw five interceptions and only one touchdown in those Georgia losses.

With Auburn and Georgia Tech on the horizon, both the Bulldogs and Stafford needed a strong finish, and that's what they got. Against Auburn, Stafford was nearly perfect and completed 14-of-20 passes for 219 yards, one touchdown, and no interceptions as Georgia won 37–15.

Another solid performance against Georgia Tech gave Georgia a close 15–12 win over the nationally ranked Yellow Jackets and an invitation to the Chick-Fil-A Bowl to take on the Virginia Tech Hokies.

Against the Hokies, Matt Stafford rallied the Bulldogs from a 21–3 halftime deficit to a 31–24 win. Stafford threw for 129 yards and a touchdown and won the Chick-fil-A Bowl Offensive Most Valuable Player Award.

By his sophomore season, Matt Stafford was firmly entrenched as the starting quarterback. In 2007, Stafford had eight games where he threw for more than 200 yards, and he completed the longest pass of his college career. Stafford threw an 84-yard touchdown to Mohamed Massaquoi in Georgia's 42–30 win over Florida.

The 2007 season ended on a high note with Georgia whipping Hawaii 41–10 in the Sugar Bowl and earning a No. 2 ranking in the final Associated Press college football poll.

Plenty was expected from Stafford and the Georgia Bulldogs for the 2008 season. All the top awards for college quarterbacks had Matt Stafford on their watch lists—even the Heisman Trophy folks were keeping an eye on the Georgia quarterback.

Stafford came out of the chute throwing for a then-career high 275 yards in the 2008 season opener against Georgia Southern. It was the beginning of Stafford's best season wearing the red and black.

Eleven times Stafford threw for more than 200 yards. Against Kentucky, Stafford broke out with 367 yards passing and three touchdowns. But his best performance as a Bulldog came in his final regular-season game against arch rival Georgia Tech. Against the Yellow Jackets, Stafford threw for career highs in passing yards with 407 and touchdowns with 5—the latter tied a school record. While Stafford had a career game, it ended in disappointment as Tech took care of Georgia in a shoot-out 45–42.

Stafford closed 2008 with a Capital Bowl MVP performance where he threw for 250 yards, and he tied a Georgia bowl record with three touchdowns passes in the Bulldogs' 24–12 win over Michigan State.

Matt Stafford threw for 3,459 yards in 2008, which was second best in school history for a single season. But his 25 touchdown throws that season are a school record. Stafford's 7,731 career passing yards is third all-time at UGA.

With a year of eligibility remaining, Stafford chose to enter the NFL draft. He was the top overall pick by the Detroit Lions, following the career path of Bobby Layne once more.

76 "My God...Massaquoi!"

Georgia fans revere the now-retired Larry Munson, the legendary voice of the Bulldogs. Though he departed after the 2007 season, his voice, the gravely signature of Georgia football, reverberates throughout the community. One of his last great signature calls happened in the traditional last game of the season—the rivalry game of all rivalry games—the annual Georgia–Georgia Tech game.

The 2006 season was not a great one for Georgia football. Though not a bad one, it was somewhat similar to the 2009 season where the expectations were high, the team struggled for a stretch to find its identity, and then finished pretty strong. Including the win over Virginia Tech in the Chick-fil-A Bowl, the Dogs finished 9–4.

The 2006 version of the Georgia Bulldogs was a transition year. Joe Tereshinski III was slotted to be the quarterback, with hotshot freshman Matthew Stafford ready, willing, and learning. By Week 2, Tereshinski was injured and Stafford led the Bulldogs to an 18–0 shutout of the South Carolina Gamecocks. Tereshinski would never play again.

Typical of a team with a true freshman at quarterback, the Bulldogs were inconsistent early that season on offense. With Kregg Lumpkin, Danny Ware, and Thomas Brown at running back, they had some depth and moved the ball. Wide receiver, however, was a different story. Several guys had playing time during the season— Kenneth Harris and Demiko Goodman were among the guys who made plays—but none had stood out. Interestingly, one of 2006's leading receivers was the tight end Martrez Milner.

Mohamed Massaquoi was the other leader, tying Milner with 30 catches that year. Massaquoi was a quiet sophomore from the Charlotte area who the coaches felt had all of the ability in the world, but they were concerned that he was hesitant, quiet, and almost too shy to be a standout. But the slender wideout had a knack for catching anything remotely near him and making plays when they were most needed.

The Georgia–Georgia Tech game is always played two days after Thanksgiving. The game alternates between Atlanta and Athens and is one of the most intense and best rivalries that college football has to offer.

November 25, 2006, was much like most days that time of year in Georgia, overcast and cool. The game was set for a 3:30 PM kickoff on CBS in front of a sold-out Sanford Stadium crowd. Ranked No. 16 coming into the game, Georgia Tech was the favored team and featured the hot hands of Calvin Johnson, perhaps the best receiver in college football that season.

Georgia, on the other hand, wasn't quite that good. They had surprised the fifth-ranked Auburn Tigers just two weeks before. Though impressive, the win was achieved primarily with a ball-hawking defense and just enough offense to get by.

The Tech game wasn't pretty, either. The "tons" of predicted offense didn't happen. Both teams fumbled twice, and Tech was intercepted once. Arguably the biggest play early in the game was Bulldog Tony Taylor's somewhat controversial 29-yard fumble return for a touchdown.

As the game wound down in the fourth quarter, you could sense the tension in Munson's voice. The Bulldogs had won the previous five games against Tech, but this one was different. The Yellow Jackets were up 12–7 with a little less than 9:00 left. That is when the game changed.

All of a sudden, Stafford, who had struggled for most of the game, found his rhythm. He found Massaquoi several times on the final drive. The drive was the longest of the season, 12 plays, 64 yards, and ate up 7:05 of clock time. The drive ended with about 1:45 left to play in the game.

From the 4-yard line, Stafford dropped back. Massaquoi, the primary receiver, ran a flag route toward the corner. Stafford lofted a pass that went just over the outstretched defensive back and hit Massaquoi smack dab in the hands.

That's where Munson's call turned this play into a classic. God knows how many game-winning plays Munson called during his career. He didn't have many calls left, and he knew it. But as he was prone to do with calls like "Run Lindsay, run!" and though he couldn't see nearly as well as he used to—he saw this one—and you could hear it in his voice. Even with 92,000 fans roaring in the stadium, you could hear him:

"My God…Massaquoi! Massaquoi!"

He didn't say anything else. He didn't have to.

You *knew* just listening to him, even if you didn't see it, that something crazy had happened at the end of the game. A game that wasn't pretty for Georgia fans, it looked and sounded great at the end. Despite the 15–12 score, it was certainly one of the most entertaining games in the Georgia–Georgia Tech series.

77 The Edwards Brothers

Robert and Terrence Edwards grew up in the town of Tennille in middle Georgia. They attended Washington County High School in neighboring Sandersville, and Terrence always referred to both towns as the "twin cities."

After leaving their Golden Hawk roots, the brothers made their marks between the hedges and in the pro ranks. Their roads to the pros led them both to Canada, and it's a long way from

SEC Top 10 Career Receiving Yards

1. 3,093 Terrence Edwards, Georgia (204 catches) 1999–02
2. 3,001 Josh Reed, LSU (167 catches) 1999–01
3. 2,964 Boo Mitchell, Vanderbilt (188 catches) 1985–88
4. 2,923 D.J. Hall, Alabama (194 catches) 2004–07
5. 2,899 Craig Yeast, Kentucky (208 catches) 1995–98
6. 2,884 Fred Gibson, Georgia (161 catches) 2001–04
7. 2,880 Dan Stricker, Vanderbilt (182 catches) 1999–02
8. 2,879 Anthony Lucas, Arkansas (137 catches) 1995–99
9. 2,852 Earl Bennett, Vanderbilt (236 catches) 2005–07
10. 2,814 Joey Kent, Tennessee (183 catches) 1993–96

Tennille to Montreal and Winnipeg. But they almost never made it to Athens.

"When Robert and I would talk going into his senior year, he was just hoping to be a prospect," former Washington County and current Effingham County High School head football coach and athletics director Rick Tomberlin said. "He was thinking, maybe, Fort Valley State or Georgia Southern. He loved to play and compete. He would block PATs and field goals, intercept passes, or even make the clutch catch. He was one of the nicest kids in the world."

Robert played both basketball and football at Washington County High. He was recruited by John Reaves to come to Florida, and since Robert didn't really grow up a Georgia fan (gasp!), the Gators were in play. He received more offers after their state title game, but there was a problem.

"He had a hard time scheduling visits because of basketball," Tomberlin said. "And his dad, Robert Sr., really didn't understand what an 'official visit' was. I told them that it meant they'd have a great time at the stadium and they would show you around town over the weekend...show you a good time."

But Tomberlin also told them that it meant that before they left Gainesville, Florida, head coach Steve Spurrier would want Robert to commit.

Florida's Anthone Lott, No. 9, grabs Georgia's Robert Edwards, No. 47, with less than a minute in the first quarter during their matchup at the new Jackson Municipal Stadium in Jacksonville, Florida, on Saturday, November 2, 1996.
(AP Photo/Frank Niemeir, *Atlanta Journal-Constitution*)

Robert's high school coach had a suggestion, "I told him to tell Coach Spurrier that, since only your dad was here, that you had to call your mom first. He could call back Monday morning with his answer. But if you love it without a doubt during your visit, go ahead and commit to Florida. Otherwise, don't make a fast decision and think about it."

Spurrier did as Tomberlin predicted. Robert told the coach about calling his mom, and that following Monday back in Sandersville, he decided he was going to Florida.

"The phone rings," Tomberlin said, "and it's Reaves. He said that they were full and that they didn't have anything left. I hang up the phone with Robert there in my office, and the phone rings again."

It was Ray Goff. Goff asked Tomberlin if Robert had committed. Tomberlin told him, "No."

The University of Florida did call back a few days later. They wanted to let Coach Tomberlin and Robert know that one of their commits had cancelled, and the open slot was Robert's if he wanted it.

Robert was heading to Georgia. Thanks, but no thanks.

That was how the high school wingback/inside linebacker/Defensive Player of the Year ended up in Athens. When Tomberlin was asked what position he thought Robert should play, he told the Georgia coaching staff strong safety and tailback.

Coach Goff tried Robert on offense—even after he was All-SEC as a freshman at defensive back. In the spring game his sophomore year, he couldn't be stopped, and that was where he stayed.

"The *Atlanta Journal-Constitution* called and asked me what I thought about that, and I said 'That was where he shoulda been all along!'" Tomberlin said.

Robert led the Dawgs in rushing in 1996 and '97 and was the New England Patriots first-round pick for the '98 season. As part of Pro Bowl week activities in Hawaii, Edwards participated in a flag football game on sand. He blew out his knee, and it was questionable as to whether or not he would ever walk again much less play football.

After a long rehab, he came back to play for the Miami Dolphins. By 2005, he was the leading rusher for the Montreal Alouettes of the CFL. He remained there until the 2008 season.

As for Robert's younger brother, "Terrence?" Tomberlin asked with a laugh. "I'd adopt him."

Tomberlin knew Terrence as a seventh grader initially. He started as a sophomore as a part of the team's 30–0 run during his junior and senior seasons. When Terrence was being recruited, every school wanted him at quarterback to play a West Virginia Pat White–like role. Georgia put him at wide receiver instead.

Jimbo Fisher came to Sandersville to recruit Terrence in an attempt to get him to Auburn as a quarterback. But the fact that his older brother had gone to Athens was huge.

"He and Coach Donnan connected really well," Tomberlin admitted. Well enough for Terrence to lead the Bulldogs in receptions and yards in all four years he played in Athens.

"He had broken every record at UGA," Tomberlin said. "He was, what, second in receptions in the entire history of the SEC. With what Florida, LSU, and Tennessee do on offense, and Terrence Edwards is second? That is amazing to me."

Not bad for a guy who never weighed more than 165 pounds in high school but could dead lift 500 pounds. Terrence still holds the SEC record for total receiving yards and is littered throughout the Bulldogs record book in plenty of receiving categories. He's spent his last six seasons playing in the Canadian Football League for Montreal and Winnipeg.

He has two 1,000-yard seasons to his credit up there, and Coach Tomberlin would like for Terrence to someday come and be his offensive coordinator.

Robert will be his own boss starting with the 2010 football season as the new head coach at Arlington Christian, a small school in the suburban Atlanta city of Fairburn. The school is a member of the Georgia Independent School Association (GISA).

"I get an opportunity to stay around the game that I've played for…probably over 20 years now," Edwards said in an interview with the GHSF Daily website in late March. "I'm definitely excited about the opportunity to give back to young kids and give them the opportunity to develop and grow."

You can bet that Edwards will have Rick Tomberlin's cell phone number on speed dial all season long.

78

The 2007 End of the Season Run

In college football, you can still finish strong after a weak start. Although 2007 wasn't a national championship year for the University of Georgia, it was one of its greatest seasons.

In 2007, Georgia didn't really give anyone the impression they'd knock someone's socks off. Sure, the season started well enough with a 35–14 win over Oklahoma State in Athens, but it was followed by an ugly 16–12 loss to South Carolina. A nice win over Western Carolina and a last-second overtime win at Alabama were next on the slate, followed by a relatively easy win against Ole Miss.

At that point, the Dogs were 4–1 and riding high when they made their biannual trip to Knoxville to face the Tennessee Volunteers. Tennessee took it to them with a 35–14 trouncing that led many of the Georgia faithful to wonder if this team was a pretender or a contender. With two SEC losses already, there wasn't a great chance Georgia would win the SEC title.

One week after Tennessee, all really did look lost. Georgia trailed Vanderbilt for most of the game and tied it in the fourth quarter on a Brandon Coutu field goal. Vandy drove down the field and appeared ready to take the lead as the clock wound down, but Darryl Gamble made a play that most observers say turned around the Georgia season. Gamble stripped Vandy running back Cassen Jackson-Garrison of the football. Dannell Ellerbe fell on it with just less than three minutes to go. Matthew Stafford drove the Bulldogs down the field and Coutu drilled the game-winning field goal at the final gun.

Two weeks later, the Dogs took on Florida. Most will remember it as "The Celebration Game"—after Knowshon Moreno scored the game's first touchdown, the whole team came onto the

2007 Dogs in the NFL
RB—Thomas Brown, 6th Rd. pick, Atlanta Falcons 2008
OT—Chester Adams, 7th Rd. pick, Chicago Bears 2008
DE—Marcus Howard, 5th Rd. pick, Indianapolis Colts 2008
PK—Brandon Coutu, 7th Rd. pick, Seattle Seahawks 2008
RB—Knowshon Moreno, 1st Rd. pick, Denver Broncos 2009
QB—Matthew Stafford, 1st Rd. pick, Detroit Lions 2009
DE—Brandon Miller, FA Signee, Seattle Seahawks 2008
RB—Kregg Lumpkin, FA Signee, Green Bay Packers 2008

field to celebrate. The emotional game was never close, and Georgia won for the second time in 10 tries against its most storied rival.

That celebration got everyone's attention. Georgia became the most talked about team in college football and at 6–2 became a fixture on the national scene.

The next motivational ploy from Coach Mark Richt happened two weeks later versus Auburn. Word leaked out that the team was going to wear all-black uniforms for the game. The coach and players all denied it, but the fans all bought into it. Most suspected something was afoot, but nobody knew exactly what. Even the players, who came out for warm-ups in their usual red uniforms, had no idea.

Richt sent out the captains for the coin toss alone, wearing the home red jerseys. A few minutes later, there was chaos.

The Sanford Stadium roared as the Bulldogs took the field dressed head to toe in black with AC/DC's "Back in Black" blasting through the sound system. Needless to say, the game, though emotional, was never particularly close. Georgia won 45–20.

The Bulldogs finished the season with wins over Kentucky and Georgia Tech, and they were now important in the BCS discussions. They were 10–2, ranked No. 6 in the country, and the trendy hot team. However, they were not the SEC champions. Nor did they play in the SEC Championship Game—LSU and Tennessee did. Despite having two losses, LSU was the prohibitive favorite not only to win that game, but play in the BCS Championship Game. They beat Tennessee, and that is exactly what happened.

That is where it got interesting.

Traditionally, the loser of the SEC Championship Game goes to the Florida Citrus Bowl, and that is where Tennessee was headed. With LSU heading to the BCS Championship Game, it left the Sugar Bowl, which traditionally gets the SEC champion, without the SEC champ. They decided to take an at-large team, Georgia, to play against another at-large team—Hawaii.

The Georgia-Hawaii game was never close. Georgia ran right by the Fighting Rainbow Warriors for a 41–10 win to finish the season with its seventh straight win and an 11–2 record. Because of that streak and a combination of other teams losing, Georgia, whose season almost ended before it got on track, finished with the highest non-championship ranking they could—No. 2 in the Associated Press final poll. The team was No. 3 in the Coaches Poll.

Most current or recent Georgia alumni would be more than happy to tell you the story of this team. It was one of the more surprising successes in Georgia football history. One that brings a smile to not only the fans, but the coaches and players involved in it, as well.

79 D.J. Shockley

There is a commonly used saying that some people "just have *it*."

Nobody knows exactly what that *it* is, where *it* comes from or why they have *it*. Those people are the ones who everyone just seems to gravitate to. Quarterback D.J. Shockley, class of 2005, is one of those people.

Although you probably can't define *it,* the players on the Bulldogs football team listened to and followed D.J. without question.

Strangely, D.J.'s story didn't begin the way you would think it would have. Sure, he was a heavily recruited high school star who played for his father at North Clayton High School just outside of Atlanta. But when he showed up on campus as one of new head coach Mark Richt's first recruits, he wasn't an instant star.

He began his college career in 2002 as a backup because he was beaten out by redshirt freshman David Greene—the same David Greene who set a record for most career wins by an NCAA quarterback, a record recently broken by Colt McCoy.

But Shockley didn't sit the whole season. He got some game time, playing in 10 of the Bulldogs' contests that season. The same thing happened the next season, though the 2003 season was cut short when Shockley hurt his knee early in the season and missed eight games.

After that season, there was a lot of discussion regarding his future. Though not widely discussed outside of Georgia, there was a lot of talk that Shockley might want to consider leaving Georgia and go to a school where he would get to play regularly. Most in Athens felt that he had tons of talent, but Greene had proven to be a wildly successful quarterback and leader, and the coaches were reluctant to change that. Shockley eventually made a decision that would forever endear him to the Bulldogs faithful, declaring he would stay at Georgia and wait his turn.

Shockley got more playing time in 2004 and was rotated into games for a few series. Coach Richt had decided that he was a good change of pace from Greene and that it would help prepare D.J. if he was needed. The preparation and playing time certainly helped, but nobody including the coaches could have foreseen what Shockley would do in 2005 when he became the starter.

Most observers thought that Georgia would struggle in 2005. It was replacing the two Davids—Greene and star defensive end

David Pollack. Little did the folks in Athens know that another SEC title was in their future.

Shockley came out in his first game as a starter and made quite an impression with five touchdown passes, a rushing touchdown, 289 yards passing, and 85 more running as the Bulldogs torched Boise State 48–13 in front of a national television audience.

The next game against South Carolina wasn't quite so pretty. But the Bulldogs won 17–15, started the season 7–0, and were ranked No. 4 in the country. However, in the seventh win versus Arkansas, Shockley was taken from the field with a sprained knee, unable to return. He was unable to play in Game 8—the game against Florida that Georgia lost 14–10.

Shockley returned for the following game against Auburn, though the Bulldogs were beaten 31–30 on a last second field goal. The following week they clinched the SEC East title with a 45–13 win over Kentucky.

The magical run continued in the SEC Championship Game. Shockley, the game's MVP, threw for two TDs and ran for another as Georgia routed LSU 34–14 and secured a date at the Sugar Bowl. Shockley threw three more TDs in the Sugar Bowl, tying Eric Zeier's record of 24 TD passes in a season.

The 2005 Bulldogs were extraordinarily focused and played very well as a team. They all looked to D.J. as their leader—the guy who set the example and did what was necessary to win.

Shockley's reputation only grew as he was drafted by the hometown Atlanta Falcons in the 2006 draft and made the team. He was on the roster for three seasons. Though he didn't play much, the Falcons saw many of the same characteristics and potential in him that the University of Georgia fans and coaches did.

D.J. left the University of Georgia as one of the most popular players ever to play in Athens. Though he only started for one season, he made the most of it, winning an SEC title and playing in the Sugar Bowl. To Bulldogs fans, he made the ultimate sacrifice for loyalty to the school. He remained a Bulldog when he could have played somewhere else. When his opportunity came, he made the most of it—a storybook season for a storied player. He was the guy who, more than any other Bulldog in recent memory, had *it*.

80 Claude Felton

Who is Claude Felton? There is a very good chance that without Claude Felton, this book would probably not be available for you to read.

There aren't many schools that can say that their sports information director is part of the College Football Hall of Fame. The University of Georgia can. The SID's role is to be the person most responsible for dealing with the various media and disseminating the appropriate messages that cast the university in the proper light.

Anyone who has worked a Georgia football game and had the opportunity to deal with Claude and his staff will tell you the same thing.

"They are the best at what they do," Bill Hartman, a longtime Atlanta TV sports anchor, said about Felton. "The best there has ever been. When you wanted to do something out of the ordinary for a story on the Dogs, Claude would find a way to help you. Most sports information folks are quick to say, 'No.' Claude was quick to say, 'Yes!'"

Claude is a low-key individual. Quick to smile yet quiet—if you speak to him once and then not again for a long period of time, he'll remember details of your conversation that you never will.

Claude was an assistant SID at the university in the early '70s and moved on to Georgia Southern as their head sports information director in 1974. When the legendary Dan Magill retired as the SID, the school's new athletic director and football coach, Vince Dooley, immediately reached out to Felton and asked him to come back.

According to Coach Dooley, "When I became AD, I thought that the hiring of Claude Felton was my No. 1 priority. I had known him as the assistant sports communications director under Dan Magill before he was recruited back to Georgia Southern as the information director for the school. Claude was a little reluctant to return to Athens in light of his position at Georgia Southern, so I've told the story many times that I recruited him just a hard as I did Herschel Walker. I had the late, then-president Fred Davidson call him as part of the recruiting effort."

Fans of other schools in the state wonder just how Georgia football gets so much press coverage during the course of the year. It is quite simple.

Members of the sports media who cover the team will tell you the same thing—it's because of Claude. It's rare to work with someone who will always have the best interest of his superiors in mind but will be as fair as he can possibly be with you. Good news or bad, you will get the information that is available and can be released. If there is something that he can't tell you, he'll tell you that. And if it is a feature that you want, he or his staff will do all that they can to make it happen.

Claude was the 2008 winner of the Bert McGrane award from the Football Writers Association of America. With that comes a place within the rotunda of the College Football Hall of Fame. When the video of that induction was aired on the Atlanta television sportscasts, Claude was a bit surprised.

The local TV stations told him, "It was the least that we could do."

Vince Dooley said of Felton, "During my 25 years as the athletic director, he was the most important staff member throughout that time. As an example to the high regard that I have for him, the last three days before I officially retired were spent at the National Convention of the Sports Information Directors to see Claude being honored by being inducted into their Hall of Fame. I couldn't think of a better way to spend my last days in office than with someone who I held in such high esteem. He is the best in the business."

Really, there isn't a better way to state it. Claude is to this day an integral part of the football program, and he is rarely far from Coach Mark Richt's side. Be it on travel days or game days or even practice days, he is always there.

We would normally suggest that you make the trek to the Butts-Mehre Heritage Hall and track down Felton and meet one of the people who make the athletic department what it is. But we know Claude very well. He would ever so politely smile, bend his head down just slightly, thank you very much for asking, and tell you that there are many more important people that you should be talking to.

That, quite honestly, isn't true.

81 "Boss Hog" Terrell Davis

A lot of Georgia fans ask, "What is it with Ray Goff and tailbacks?"

You've read about Hines Ward and the move from scatback to wideout and/or quarterback. You've read about what it took to get Robert Edwards to the tail. And then there's the story of Terrell Davis.

Running back Terrell Davis carries the ball during the game against Clemson in Athens, Georgia, on Saturday, October 8, 1994. (AP Photo/Curtis Compton, *Atlanta Journal-Constitution*)

Lincoln High School's Hornets football team in San Diego, California, had Davis playing six different positions, including nose guard and kicker. He had only played one other year of football in high school, so it took a little encouraging by his older brother, Reggie Webb, to get Davis a place at Long Beach State. He was red-shirted but never got the chance to play for the 49ers. Long Beach head coach George Allen died of a heart attack after the end of the season, and the university blew up the program because of financial problems on campus shortly thereafter.

Two schools called with interest: UCLA and Georgia.

Davis, in an interview with Austin Murphy in *Sports Illustrated*, explained his lack of geographical knowledge. "If you'd have given me a puzzle of the 50 states," he said, "I wouldn't have known where to put Georgia. But it was a free trip, so I went."

Davis was blown away with the school's presentation to him, and when he was given a jersey with his name on the back, he was hooked. He backed up Garrison Hearst in the 1992 season when the Lincoln County grad finished third in Heisman Trophy voting, and Davis was given his chance in 1993, wrapping up the year with a little more than 800 yards on the ground.

Depending on who you talk to, the injuries Davis sustained to his hamstring during his senior season were either because he wasn't tough enough or that he really had shredded the muscle and couldn't run on it.

A disappointing 1994 season numbers-wise led to a deep-draft sixth-round selection by the Denver Broncos. But what they got was a running back with purpose that was either driven, mad, or both because of what happened in Athens.

In his defense, Coach Goff told Tony Fabrizio of the Morris News Service about that season, "I had a job to keep. I might be accused of not being the smartest guy in the world, but [I'm] not crazy enough to not use my best player [Zeier]. Terrell got hurt two years in a row."

Davis was so mad that at one point in his life, when he was asked what Athens meant to him, he said that it was a "city in Greece."

Davis rushed for more than 1,100 yards as an NFL rookie and even made a return trip to Athens during the Broncos bye week. Goff was fired in the off-season. Davis saw Goff while he was on campus but didn't engage in any conversation—polite or otherwise.

Davis told Murphy, "I'm afraid I might have been kind of rude to him."

But given the chance to do it all over again, Davis later admitted he would have gone back to Georgia to play football given the choice. It made him a mentally tougher athlete.

Davis would need that mental toughness later on in his career as he battled migraine headaches and knee injuries. Both would take their toll on him and cut short his now constantly argued possible Hall of Fame career in the pros.

He has suffered from migraines all of his life, but it wasn't until the 1996 season that he couldn't play on the field because of them. They even affected his performance in Super Bowl XXXIII. He had to sit out the second quarter and required medication to be able to even return for his three-quarter, then-Super Bowl record 157-yard, three TD performance in the victory over Green Bay.

In 1998, Davis set franchise records for rushing yards in a season with 2,008, rushing touchdowns with 21, and most 100-yard games in a season with 11.

Davis ran for more than 7,600 yards in his seven seasons in Denver before he was placed on injured reserve before the 2002 season. A degenerative condition in his knees forced a premature retirement before the 2004 season.

82 Jake Scott

Defining the qualifications of a football legend isn't easy to do. Most Georgia football fans know names like Herschel Walker, Knowshon Moreno, Matthew Stafford, Buck Belue, Lindsay Scott, and Hines Ward, but one name that may not immediately come to mind really should.

He was a star in his own right—Jake Scott.

Jake Scott was born in South Carolina and raised in Athens, though his family moved to Virginia halfway through his high school career. As a standout athlete in high school, when it came time to decide where he wanted to play college football, Scott knew that he wanted to come back to the town where he was raised and play for Georgia. He played through the 1968 season. He spent the next year in Canada playing in the CFL. In 1970, he was picked in the seventh round of the NFL Draft by the Miami Dolphins.

You might be surprised that with all of the quality defensive backs that have played for the Bulldogs, Jake Scott is the all-time leader, not only in interceptions, but in interception return yards. He is also among the all-time leaders in punt returns. Twice an All-American and twice and All-SEC football player, he was among the most decorated Bulldogs of his time. He was an academic All-SEC performer after beginning his time in Athens on academic probation.

Scott obviously left a big impression during his days in Athens. From being selected to the 1960s All-SEC team to the All-Time SEC team, he was recognized as one of the best safeties to ever play in the league. A story in the *Athens Daily-Banner* written in 2000 on Scott, had this quote from Coach Dooley: "If I was going to list a handful of athletes, Jake Scott would be on that hand, if not be the one or two, because he was able to do so many things. I don't ever remember a player do as many things as he could. He was a marvelous athlete, and he studied the game. He was a smart player."

Jake was instrumental in Georgia's run to the 1968 title. He intercepted 10 passes, two of which he returned for touchdowns, along with leading the conference in punt returns.

He got better in the pros. He teamed with Dick Anderson to form one of the best defensive safety tandems in the history of the NFL. The two helped lead the Dolphins' "No Name Defense" in 1972. The team that year was an undefeated 17–0—the last squad to run the table as an undefeated team.

They're the gentlemen every year who crack open the champagne bottles when the last undefeated team loses before the season is over.

Scott was named the Most Valuable Player in Super Bowl VII, with two interceptions as the Dolphins finished the season defeating the Washington Redskins. A three-time NFL All-Pro, he played in the Pro Bowl five straight years. Scott went on to play for three more seasons with the Redskins and finished his career with 49 interceptions and 13 fumble recoveries.

After he retired from football, Scott went somewhat into seclusion, according to a story in the *Fort Lauderdale Sun-Sentinel* that was written in 2006. He settled in Hawaii living a quiet, happy, and isolated life.

He occasionally surfaces. In late in 2006, he was the guest captain at the Georgia–Georgia Tech game in Athens. He also has contributed signed memorabilia to the preseason Kickoff Classic fundraiser. He has been elected to the Georgia Sports Hall of Fame and the Athens Athletic Hall of Fame.

Jake Scott certainly is not one of the most widely discussed of all the Bulldogs legends, but he definitely qualifies as one of greatest, if not the greatest all-around athlete to play football at the university. It may take a little digging to find some information on him, what he did, and what he is and was about, but it would be well worth the time. Scott is someone who has never quite been duplicated and probably likes it that way.

As Betty Cuniberti of the *Washington Post* once described Scott, Jake is "a baffling and fascinating recruit, a one-edition museum piece that ought to be cherished for its oddity, even if the sight of it confuses the eye."

Especially if the story about Scott, a motorcycle, and Stegeman Coliseum is true. Going into detail may be dicey. We don't want to endanger any statutes of limitations about trespassing, so we'll just leave it at that.

83 The Ramsey Center

You found out a little earlier in the book about the donation Bernard Ramsey gave to the University of Georgia, thanks to Bill Hartman. Part of that donation was focused toward a 5½-acre, $40 million structure called the Bernard B. and Eugenia A. Ramsey Student Physical Activities Center.

Sports Illustrated gave the building the title of "Best Recreational Facility in the Country" in 1997. Under its roof are 420,000 sq.-ft. of five arenas, three swimming pools, three multipurpose rooms, a climbing wall, 10 racquetball courts, two international squash courts, a strength and conditioning room, a ⅛-mile jogging track, an outdoor equipment rental room, and something called an outdoor resource center. Does your health club membership give you all that every month for the cost of a student's activity fee?

Probably the most well-known part of the Ramsey Center is the Gabrielsen Natatorium—that's a fancy word for the place where all the Bulldogs swimming and diving events are held.

Coach B.W. Gabrielsen, otherwise known as the "Shrewd Norwegian" during his tenure on campus, was the swim coach in Athens from 1948–66. In his 18 seasons, he won 118 meets, but his impact was with the athletes who entered and left their mark on the program by the time they graduated, including 70 SEC championship swimmers, three conference team championships, six All-American swimmers, one NCAA champion swimmer, and the Bulldogs' first U.S. Olympic Team member, Reid Patterson, who represented the United States in the 1956 Melbourne Games.

The natatorium has three separate pools. The 50-meter pool can be laid out in four different ways. The seating capacity for any crowd watching a meet can be up to 2,000. There are five separate platforms for competition diving and four springboards in the second pool. The third pool is used for instruction, and the three pools can support a total of almost a million-and-a-half gallons of water among them at any one time. The facility has hosted multiple men's, women's, and SEC swimming championships. U.S. Diving even used the facility for its 1997 world championship trials.

Why include the capacity figure for the meets that are held at the natatorium? That way, you can catch up with one of the true legends of the sport—UGA head swimming coach Jack Bauerle.

Bauerle just wrapped up his 30th season as head coach for the men's and 26th for the women's team on campus. He finished the 2009 season third on the all-time collegiate wins list with 415. A 1975 graduate of the school, Bauerle was a four-time letterman. He also held three school records and was team co-captain in his junior and senior years.

Bulldog Olympians

Speaking of Olympians, how many Bulldogs have spent time as Olympiads?

A total of 115 athletes and coaches have represented their country and have ties to Athens.

Nine different sports are represented: swimming, diving, track and field, gymnastics, basketball, equestrian, weightlifting, baseball, and Herschel Walker's foray into bobsled (or "bobsleigh" as it's called internationally).

Bulldogs have worn the colors of 28 different countries on the world stage: United States, Antigua, Jamaica, Canada, the Bahamas, Gambia, Sweden, Great Britain, Malaysia, Iceland, Denmark, Germany, Suriname, France, Croatia, Argentina, the Virgin Islands, Barbados, the Philippines, South Africa, St. Lucia, and Grenada.

With 205 National Olympic Committees recognized by the International Olympic Committee, that means that almost 15 percent of the nations participating in the four-year competition have red and black ties.

As coach, Bauerle's squads have garnered four team national titles and six Southeastern Conference top-steps with the Lady Bulldogs. He has been chosen as the SEC Coach of the Year 13 times—11 with the women and two with the men—and the National Women's Coach of the Year five times. He's the SEC's winningest coach, his swimmers have consistently picked up All-Academic team honors, and the program boasts three NCAA Woman of the Year winners—Lisa Coole in 1997, Kristy Kowal in 2000, and Kim Black in 2001.

No other school can name more than one for the honor.

One other honor that you might recall from recent memory is that Bauerle was named head coach for the U.S. Women's Swim Team for the Beijing Olympics in 2008. The United States delegation won 14 medals during the time they spent at the Water Cube, including two gold, seven silver, and five bronze medals. That total was the largest haul of any nation present. Two of his own swimmers, Lady Bulldogs graduate Kara Lynn Joyce and 2008–09 freshman Allison Schmitt, made Bulldogs fans proud as Joyce won two silvers and Schmitt won a bronze.

Longtime Georgia assistant Harvey Humphreys, in an interview with Roger Clarkson of the *Athens Banner-Herald*, addressed what has contributed to all of Bauerle's successes as a coach in a career that seems like it's humming right along without an end in sight:

"He always made the underdog feel special. I was a walk-on; I was not recruited. So walking in and having Jack give me the same amount of attention as the top guys made me ready to lay down my life for the guy. I'd do anything in a practice.

"Even at the world-class Olympic level, certainly there's a depth chart even on an Olympic team. There's always an underdog that Jack usually clicks with. There's always somebody who outperforms everybody's expectations because of their contact with Jack."

It's that attention to detail, no matter how large or small, that has contributed to Bauerle's long and successful resume. On a campus filled with championship coaches and histories, Bauerle has made one of the biggest splashes.

84 Stegeman Coliseum, The "Stegasorous"

Just because local Atlanta television sports anchors may give the place a dinosaur's nickname doesn't mean the building is a dinosaur. The uniqueness of the building aside, it's another place to visit during your trips to Athens.

Taking the place of 3,000-seat Woodruff Hall on campus, the Steg was initially the Georgia Coliseum when construction began in the summer of 1961. Coach Magill, in a 2007 column in the *Athens Banner-Herald* relayed a story of a boyhood friend, Herschel Carithers, who tested the roof of the building when the "clam shell" was the only part standing: "He flew a small airplane smack through the building—a tremendous feat which he never admitted because it was against the law. I know he did it because I saw it. But, no matter. If he were still living, he'd be protected by the statue of limitations." With a capacity of a little more than 10,500, it opened February 22, 1964, for a rivalry game against Georgia Tech. The head coach for the Bulldogs was Harbin "Red" Lawson, and his team earned the 81–68 upset over the Yellow Jackets in front of the largest crowd ever to see an event in the building.

As a nod to opening night for the "Jewel of North Georgia," anyone who walked up to the doors of the Coliseum was allowed inside—to the tune of a recorded 13,200 people. That number is a Bulldogs best, a Bulldogs first, and a Bulldogs last. Standing room is good for another 1,000 people nowadays. But that's all the fire marshals in Clarke County will allow.

The design of the building is two separate pieces: the roof and the coliseum proper. The ceiling is barrel-shaped, so the inside seating looks more like a "U" design. The flat end is where the scoreboard is seen, and as a result, there is no upper-deck seating. The roof is connected by aluminum bellows which allow the roof to rise and fall when the temperature drops below certain levels. There are four outward supports that were once used by fraternities in their initiations, but that practice ceased when the supports were gated and locked.

In March 1996, the Coliseum name was changed to reflect the contributions of Coach Herman Stegeman. Stegeman was involved with the Georgia program from 1919–39. He helped develop college basketball in the South in the 1920s and even originated the first big basketball tournament in the South when he started the Southern Conference tournament. It ran in Atlanta from 1921–32.

Stegeman Hall on the UGA campus was named for Coach Stegeman in 1946 and was the original home of the university's athletic and physical education departments. The athletic department moved to the new coliseum in 1964. Stegeman Hall was demolished in 1995 when the Ramsey Center was completed.

Stegeman has undergone renovations—some in concert with hosting the rhythmic gymnastics and volleyball competitions held in Athens for the 1996 Olympics. The Southeastern Conference's first video replay board was unveiled there in time for the games in addition to a new scoreboard system. In 1998, a new basketball floor was installed, and two years later, the old wooden seats in the lower level were replaced with cloth ones.

The building will undergo some more changes in the near future.

In September 2009, almost $2 million was approved to examine how to add an additional 10,000 square feet of walking space in the concourses and modernize some of the other amenities.

"I want, when you walk up to that coliseum, for it to look a little bit more modern and have more modern amenities," AD Damon Evans said. "The concourses are not only going to be bigger, but there [will] be more concessions and more restrooms and more interactive displays where we can really showcase our programs."

Head gymnastics coach Jay Clark agreed with the assessment and knows what that kind of change can do for his program because the GymDogs have been bringing in capacity crowds for some time—bigger crowds than some of the basketball games the building hosts.

"I've never heard anybody say that the thing needs to be bull-dozed," Clark said. "That roofline with the archway, it has a brand of its own. As long as I can remember, even back when I was a kid, I always thought that was the neatest building. There are so many stories about people riding their motorcycles over it or people climbing the arches before they put the gates up there.

"The roofline and general look of the structure itself has so much history here at the University of Georgia. I'd hate to see that they even attempt to bulldoze it."

Looks like they won't be doing that anytime soon—in February of 2010, Evans announced that the Athletic Association will spend close to $12 million on those renovations. They are supposed to have started after commencement in May of the year and be wrapped up by November 19 for the start of basketball season.

UGA Campus Architect Danny Sniff will definitely have his work cut out for him.

85 The 40 Watt Club

Suppose you had a band in the late 1970s or early 1980s and you had what people are referring to as that "alternative" sound. Your sound was different than anything else the rock-and-rollers had ever seen in concert or heard on a cassette tape.

The biggest question, if you were in the South or just wanted to make your mark was, "Where do we play to really get noticed?" The answer is the 40 Watt club in Athens.

Guadalcanal Diary, Pylon, R.E.M., The B-52's, Widespread Panic, Vic Chestnutt, and Love Tractor were part of the "Athens sound" and launched gold albums and golden careers at the 40 Watt. The 40 Watt was Athens' answer to CBGB's in New York City and the Whiskey a Go Go in Los Angeles.

Pylon's Curtis Crowe is credited with the first version of the club—it was housed in his apartment. The name "40 Watt" came from the wattage of the bulbs that lit the apartment on College Street. The first show on Halloween Night in 1978 featured (naturally) Crowe's Strictly American band.

In May 1980, the club moved across the street into an actual building as Crowe partnered with Paul Scales to make the dream a reality. The club has had several residences—one on West Clayton Street, one at the "uptown" address of 382 East Broad, back at the West Clayton address when the rent got too steep on Broad, and its current address on Washington Street as of 1990.

The current version of the 40 Watt seats 500 people and has always kept its ideal of catering to acts with potential, as well as those with solid club followings, for their crowds—unless, of course, R.E.M. drops by. The band broke out an acoustic set in 1991 to promote their *Out of Time* album.

So if you're looking to make your mark in the music industry or pack a house with your act, your career can't be complete without playing the 40 Watt. For more information, go to their website: www.40watt.com.

86 Weaver D's

One of the beautiful things about life in the South is finding the out-of-the-ordinary, home-cooking, soul-food restaurants that you just can't find anywhere else.

Perhaps one of the most famous of these places is Weaver D's in Athens, or as the sign says out front, "Weaver D's Delicious Fine Foods—Automatic for the People."

As good as the food is, it's the last line on that sign that truly made this place famous. For those of you familiar with the Athens music scene, you'll recognize this as the title to R.E.M.'s Grammy-nominated album from 1992.

Chances are if you find your way to Dexter Weaver's ubiquitously named restaurant right off Broad Street, you'll find out exactly what the hype is about. There isn't anything particularly fancy about the building inside or out. It is painted an interesting shade of green, making it very hard to miss. With only 40 seats, it isn't a big chain restaurant. But if you are looking for one of those, you probably should go somewhere else.

The food isn't fancy, but it sure is good. Traditional Southern favorites like eggs, sausage, country ham, and grits are served. Lunch and dinner bring more of those staples: chicken, barbecue pork, meatloaf, and steak and gravy complimented by homemade mac and cheese, greens, and cornbread.

No, it isn't health food—it is food that makes you feel good, makes you comfortable, and makes you feel like you are at home.

Dexter Weaver's restaurant isn't just another restaurant. It is part of the history of the city. It wasn't always that way. But when Michael Stipe of R.E.M. came in one day with a lawyer to cut a deal for the right to use the name on their album, everything changed.

All of a sudden, television networks and magazine reporters began showing up at the door—not just to eat, but to check out this place with the interesting slogan. They had to meet Dexter Weaver and find out what "Automatic for the People" was all about. In time, that notoriety just helped build the reputation and solidify what the locals already knew about the food. Heck, even the James Beard Awards, one of the most prestigious food organizations in the country, recognized the little restaurant and bestowed one of its America's Classics titles on Weaver D's.

Dexter has written a book, appropriately titled *Automatic Y'all*. It's a book of some of his best recipes. In the book, Weaver also speaks about being raised in Baltimore, Maryland, and how he landed in Athens and came up with the idea for his now-famous restaurant.

You can look through all of the food websites and read all of the "best of" books and stories that you want. All of them will mention Weaver D's, and it is very hard to find someone who can say anything bad. If you wander in, you'll find people from all over. Tourists, local businessmen, students, professors, and occasionally a musician or two can be spotted in the booths. The diversity of the clientele is part of the atmosphere.

It is somewhat difficult to explain to non-Southerners the endearing nature of Southern comfort food.

Maybe it's the way it is cooked. Maybe it is just the love put into it. Either way, it makes an impression on your stomach and in your heart. If you find yourself in Athens on a game weekend, or any other weekend for that matter, take a ride down Broad Street, go through downtown, and start heading toward the loop. Look for that lime-green building with that sign hanging from it. No trip to Athens would be complete without stopping for either lunch or dinner here. It's a meal you don't want to miss.

87 The Uga Suite

Every dog may have his day, but not every dog has his own hotel suite. In the case of the University of Georgia's famous Uga, the bulldog mascot, not only does he have his own room, he has his own hotel suite. In fact, he and his handlers use the suite during the football season. During the rest of the year, if you choose to stay at the Georgia Center on the university campus, upon request, you might be able to stay in the same room.

First and foremost, the room is definitely a suite. It's two rooms: one a bedroom and one a parlor room that can, for an extra charge, connect to additional bedrooms. Three people can easily spend the night with a rollaway bed.

The master bedroom has a king-sized bed, a flat screen TV, and it can connect to an extra bedroom if it should be needed. The parlor room has the typical hotel amenities: a sofa and arm chair, a coffee table and another 32-inch flat screen TV, a microwave and refrigerator, connection to the separate bathroom, and an in-room safe.

So you say, "Well, it sounds like a Hampton Inn or some other suite hotel."

Well, dearest reader, if you said that, you would be wrong.

The experience starts when you arrive. All Uga Suite guests receive a stuffed bulldog and a photo of the current Uga. It continues when you walk into the "Parlor" room, a room that is decorated in Georgia colors (red and black) and has memorabilia scattered throughout the room, provided by the Seiler family who have raised all of the bulldog mascots.

The Georgia Center itself is in a great location. Right near the center of athletic activity on campus on Lumpkin Street, it sits caddy corner to the Stegeman Coliseum. A very short walk puts you out near the football practice fields. You are also within a mile of Sanford Stadium.

The Center does have more than 200 rooms—11 of them unique suite-level rooms—and has hosted all levels of dignitaries. The hotel features four different restaurants, banquet facilities, a business center, and many conference rooms. They offer multiple packages and have special deals available to families of students and guests of the university.

Check out the Center's website if you are interested in the Uga Suite. The price is pretty reasonable, and for many Georgia fans, it is a unique campus experience.

88 The Grill

It's the second-oldest restaurant in downtown Athens, just shy of its 30th birthday, but the look hasn't changed and the approach hasn't changed to ensure that when you visit The Grill, it's always as you remembered it.

In 1981, legendary Athens restaurateur Bob Russo opened the first version of the place over on East Broad Street—where the Five Star Day Café now sits. He wanted the look to reflect his New York upbringing, so the inside colors were a basic black and white, and neon was added to give it an art deco look. The word the kids use today is "retro."

The story goes that The Grill was so popular in its early days, waiters and waitresses took orders while people waited outside so they could have their food ready when they actually got the chance to finally sit down at a booth.

Two years in, Russo sold the place to Steve Sgarlato, a Grill employee. And the variety of the menu has always kept the clientele coming back—including Michael Stipe, who actually thanked Sgarlato once for including vegetarian items on the beef-based menu.

Sgarlato moved The Grill to its current location on College Avenue in 1989. He eventually sold it to Jeff Weinberg, another Grill employee, who graduated from the University of Georgia with a mathematics degree. Weinberg worked there through school and agreed to stay when Sgarlato promised to sell the restaurant to Weinberg when Sgarlato was ready to go.

That was in 1994.

Weinberg held on to the place until early 2009, when he sold it to another employee who came up through the ranks, Mike Bradshaw.

Bradshaw had learned the ins and outs for a dozen years, starting as a cook and working his way up to being a manager. Bradshaw came down from the town of Toccoa to go to school in Athens, and one thing attracted him to the eatery at first—the noise.

"It was a real racket at night," he said in an interview with the *Athens Banner-Herald*. "I couldn't sleep, so I'd come down here and eat."

He would get tired of working the night shift, and Bradshaw actually quit for a time. But Weinberg set up a basketball game to lure Bradshaw back, promising a day shift if he'd return.

"If we sold it to another buyer, they'd probably turn it into a Johnny Rocket's or something," Weinberg said when he sold to Bradshaw. "We felt like we'd created a lot of traditions here."

Those traditions include being open 24 hours a day, the 5-oz. burgers, the Wurlitzer jukebox, fresh-cut fries, and the décor that came from a lot of different directions to add to the charm of the building.

Just be prepared, though, if you go during the late night and overnight hours. A thing or two out of the ordinary might happen. Bradshaw once saw a UGA football player (who shall remain unnamed) see a brawl start outside The Grill. He walked outside, beat up everyone in the fight, and came back inside to finish his meal. Then there was the instance where members of Elephant 6, a collective of experimental pop bands in the area, tried to do their impression of the Redcoat Band by working laps around the building, playing whatever instrument they could find in whatever shape it was in.

No one cared as it was another round of joyful noise in the downtown Athens party district. But that's what always comes out of The Grill in the first place.

"It's the only 24/7 diner downtown," Kathryn Lookofsky, director and CEO of the Athens Downtown Development Authority, added. "It's an Athens icon. I would suggest the patty melt or a Rueben with The Grill's famous fries with feta and a deliciously thick, old-fashioned chocolate malt."

Save for Thanksgiving and Christmas day, The Grill serves just that all year long. In the daytime, it's a family place with parents and kids. The bars let out at 2:00 AM, and there's a good bet that the daytime crowd won't recognize the place at that time of night.

The family atmosphere even applies to the workforce—past and present. Bradshaw always tells people that the students, as long as they leave the place on good terms, can always check back in and see if anything's happening should they return to town.

"It's been really important to me that the restaurant people enjoyed 15 years ago [is] the same one today," Bradshaw said. "There's no point, from a business standpoint, to noodle around with it."

89. A.J. Green

It's not often that a high school football star commits to play at a college as a junior and sticks to that commitment. These days, with all of the pressure and constant badgering and posturing by coaches and recruiting coordinators, it makes the decision very difficult for a teenager. It's an even bigger surprise when that recruit is in a different state and does not choose the hometown and home state schools. That and the friends and supporters who are all around, begging and pleading for you to "stay at home" make the recruiting process nothing short of crazy.

A.J. Green stood by his commitment.

He wanted to be a Georgia Bulldog early in his high school career, and he never wavered from that dream. One of the most nationally recognized wide receivers ever to play in high school, Green was a star at Summerville High School where he was fortunate enough to play for one of the winningest coaches in the history of high school football, John McKissick.

Green makes our list not for how he finished his college career but because he was such a highly touted recruit and the impact that he has made early in that career. He instantly changed the Bulldogs offense in 2008, giving it the receiving threat that had been lacking the previous four years. He immediately teamed with Mohamed Massaquoi to form one of college football's best receiving tandems.

Four games into his freshman season, Green, in front of a national television audience on ABC/ESPN, had eight catches for 159 yards and a touchdown versus Arizona State. He led the entire SEC in receiving yards and was the SEC Freshman of the Year in

2008. He set a freshman record at Georgia with 56 catches for 963 yards and eight touchdowns.

Not a bad start.

There haven't been many freshmen outside of Herschel Walker who put on that kind of performance and get that kind of recognition. Green, a soft-spoken young man, when asked about it would normally smile and say, "I got to learn from MoMass [Mohamed Massaquoi], who taught me the right way to play."

Green became a "do it all" player for the Bulldogs in his sophomore year. Not only was he a national semi-finalist for the Biletnikoff Award as the nation's best wide receiver, he also did the little things to help his team win. His game against Arizona State cemented that reputation. Sure, Green had eight catches for 153 yards and a touchdown, but that wasn't nearly as important as the field-goal attempt he blocked that would have won the game for Arizona State. The Bulldogs came back and won that game, 20–17.

The 2009 season was a tough one for both the Bulldogs and for Green. The primary threat on offense, Green was injured for a good part of the season, unable to play in three games. Yet he still managed 53 catches for 808 yards and six touchdowns.

Georgia has had several talented receivers come through the program. Terrence Edwards, Hines Ward, Andre Hastings, Reggie Brown, and Mohamed Massaquoi were all drafted or spent time playing in the NFL. Most expect that not only will he play in the NFL, but the general consensus is that at 6'4" and 200-plus pounds, the speedy, sure-handed Green will be drafted early when he decides to turn pro. The expectations are such that most scouts and observers feel he will be a remarkable pro.

High expectations? Sure, but for the kid who always wanted to be a Bulldog, those goals can be achieved.

90 Suzanne Yoculan

A gymnastics coach? Certainly. You can't understand the fabric of campus life without some familiarity with its icons. If there was a Mount Rushmore of collegiate head coaches, then former Georgia Gym Dogs head coach Suzanne Yoculan's image would be carved in stone with John Wooden of UCLA, Pat Summitt at Tennessee, and Paul W. "Bear" Bryant at Alabama.

During her 26 years as head coach of the Gym Dogs, Yoculan had a knack for collecting championship hardware. Georgia won 16 Southeastern Conference championships and 10 NCAA championships, including five in a row from 2005 through 2009.

Yoculan, a Penn State alum, owned a private gymnastics school in Pennsylvania when she received an offer to coach the Georgia team.

"Liz Murphy, who was the women's athletic director, was the person who actually hired Suzanne Yoculan. But as the athletic director, I endorsed the hiring," former Georgia athletic director Vince Dooley said.

The Georgia Gym Dogs had enjoyed modest success before Yoculan arrived in Athens in 1983. Georgia's best postseason finish was third place in the SEC Championships in 1981.

Ever driven, Yoculan took the Georgia job by the reins and set a path toward winning championships.

"Suzanne's tremendous passion for the sport, her athletes, and the University of Georgia made her a champion," former Georgia Gym Dog Lori Strong-Ballard said. "She had that internal drive in every area. And year in and year out, she wanted that national title just as bad as the last. It was her passion and desire that motivated us. Suzanne always expected success, and she wanted every one of us to experience the emotion and glory of winning a national title at the University of Georgia."

Yoculan's first Georgia team finished second at the SEC Championship and qualified for the NCAA Championship for the first time, finishing ninth.

The Gym Dog Express had left the station.

From that fast start, Suzanne Yoculan found the most talented gymnasts and used her confident leadership to recruit them to the program. Once students became part of the Gym Dogs, Yoculan's role as head coach was to mold minds.

"Over the years, Suzanne honed her exceptional ability to bring out the best in her athletes by making them mentally tough and confident," Strong-Ballard said. "Each gymnast responds to a different approach, and Suzanne understood and uncovered that connection. Some needed a stern yell or the threat of 6:00 AM bars to get the job done, while others needed a more rational discussion to make the change."

As the talent level rose, the success of the program followed. Georgia won its first SEC Championship in 1986, Suzanne Yoculan's third season as head coach, and took its first NCAA Championship in 1987. Georgia closed the 1980s with the program's second NCAA Championship in 1989.

As a young head coach, Suzanne Yoculan was a coach with a mission to accomplish. When things didn't go her way, Yoculan could let her emotions get the best of her.

"Back in the early 1990s or late 1980s when I would get mad, I would throw a shoe across the gym or walk into the locker room and throw a handful of M&M's at [a gymnast]," Suzanne Yoculan told the *Athens Banner-Herald* in January 2009. "I think they know that I was frustrated, and I didn't know how to deal with it."

Lori Strong-Ballard added, "I have been to many alumni functions where we laughed long and hard about the early 'shoe throwing' days of Suzanne. But by the end of her career, she told me she learned never to deal with situations in the heat of emotion and that she always waited 24 hours before discussing the issue."

Even as the championship success continued through the 1990s, Yoculan's unpopularity began to grow. "She's an aggressive female," former Georgia Gym Dog Terri Eckert-Smith told the *Athens Banner-Herald* in 2009. "She's going to go after what she wants."

Playing the role of the villain was just fine with Yoculan, and she didn't mind wearing the black hat. Yoculan has even likened herself to Darth Vader. "I think what I've learned the most is that I would much rather be respected than liked," Yoculan was quoted in the *Athens Banner-Herald* in January 2009. "I know I'm not that popular in the athletic department or around the country in gymnastics because of my style, but I feel like you can't question results. What is more important to me is that the team respects me."

During the 2007 season, Yoculan announced that 2009 would be her last year as the head coach of the Georgia Gym Dogs. It was in the middle of the program's most impressive run of national championships.

In 2005, the Gym Dogs lost four dual meets in a row, three in the SE—a first during the Yoculan era. By the time the SEC Championships came around, Georgia had righted the ship. When freshman Katie Heenan stuck her beam landing in the Gym Dogs' final apparatus of the meet, Georgia nailed down another SEC Championship. A month later, the Gym Dogs won the NCAA Championship.

The next season Georgia enjoyed its fourth undefeated season and won the SEC and NCAA Championships.

Two more NCAA championships and one SEC title followed coming into the 2009 season. Georgia's goal was to send Suzanne Yoculan out on top with her 10th NCAA Championship.

The only loss of the 2009 season was losing to arch-rival Alabama in the SEC Gymnastics Championship in Nashville, Tennessee, but the drive for the Perfect 10 was still on schedule.

The NCAA's were staged in Lincoln, Nebraska, and it took a pair of perfect 10s by Courtney Kupets on uneven bars and vault for Georgia to earn NCAA Championship No. 10. Suzanne Yoculan ended her 26-year Georgia coaching career on top.

"I can't even put it into words," Yoculan said after the 2009 NCAA Championship. "We came into this competition saying zero regrets and leave it all on the floor."

Suzanne Yoculan did just that in 26 years.

Yoculan's career accomplishments are ones her former boss admires.

"Of course her record is not only amazing but unmatched, and she will go down as one of the best, if not the best, gymnastic coaches of all time," Dooley said.

91 Marcus Howard and the 2008 Sugar Bowl

There are some college football players who will always be remembered for their body of work. There are also those select players who are remembered for specific plays—plays that either defined a game, a season, or a career. In the case of former Georgia Bulldog Marcus Howard, his college career will be remembered forever for a game—a game for the ages—the 2008 Sugar Bowl versus Hawaii.

For three years, Marcus Howard was a contributor to the Bulldogs defense, but he was never really a standout. He was quick—perhaps one of the fastest defensive linemen/linebackers on

Marcus Howard the Pro

Marcus Howard has not been able to translate the success of his 2007 season at Georgia into success at the professional level. Undersized for a professional defensive end, he was picked in the fifth round of the 2008 draft by the Indianapolis Colts with the hope that they could develop him as an outside, defensive speed rusher. He played in nine games in 2008 and had 14 tackles and 1.5 quarterback sacks.

Waived right before the season started, he didn't play for the Colts in 2009. Howard did sign a developmental contract with the Tennessee Titans in 2010, but it appears that his success in college was not able to carry over to the next level.

the Georgia roster during his stay in Athens, but he never really excelled like the coaches thought he might.

As a redshirt freshman, Howard was a linebacker. At slightly over 6' and 220-230 pounds, the defensive coaches initially thought Howard would progress to be a solid contributor at linebacker.

By 2005, he had been moved to defensive end, a position where his speed would come into play, but he still didn't accomplish a lot. He was part of the rotation and would make an occasional sack or tackle, but he didn't do much to stand out. Playing behind guys like Quentin Moses and Charles Johnson, however, began to rub off on him.

In 2007, Howard became a force with 10½ sacks and 41 tackles over the course of the year, along with three forced fumbles. He was a tough matchup for the bigger offensive tackles he faced because of his speed, and he had finally learned how to utilize it.

In 2007, the Georgia Bulldogs had a very memorable end to their season. They didn't win the SEC title, but they played so well at the end of the year that they earned a trip to the Sugar Bowl to face the University of Hawaii.

The Sugar Bowl, played on New Year's Day 2008, was a game that drew a lot of national interest. Georgia came in ranked fourth and was the talk of the country, finishing 10–2 on the season. Hawaii was the upstart—the BCS crasher—and they had a high-flying offense. Many of the so-called experts thought that the Rainbow Warriors would give the Georgia defense fits because of their precision passing game.

Well, anyone who saw the game knows that didn't happen. The Hawaii offensive line had no answer for the Georgia blitz package and, more importantly, they couldn't block the Bulldogs defensive line.

Marcus Howard had the game of his career—three quarterback sacks, two fumbles caused, one of which he recovered for a touchdown. He was the Rainbow Warrior's worst nightmare. Howard lined up all over the line, and at times it seemed as though there were three of him rushing Hawaii quarterback Colt Brennan.

Howard was voted the game's Most Valuable Player as Georgia easily defeated Hawaii, 41–10. Those who were at the game will tell you that it was never close. Howard had outshone Georgia's other stars, Matthew Stafford and Knowshon Moreno. He was in tears on the stage as the award was announced.

After the game, Brennan was heard asking, "Who was that guy?"

That guy was, because of that performance, able to increase his stock in the NFL—so much so that he was drafted that April in the fifth round by the Indianapolis Colts.

92 The Countdown to Kickoff

No, this isn't a football game, nor is it a pregame show before a game, although it involves quite a few football players. It isn't a clock that counts down, nor is it the moment before the start of a football game.

It is an event that has, in just a few short years, become the unofficial official start to the football season. The Countdown to Kickoff was dreamed up by former Georgia football players and brothers Jon and Matt Stinchcomb as a way to get former and current players out in front of the fans during the summer, to get the fans excited for the fall and, most importantly, to raise some money for local charities.

The Countdown to Kickoff is a fairly simple event. There are sponsor booths, games, and play areas set up all around the practice fields. The big draws for fans are the autograph lines. Bring your camera, and be prepared to wait on line. The appeal is the lengthy list of both Georgia football alumni and current players who appear and sign autographs. Along with the Stinchcomb brothers—Matt, who is an analyst for ESPN, and Jon, who plays for the Super Bowl XLIV champion New Orleans Saints—you'll have the opportunity to meet Bulldogs who played in the NFL plus stars on Georgia teams gone by who all come back to spend time meeting and thanking the fans.

As we all know, Georgia fans are among the most passionate in college football. They attend just about any kind of event involving the word "football" or "Bulldogs." This mood and the feelings from this event fit right in with that. Traditionally, a line begins early in the morning on Saturday, and by early Saturday afternoon when the gates open and it starts getting summertime-in-Georgia hot, the line drapes around the wall outside the practice fields and down past Stegeman Coliseum.

The $25 ticket price doesn't deter a lot of people. Judging by the crowds at the first four of these events, the fans seem more than eager to drop money for this opportunity. Both Jon and Matt will be the first ones to tell you that, "This isn't being done for us to make money. It all goes back to the charities."

The Georgia Transplant Foundation, the Children's Tumor Foundation, Children's Healthcare of Atlanta, and several other charities receive the proceeds from the event, and raising money for these groups is a big part of the reason that the event is held.

The event itself has already evolved. It started with just a Saturday afternoon, and it has now evolved into a full-fledged weekend. A golf outing at the university's championship golf course and an awards dinner and raffle now start the weekend on Friday.

It's a nice opportunity for fans to play with some of the former players and coaches and another way to raise some money for charity.

Between Jon and Matt and recent co-host addition and former Georgia quarterback David Greene, they have a long and lengthy list of guys that they can call on to appear at this event. July is the hottest time of the year in Central Georgia, so bring some water, light clothing, a good Sharpie marker, and a camera. You will leave with a smile and the knowledge that you have been a part of the start of another football season.

93 Georgia-Florida 1975

"Appleby, end around, he just stopped, planted his feet, and threw it. Washington caught it thinking of Montreal and the Olympics, and ran out of his shoes right there 80 yards. Stadium rocking, girders are bending now. Look at the score, look at the score!"

Another game in the Georgia-Florida series that sticks with Bulldog fans was played on November 8, 1975, and saw the No. 7 Gators enter the game with a 6–1 record, and the Bulldogs, ranked No. 19, at 5–2. Florida's only blemish was an 8–7 loss to NC State in Raleigh. The Dawgs had lost to Pittsburgh and Ole Miss.

But the story starts four years earlier.

The Five Commitments

Richard Appleby was one of the five commitments for Coach Dooley in 1971 who integrated the Bulldog football team. Who were the other four?

Horace King and Clarence Pope were teammates of Appleby's at Clarke Central High School. Larry West was from Albany, Georgia. Chuck Kinnebrew was the fifth from the town of Rome.

The five were honored before the Clemson game in 2002.

Coach Dooley wanted to integrate the Bulldogs roster as far back as the late 1960s. It took until 1971 for that idea to finally hit the field. Richard Appleby was one of the first black football players in UGA football history. He had attended Clarke Central High School in the Athens area. The Gladiators themselves hadn't even integrated their roster until Appleby's senior season. His career in the red and black was that of a solid receiver who led the team in receptions in 1973, 1974, and 1975. His total receiving numbers were 12, 23, and 13 for those respective seasons.

Gene Washington still holds the record for the average gain per catch in Georgia history at 24.6 yards during his four-year career. He was also the leading receiver for the 1976 season with 20 catches. These two connected for Appleby's first pass of the 1975 season, and that is what people really remember about the tight end and the receiver.

Florida took a 7–0 lead on the legs of Tony Green, and Georgia responded with a field goal to close the margin to 7–3 heading into the fourth quarter. The end-around with Appleby had worked previously in the game with Washington, at just 5'9" and 172 pounds, playing the lead. But Coach Dooley had called a trick play off the reverse with Georgia backed up to its own 25-yard line—something the coach rarely did.

Dudley had to do something with a little more than three minutes to go in regulation if the team was going to have a chance to tie or go ahead.

Washington faked his block and ended up behind the Florida coverage. Quarterback Ray Goff handed off the ball to Appleby. He gave the impression it was just another end-around, but then Appleby stopped in his tracks, planted his feet, and fired the ball downfield for the go-ahead score.

Florida did have one final chance for the tie after the Bulldogs took the lead 10–7, but the snap from center didn't quite make it to the holder cleanly. Georgia had its upset, and the Gators established a 1–6–1 career record for any game played on November 8.

Both players were inducted into the Georgia-Florida Hall of Fame. Appleby was inducted in 1999, and Washington was inducted during the week of the 2008 game. Washington ended up a ninth-round pick of the San Diego Chargers in 1977. He was in the NFL for two seasons, dressing for the Lions and the New York Giants.

Washington never caught a pass in the NFL.

94 Spec Towns

Here's a trivia question that will stump even die-hard Georgia fans—name the first Georgian to be placed on an Olympic team?

Track and field puts you in the ballpark. But it's the pride of Fitzgerald, Forrest "Spec" Towns, who is the correct answer. Towns was the world-record holder in the 110-yard hurdles and was only one-tenth of a second off that time in Berlin for the 1936 gold medal performance, finishing in a time of 14.1 seconds.

Towns held the world record in the event with a sub-14 second time for almost fourteen years when Harrison Dillard bested the time.

But the hurdles was not the event that was Spec's initial strength—it was the high jump. And were it not for a local Augusta sportswriter, Towns may have gone somewhere else for his record-setting time—or even worse yet, he may have gone completely unnoticed as a talent.

As the story goes, Towns' father and brother-in-law were standing in their backyard. Both were about 6' tall and placed a bar across themselves. Towns cleared the bar. Tom Wall was the local sports writer. He was visiting friends next door, looked out their window, saw what Towns was doing, and wrote a story saying that it would be a shame if this kid wasn't going to have a college career somewhere.

The article made its way to UGA track coach Weems Baskin in 1933. Baskin tried Towns out, and it was the beginning of a 40-plus year association with the Bulldogs program.

"'Coach Baskin looked at him, and he had long legs and was about 6'2", 6'2½", and coach Baskin said, 'Do you want to try run these hurdles?'" Spec's widow, Martha Eberhardt Towns, told Adam Minichino in an interview with onlineathens.com, "The first time he ran the hurdles on a cinder track, he fell and had cinders from his shoulders to his ankles. He got up and asked Coach Baskin if he could try it again and Coach Baskin said at that moment I knew I had a hurdler."

Towns' accomplishments in the SEC:

1935: SEC title in the 120-yard hurdles

1936: All-American in the 110- and 120-yard hurdles. Won the NCAA Outdoor Championship and the SEC title in the 120-yard and the 220-yard hurdles.

1937: Won the 110- and 120-yard hurdles (again), the NCAA outdoor title in the 120-yard hurdles, and the SEC version of the 120- and 220-yard hurdles.

His win streak was more than 60 straight races in that time frame.

In 1938, Towns started his 37-year run as head track and field coach at the University of Georgia. He was inducted into the U.S. Track and Field Hall of Fame in 1975. The track and field facility at the University of Georgia was named in his honor in 1990, and in 1997, he was inducted into the UGA Athletic Association Circle of Honor.

Towns passed in April 1991 at the age of 77, and athletes make a yearly appearance at the track that bears his name during the Spec Towns Invitational.

95 The One-Shot Deal

Ever heard of a double-barreled cannon? You can find one out in front of city hall.

If you go to Athens, you'll actually see the firearms equivalent of a one-hit wonder band, the Tucker and Edsel automobiles, and Sensurround all rolled into one.

In April 1862, John Gilleland was set to display his idea that was supposed to revolutionize war and any kind of aerial assault associated with it. From a distance, Gilleland's invention looked like a normal cannon. But at the discharge end, there were two muzzles that could fire two cannonballs attached by a chain link, or each barrel could be independently.

Gilleland was a member of the Mitchell Thunderbolts outfit—a group of individuals who were considered by the Confederacy too old to fight. So the carpenter (one of his reported occupations at the time) decided to create this monster of offense with a 10' chain option in the middle that was supposed to take down an opponent like a clothesline.

He knew that his fellow soldiers were often outnumbered in battles against the Union, so thinking like the 17th-century French, Gilleland wanted to treat Union soldiers like ship's masts. It was a good idea in theory.

When the time came for actually demonstrating the idea, it didn't go so well. Since the results of the test-firing were 50-50 at best, and the subsequent attempt at fine-tuning in an Augusta arsenal didn't improve the odds, Gilleland's invention was stamped "return to sender."

Undaunted, Gilleland sent letters to both the Confederate government in Richmond and to his governor, Joseph E. Brown. That effort met with the same level of success.

The cannon was placed in front of the city hall in Athens as a rather loud warning beacon for enemy attacks, but it was brought out of its government-imposed retirement for an incident in August 1864.

Brigadier General George Stoneman was on his way with his forces. Gilleland's pet project sat with other cannons as a welcoming committee and, once it was fired (as legend has it), the Union troops withdrew from the area. The double-barreled cannon was put into permanent retirement with an undefeated record.

After the War Between the States, the gun was sold. It was missing in action until the 1890s when it was rediscovered, refurbished, sold twice for a total of $9, and moved to its present location in the City Hall Plaza at the corner of College Avenue and Hancock Street.

It has even been featured in the *Ripley's Believe It or Not* series, demonstrating Gilleland's intuition as he was way ahead of his time.

96 An SEC Tournament Run for the Ages...in Another Sport

The University of Georgia fielded its first men's basketball team in 1905, and in more than 100 years on the court, the Bulldogs haven't enjoyed the overwhelming success of the football team.

The greatest player to put on a Georgia basketball uniform was Dominique Wilkins, who was a two-time All-American in the early 1980s. He still holds the school record for points in a season when he scored 732 points as a sophomore in 1981. The No. 21 Wilkins wore as a Bulldog is the only number to be retired by the school.

The 1982–83 Georgia Bulldogs were the most successful. That team featured All-American guard Vern Fleming, forward James Banks, and All-SEC Terry Fair in the post. The Bulldogs trio averaged double figures in points per game and led Georgia on an unprecedented postseason run.

At the 1983 SEC Tournament in Birmingham, Alabama, the Bulldogs defeated Alabama in the final 86–71 to capture the program's first SEC Tournament title in school history.

Next, Georgia made an improbable NCAA Final Four run beginning with a close 56–54 win over Virginia Commonwealth in the first round to advance to the NCAA Regionals in Syracuse, New York. Georgia faced a very good St. John's team in the Regional Semifinals and defeated the Redmen (as they were called then) 70–67.

Next up for the Bulldogs in the Regional Final were the defending national champion North Carolina Tar Heels, who featured Michael Jordan. Georgia prevailed over North Carolina 82–77 to win the program's first NCAA Regional and a trip to the Final Four in Albuquerque, New Mexico.

It was there that Georgia's Cinderella run ended against North Carolina State—a team that would be known as the "Cardiac Pack." The Wolfpack won 67–60 and went on to win an improbable national championship two nights later.

Other than the program's only outright SEC regular-season title in 1990 and the buzz of Tubby Smith's two years of success in Athens, the program was very mediocre.

By the time the 2007–08 season began, Dennis Felton was entering his fifth season as head coach of the Bulldogs following a 19-win season and postseason play in the NIT. Although Felton's Bulldogs had steadily improved from an eight-win season in 2004–05, fan apathy and disinterest in the program was spreading.

The Bulldogs didn't inspire the fan base by going 8–5 in non-conference games including losses to East Tennessee State and Tulane in a pre-Christmas tournament held on the Hawaiian Islands. However, the Bulldogs created some buzz by defeating arch-rival Georgia Tech 79–72 in front of more than 10,000 at Stegeman Coliseum. The win over the Yellow Jackets came at the right time to generate momentum heading into SEC play.

Georgia got off to a 2–1 start in conference play with home wins over Alabama and Arkansas. Then Georgia struggled, losing the next five SEC games before (temporarily) reversing course with an 18-point win over South Carolina at the Steg.

At this point, there were rumblings that Dennis Felton was on the hot seat. The Bulldogs didn't help their embattled head coach by losing six of their last seven games in the SEC to finish 4–12 and in last place in the SEC East. The Bulldogs, and perhaps Dennis Felton's Georgia career, had one lifeline left—to win the SEC Tournament down the road at the Georgia Dome in Atlanta.

Georgia opened the SEC Tournament matched up against SEC Western Division champion Ole Miss in a game that set the tone for Georgia's tournament run. The Bulldogs were playing their best basketball of the year led by senior captains guard Sundiata Gaines and center Dave Bliss. Terrance Woodbury played the game of his life and contributed to Georgia building a double-digit lead early in the second half.

Ole Miss went on a run and came back led by David Huertas, who led the Rebels with 29 points and sank three free throws with seven seconds left to send the game into overtime.

It set up a dramatic overtime period and a classic ending. With time running out in overtime and the score tied at 95, Corey Butler took the inbound pass, went the length of the floor, and fed Dave Bliss, who banked home a short jumper with four-tenths of a second left to win it for Georgia 97–95. The Bulldogs were still breathing, but little did they know what was in store.

Georgia drew Kentucky in the quarterfinal round of the 2008 SEC Tournament, which tipped off as the second game of the night session on March 14, 2008. Alabama and Mississippi State preceded the Bulldogs' game and went to overtime, pushing back the tip-off past 9:00 PM EST.

During the overtime period, a tornado roared through downtown Atlanta where the Georgia Dome is located and delayed the Alabama–Mississippi State quarterfinal game. The game soon resumed, and Mississippi State won 69–67.

Kentucky and Georgia would not take the floor that night. SEC officials decided not to risk playing the game and postponed it until the next morning. Due to the unique situation, either the Wildcats or the Bulldogs would have to play two games in one day.

Head coach Dennis Felton knew this was the hand that was dealt to his team but he vehemently objected. Felton knew winning the SEC Tournament was the Bulldogs only shot at a bid to the NCAA Tournament—plus he felt the added burden of having his job on the line.

Playing two games in one day was asking a lot.

Georgia did catch a break when the SEC decided to move the tournament to the much smaller and intimate Alexander Memorial Coliseum on the Georgia Tech campus because of the damage sustained by the Georgia Dome during the violent weather the night before.

In front of an official attendance of 1,458 in the Georgia Tech facility, the Bulldogs continued their miracle run with a new hero, Zac Swansey. The freshman guard hit two big baskets late in overtime, including a spinning 3-pointer under heavy duress, to give Georgia its first SEC Tournament win over Kentucky 60–56.

Next up for the Georgia Bulldogs later in the day were the Mississippi State Bulldogs, the top seed from the SEC West. This time, Billy Humphrey was the top dog. Humphrey had struggled earlier in the day against Kentucky and had missed all six of his shots against Mississippi State, but he scored six points in the last two minutes of the game as Georgia surprised Mississippi State 64–60 to earn a trip to the SEC Tournament Final.

All that stood in the way of Georgia completing its miracle SEC Tournament run was the Arkansas Razorbacks. With all the emotion and momentum favoring the red and black, the Bulldogs dominated the Hogs. Led by Terrance Woodbury's 16 points and the steady leadership of senior guard Sundiata Gaines, who added 11 points and earned SEC Tournament MVP honors, the Bulldogs did believe in miracles as they defeated Arkansas 66–57 to claim the program's second SEC Tournament Championship.

Fan apathy was swept aside during the SEC Tournament run. There were no seats left on the Georgia bandwagon after the Arkansas win. It was on to the NCAA Tournament.

Head coach Dennis Felton breathed a sigh of relief; his job was secure.

"Dennis Felton is our coach," Georgia athletic director Damon Evans was quoted in the *New York Times*.

The magic ran out on the Bulldogs in the NCAA Tournament. Georgia played a very good Xavier team that defeated the Bulldogs 73–61, ending Georgia's season.

While Georgia's 2007–08 season of 17 wins, 17 losses overall and 4–12 in the SEC may look ugly, the SEC Tournament Championship banner that hangs in Stegeman Coliseum looks great.

97 The Iron Horse

The Iron Horse somehow has become a must-see item in the Athens area. The history of it is rather simple. It was built in 1954 by university artist Abbott Pattinson and was placed in front of the Reed Hall dormitory. The sculpture itself is 10' tall and weighs more than a full ton.

For some reason that has never been fully explained, the students at the university did not care for the sculpture—so much so that it was set on fire multiple times (though it is iron, and a fire wouldn't do much damage). There were parties held around it and graffiti placed on it. Paint was thrown on it, and the fire department was called to put out the blaze and eventually to disperse the students who had gathered and rallied into a frenzy.

The school quickly realized that it needed to move the Iron Horse.

The first solution was to make it disappear. The sculpture was put into hiding and was not seen for five years. Eventually, a professor from the university's Horticulture Department agreed to have the sculpture placed on his farm between Watkinsville and Greensboro, where it still stands. As the story goes, Professor L.C. Curtis had to have it loaded onto a flatbed truck and driven out of Athens in the middle of the night. He waited until downtown had cleared out for the evening before moving it.

There have been a few attempts over the years to have the sculpture returned to the campus, but they have been unsuccessful. The family of the professor who adopted it are also opposed to moving it. According to several news and feature articles, they, "judge their corn crops on whether or not they can see the horse."

Logical, as the horse sits in the middle of their cornfield.

Word eventually got out that the Iron Horse had relocated. Nobody knows exactly how, since it had been in storage for several years. But the students and others found it. The reaction this time was not quite so violent. It's actually become a bit of a tourist attraction and the topic of photo ops and conversation. Most of the time, people will ask the Curtis family for permission to go out and take their picture on or with the sculpture. Though a few incidents have happened, by and large the family is pleased that people have gotten so much enjoyment out of it.

Yes, there are multiple ways to get to Athens. And if you find yourself heading to a game via Highway 15, take a look as you start getting closer to town. You'll round a nice, sweeping curve about 18 or so miles away from town and see it standing in the middle of the cornfield.

It may look a bit out of place and might cause you to do a double take, but your eyes won't be deceiving you. It really is a 10' 1-ton sculpture of a horse staring back at you.

98 Terrapin Beer

The beauty of this country is that when you have an idea, you can pursue it and satisfy a goal that you may have had about conquering a corner of the world—or, for that matter, a particular industry in a particular corner of the world. When you go to Athens, you can see one of those examples firsthand, Terrapin Beer.

Back in late 2001 and early 2002, John Cochran and Brian "Spike" Buckowski met while working in a brewery in Atlanta. They figured they should go ahead and start their own in Athens. All they had was a recipe and an idea as they looked for the funding to put it all together.

By April they had a couple of accounts in town and were just making enough of the product to service those establishments on draft. Terrapin Rye Pale Ale won its first gold medal, the American Pale Ale Gold, in October at the 2002 Great American Beer Festival. With success came demand and more people willing to invest in John and Spike's product.

In early 2004, Terrapin released its second idea, Terrapin Golden Ale. The Golden version won a silver medal at that year's World Beer Cup, and the unofficial motto inside the building became, "Two years, two beers, two medals!"

One way growing businesses get noticed is through their packaging. Because, as a lot of you know, if something catches your eye, you're more likely to stop and check out what the pretty pictures are about. It's also another way to make a name for yourself.

The fancy title for that is "brand identification." If a product is known for a particular look, logo, or approach to presenting its work, then the conversation starts with the look and moves on to word-of-mouth about the actual item.

Terrapin's distinctive look was established by Richard Biffle and still is to this day. Biffle has done some poster work for the Grateful Dead in the past, and when Spike hooked up with Biffle at a Bonaroo festival, John and Spike's vision merged with Richard Biffle's ideas onto paper and the sides of carrying cases around the southeast. Their combined ideas have even been awarded a Best Overall 6-Pack Design by the Beverage Testing Institute at the 2004 World Beer Championships Packaging Competition.

Terrapin unveiled its third full-time production in 2007 with the Indian Style Brown Ale, and Spike has even gone as far as having what is called a "Side Project Series." Think of them as the "one-shot deals" for beer-making to go along with the Terrapin tradition of creating seasonal brews and the three 12-months-a-year productions.

Here's where faithful Athens visitors come in. You can actually see the folks at Terrapin make their creations. The brewery runs tours with live music while you walk through. The tastings run Wednesdays, Thursdays, Fridays, and Saturdays from 5:30 to 7:30 PM.

John Cochran knows how important Athens is to Terrapin's success. "It's been our ultimate goal to have a facility here in Athens from the beginning. Athens is a special place and the only place we would want to put our brewery."

Terrapin has gone from just an idea to distribution in nine states, reaching as far north as Pennsylvania with its creative artwork on the outside and hard work on the inside. The 17 awards it has earned in just eight years show you that much. The brewery celebrates its anniversary with a big party every April. With the success of the brew, the event has naturally grown with crowds larger than 1,500 people attending these days and lots of local Athens color.

As Spike said, "It's been a long strange trip getting here. But Athens is our home, and I wouldn't want it any other way."

If you have an idea, don't just toss it aside. John and Spike are prime examples of following their brains and their hearts. They also know that Athens has been as integral to their success as anything else.

And above all, once you've sampled the product...please recycle.

99 The Tree That Owns Itself

What's the old saying? "Possession is nine-tenths of the law?" If that's the case, then there's one Athens tree that grades out to an A-minus when it comes to controlling its own destiny and decisions.

Go to the corner of Dearing and Finley streets, and you'll find a 50' white oak that takes up less than a quarter-acre in space but is completely emancipated.

As the story goes, there was a university professor (and soldier) named William (or Colonel W.H.) Jackson, who grew up across the street from the oak tree. He played in it, as kids often do with trees, but over time he got to the point where he deeded to the tree the land on which it grew. "For and in consideration of the great love I bear this tree and the great desire I have for its protection for all time, I convey entire possession of itself and the land within eight feet of it on all sides."

The story of the tree first appeared in an article in the *Athens Weekly Banner* back in 1890, and A.L. Hull told the legend again in his 1906 edition of *Annals of Athens*.

At the beginning of the 20th century, George F. Peabody, a philanthropist and benefactor to the University of Georgia (yes, the Peabody Awards are named for him) had the posts and fence placed around that 8' perimeter. He is also responsible for the block with the words of Jackson's bequest on it.

Being in this book isn't the most recognition the tree and its property have received. It was named as one of the top 10 insider spots of interest in a Travelocity.com Local Secrets, Big Finds international poll in 2005.

Oh, and the tree you find isn't the original tree. A storm in 1942 knocked the original one down. But one of its acorns was saved by the Junior Ladies Garden Club, who planted the sapling on the original site in 1946. That's the one you see these days.

And much like the cannon we talked about a few pages back, it's also in the *Ripley's Believe It or Not* pages for the record.

100 Steve Spurrier

If you want to rile up a passionate Georgia Bulldogs fan just mention Stephen Orr Spurrier. There is no gray area how Georgia fans feel about the head coach.

They dislike him, and to use the word "dislike" is putting it kindly inside these pages.

Spurrier has a reputation for tweaking his opponents and taking it even further against rivals. Georgia fans will tell you Spurrier ups that ante on Georgia. The "OBC" once referred to former Georgia head coach Ray Goff as "Ray Goof."

During Spurrier's playing days as a quarterback at the University of Florida, Georgia won two of the three games, including the 1966 game in Jacksonville 27–10—the year Spurrier won the Heisman Trophy. That loss was a huge disappointment to the Gators; if they had won that game they would have won the SEC Championship. Instead, Georgia won easily and won the title that year, something Spurrier would never forget.

By the time Spurrier returned to Florida as head football coach, Georgia dominated the rivalry. From 1966–89, the Bulldogs had won 17-of-24 games against the Gators. By the time Spurrier returned to the Florida campus, Georgia was labeled public enemy No. 1.

What transpired next became the most dominant era the Gators have ever enjoyed against the Georgia Bulldogs. During Spurrier's Florida tenure from 1990–2001, the coach won 11-of-12 games against the Bulldogs. While that record sticks in the craw of most Georgia fans, it was the six Florida blowouts during that time that were pure Spurrier-esque.

Twice Florida defeated Georgia 38–7 (in 1990, Spurrier's first year as the Gators head coach, and in 1998), and Florida embarrassed the Bulldogs 45–13 in 1991 and 47–7 in 1996. Those games were played at the usual venue for this rivalry—The Gator Bowl (or Jacksonville Municipal Stadium) in Jacksonville, Florida.

Because of major renovations to the Gator Bowl stadium in Jacksonville, the 1994 and 1995 editions of those games were played on campus sites. Spurrier really put it to Georgia during those two editions, as the Gators put up more than 50 points in both games. The 1994 game was played at Ben Hill Griffin Stadium in Gainesville, better known as "The Swamp," and the Gators swamped the Bulldogs 52–14.

That result was enough to raise the anger of Georgia fans toward Spurrier. What transpired in the 1995 game, however, increased that contempt to the boiling point.

Florida's cleats marked the turf of Sanford Stadium in Athens for the first time in more than 60 years and proceeded to do something an opponent had never accomplished on that sod—put up 50 points on the Georgia Bulldogs. What really ticked off Bulldogs fans was the audacity Spurrier showed by reaching that magic number and the perceived enjoyment the visor-throwing coach got from embarrassing a rival.

With the game in hand 45–17 with five minutes to play, Spurrier called a flea-flicker that resulted in a Gators touchdown that elevated the score beyond the 50-point mark. When asked by the media after the game why Florida scored another touchdown that late in the game, Spurrier responded by saying he wanted to hang "half a hundred" on the Bulldogs at their own stadium because he had heard no one else had done that.

Georgia's dislike for Spurrier reached the hatred level.

After the 2001 season, Spurrier moved on to the NFL to coach the Washington Redskins for a couple of unsuccessful seasons.

In 2005, Spurrier returned to the SEC as head coach at the University of South Carolina. While Spurrier owned the Georgia Bulldogs at Florida, he has been humbled against the Bulldogs during his tenure with the Gamecocks.

As of the end of the 2009 season, Spurrier is 1–4 against Georgia as South Carolina's head coach. That lone win came in 2007 in Athens but not by a blowout.

Much to the enjoyment of Georgia fans, Steve Spurrier has found out what goes around comes around. And that's why we included him in the book but put him dead last—the one place short of hell that Bulldogs fans love to see the "OBC."

Acknowledgments

You never know who to thank individually when you do one of these things, so here goes.

First and foremost, thanks to Tom Bast at Triumph for green-lighting this project. Thanks to Adam Motin for being chief traffic cop, proofreader, and all things literary in the Chicago office, and thanks to editor Karen O'Brien.

Thanks to everyone at the University of Georgia in Athens who put up with every request, e-mail, and silly question along the way. Without them, this book would have never happened. To everyone who spent time being interviewed, from athletes and ex-athletes to coaches, business owners, and city personnel so we knew what we were talking about more than we may have going in. To my mother and father who have put up with me and my overt stubbornness over all these years when it comes to my work. To all my brothers and sisters (blood or otherwise) and to friends who actually asked me if I knew how to write—J-Dub, especially, for his research in the home stretch. And to the better half, Patty, for being a sounding board and making sure I made sense with all of this. Now that she's been mentioned in a Georgia book, I don't know if she'll be let back onto the Auburn campus…ever.

Last, but certainly not least, thanks to the two guys below—Phil Cantor and John Wilkerson—without whom this really wouldn't have been done. You can breathe now, guys.

Phil, your turn.

—Jon Nelson

Big thanks to Jon Nelson for sharing this project. Special shout out to Claude Felton and the University of Georgia Sports Information staff for helping facilitate contact with some of the folks we spoke to. Thanks to Loran Smith for agreeing to write the forward. Who knows about the stuff in this book better than him? Thank you

Coach Mark Richt and Coach Vince Dooley for contributing some quotes. Thanks to Bill Hartman for some background, perspective, and some more quotes. Also, a shout out to Gil Tyree and Mark Harmon, we experienced a lot of these events while covering Georgia football from 2000–09, and the experiences made the stories a lot easier to write.

Most importantly, thank you to my lovely bride, Michelle, for being patient with me while I worked on this and to Daisy the Wonder Dog for keeping me company in the office while I researched and wrote my part.

Wilkie, take us home.

—Phil Cantor

Having the opportunity to write this book on things that make the Georgia Bulldogs unique has been a pleasure. I got my first taste of the passion of Georgia Bulldogs fans covering the 1991 Independence Bowl when UGA defeated Arkansas in Shreveport, Louisiana.

I got a full dose of that passion when I moved to the Atlanta metro area in the fall of 1998. I found myself unconsciously tuning in to WSB Radio, listening to Larry Munson call the action. I admit it, I was hooked in.

Another great pleasure is co-authoring this book with two good friends who are first class, Jon Nelson and Phil Cantor. This is the beginning of many great opportunities for the three of us.

I would also like to extend my thanks to Vince Dooley who provided some great insight while compiling materials for this book. I could spend all day talking to Loran Smith about his vast knowledge of the Georgia Bulldogs. Mr. Smith gave me some great tidbits that only he could know. I'll always value my conversations with Mr. Smith.

I also want to acknowledge Jeff Genthner, senior vice president and general manager of Fox Sports South/SportSouth, where I am employed, for allowing me to pursue this opportunity to co-author this project. I can't thank Mr. Genthner enough for his blessing on this.

Finally, I would like to acknowledge my wife, Kathy, who put up with me while I put in time on weeknights after a full day's work and weekends working on this project. Kathy took care of the family business while I pursued this passion. She is the love of my life, and her love and support are invaluable.

Then there are my kids—son Michael, who tells me someday he's going to write a book, and daughters Amanda and Kayla, who are just wondering why daddy always sits at the computer.

—John Wilkerson

Bibliography

Georgiadogs.com

The Walter J. Brown Media Archives and Peabody Awards Collection

Larrymunson.com

MarkRicht.com

Redandblack.com

UGA.edu

Bulldogs Blog with David Hale/l-e-o.com/Columbus Ledger-Enquirer

ESPN.com

Onlineathens.com/Athens Banner-Herald

AJC.com/Atlanta Journal-Constitution

CSTV.com/CBS College Sports Television

Gatorzone.com

Collegefootball.org/College Football Hall of Fame

Footballfoundation.com/National Football Foundation and College Hall of
Fame

Lucididiocy.blogspot.com/Travis Fain Blog

Valdostadailytimes.com/Valdosta Daily Times

SPTimes.com/St. Petersburg Times

Tampabay.com/Tampa Tribune

Towntalknews.com

Alumni.uga.edu

Secsports.com/Southeastern Conference

Franklin.uga.edu

Bleacherreport.com

Athenstwilight.com

Wikipedia.org

Georgiaencylopedia.org

Georgiainfo.galileo.usg.edu

Freebase.com

USAToday.com

Pittsburgh Tribune Review, Rob Rossi interview with Hines Ward-12/17/06

Chronicle.Augusta.com/Augusta Chronicle

Savannahnow.com/Savannah Morning News

Macon.com/Macon Telegraph

NYTimes.com/New York Times

Time.com/Time Magazine

Decatur Daily Newspaper, Josh Cooper interview- 9/25/08

IMDB.com

Thevarsity.com

Georgiacenter.uga.edu

DJShockley.com

ugakickoff.com

gatransplant.org

terrapinbeer.com

alumni.uga.edu

excursia.com

billgoldberg.com

history.com

popwarner.com

pabook.libraries.psu.edu

collegefootballpoll.com

sicemdawgs.com

dallasnews.com/Dallas Morning News

attcottonbowl.com

visitathensga.com

downtownathensga.com

bands.music.uga.edu

40watt.com

fiveandten.com

starchefs.com

accessatlanta.com

signonsandiego.com

ugadog.com/UGA Alumni Association

Jacksonville.com/Florida Times-Union

DenverPost.com

Southgeorgia.inthegamemagazine.com/In The Game Magazine

Armc.org/Athens Regional Medical CenterÎÎ